THE GREAT BRITISH

BAKE OFF®

FAVOURITE FLAVOURS

THE GREAT BRITISH
BAKE OFF®

FAVOURITE FLAVOURS

SPHERE

SPICY & AROMATIC

TART & TANGY

FRESH & FRUITY

SWEET & STICKY

NUTTY & EARTHY

RICH & CREAMY

CONTENTS

A note from Paul

It's incredible what flavour can do. A single bite can transport you to another time and place entirely – a citrus kick can send you back to your last holiday, the aroma of a certain spice can get you thinking about your favourite restaurant, and the taste of a home-cooked treat can even bring you back to the kitchen of a loved one. Just the word 'flavour' is enough to get your mouth watering, and this book is all about those favourite flavours and textures that have you reaching for particular ingredients again and again.

When it comes to my all-timers, I usually like to keep things simple, really making sure I enjoy the depth I find in a few rich flavours, and the satisfying results of some time-honoured combinations. Lime, with its layered, sharp, citrus tang, is a particular love of mine; and the combination of almond and cherry in a Bakewell tart, or dark, rich chocolate and boozy cherry in a Black Forest gâteau are, for me, just perfect. I'm always surprised by how many layers a bake, even a straightforward one, can offer.

The recipes in this book are a celebration of the simple and the complex. Our fantastic bakers and our *Bake Off* team have, between them, created a collection of bakes with flavours that are both reassuringly comforting and full of surprises. I can't wait for you to try them – and, when you do, I really encourage you to stop and savour what you're eating, to really notice the way flavours work together and to begin to identify your own favourites. Who knows? Perhaps that in itself could be the catalyst for your own *Bake Off* adventure.

A note from Prue

When I'm baking or cooking, my mind at once starts to run with flavour and texture possibilities: what will go with what; would a bit of crunch be good with that? A kitchen is a playground for innovation, and every year we see that with our bakers. They are amazingly creative. I love watching a baker's face light up as they explain the combination of ingredients they've layered together for their showstopper, or the inspiration for their signature bake (as likely as not some memory of something their mum or grandmum made for them as a child). And I never cease to marvel at their excitement as week after week they come up with exceptional confections.

One of the best things about baking is watching people taking that first bite. Food is a labour of love, and there are few things as rewarding as making someone something glorious. I love flavours to be clean, deep and uncomplicated. Mixing too many flavours can confuse the palate and the tastes lose their crisp distinction. Rather like using the colours in a paint box – mix too many and you risk turning a rainbow into a muddy brown. But I do love surprising flavour combinations. One of my favourites is chilled fresh watermelon wrapped in pancetta and crisply fried!

We've stuffed this book with delicious bakes for you to devour, and I hope that you can use it as a springboard to develop new favourites of your own. Take a leaf out of our bakers' books and try something unexpected. But most of all, I hope you find the recipe that will bring you the most joy – in making it, serving it and eating it for years to come. Happy baking!

Introduction

Welcome to *The Great British Bake Off: Favourite Flavours*, a collection of sweet and savoury bakes from Paul, Prue and the team behind the show – as well as, of course, from our wonderful 2022 bakers themselves.

Over the years, our bakers have been generous in telling us what inspires them to bake. One theme that comes up time and again is that baking somehow satisfies a need. This might manifest in a hankering for flavours or textures we love, have meaning for us or simply suit the mood – a chocolate birthday cake for a chocoholic; the comfort of a creamy mash-topped cottage pie after a tricky day at work; a tangy, crisp ginger biscuit as an afternoon pick-me-up; a rich, warming slice of toffee-laced fruit cake to nurture the soul; a slice of lip-smacking lemon meringue pie to somehow counter the heat of a summer's day. Of course, not everything about this is to do with the actual experience of the flavour on the palate – memory has a lot to answer for, too. The aromas of that cottage pie might remind you of a happy gathering of friends and family. Perhaps you chose a citrus-flavoured wedding cake, and now even a simple lemon drizzle takes you back to your big day. Taste, flavour, emotion – they are powerful, inseparable and fundamental. And they provide one of the most important keys to how we choose and then how much we enjoy our food.

Inevitably over the last 13 years in the tent, flavour has played a major role in the success (or otherwise!) of the bakers' journeys. But flavour isn't just the result of a pinch of this or a swirl of that. When Paul and Prue come to judge a bake, they start with how it looks. Like so many clichés, there is much truth in the adage that 'eating begins with the eyes'. Science tells us that the look of our food (both its colour and its presentation) can influence how we perceive its flavour. Researchers also believe that presentation, and our subsequent enjoyment of the flavour, goes on to influence the foods we might choose in the future. In the simplest terms: if you eat something orange and you love it, you are more likely to seek out orange-flavoured foods as among your favourites in the future.

Of course, the significance of a bake's presentation is only part of the flavour journey. When our judges take their first bite, they want something that lives up to the presentation. Layering flavours – bringing together different but complementary ingredients, and even adding or cooking them in an order that best suits the twist they bring to the bake – will have a much better chance of eliciting the elusive Hollywood Handshake than something that has focused on style over substance. With every chew, Paul and Prue look for an added dimension to that first mouthful, and a lingering delight that begs for more when the first mouthful has gone.

Our bakers know this, of course, and perhaps that's exactly why the tent has been such a hive of exciting (dare we say it *groundbreaking*) flavour-layering over the years. With every series, established favourite flavours meet new and exciting ingredients, often from all over the world. In this book, fragrant rose pairs with juicy raspberry in a sumptuous vegan drip cake (see page 33), and appears again with warming spices in a Sri Lankan fruit cake (see page 45); nutty, earthy tahini lavishes a chocolate and caramel tart (see page 227); citrussy yuzu (think lemon, lime and grapefruit all in one) hunkers down with blackberry (see page 129) – and so much more. Where once flavour pairing was limited to ingredients that grow together in the same soils and climates, our global community enables us to try combinations that reflect our mingling culinary heritage – and our *Great British Bake Off* bakes are all-the-more interesting for it.

If this book is to be a celebration of *Bake Off*'s favourite flavours, though, there have to be some classic flavour pairings, too: pistachio and rose, strawberry and cream, chocolate and vanilla, chocolate and cherry, coffee and ginger, lemon and coconut, plum and custard, banana and caramel, blue cheese and apple… the list goes on. Throughout the book, the 80 recipes – some from the series, some from our dedicated behind-the-scenes team and some from the homes of our 2022 bakers – make sure that flavours are not only perfectly matched, but delicately balanced to bring a tingle to the tongue of even the most hard-to-impress judge.

USING THIS BOOK

How do you break down flavour so that you can have neat chapters in a book? At *GBBO* Book HQ this question perplexed us for a good while before we settled on the collection you have today: Spicy & Aromatic (think spices, herbs, flowers…), Tart & Tangy (sour fruits, sourdough…), Fresh & Fruity (soft fruits, dried fruits, stone fruits…),

Sweet & Sticky (toffee, caramel, honey…), Nutty & Earthy (root veg, nuts, seeds…) and Rich & Creamy (custard, tres leches, cheeses…) – a line-up that we hope broadly covers the favourite flavours from the *Bake Off* tent.

Of course, though, none of these is truly independent of another – throughout the book the bakes' main flavours mingle with flavours from other chapters to make sure that every recipe results in something beautifully layered and balanced. To help with this notion, each recipe is given three complementary flavour notes that appear in the footnote of every page. We hope this means that even if half your family is aching for sweet and sticky and the other half for something to give a tang, you'll be able to find a single bake to please everyone.

Throughout the book you'll find gluten-free and vegan labels at the top of the recipe lists to signpost the relevant free-from bakes. Even if you aren't specifically looking for a free-from idea, we really encourage you to try these recipes – they have been developed with every taste bud in mind and are no less flavourful than the other bakes.

Finally, at the end of the book, as well as a standard index, we've provided a visual thematic index – all the recipes re-grouped by type of bake, so that if, in the end, it's a citrussy biscuit you're looking for, you'll know at a glance where to find it. Happy baking!

A BIT ABOUT FLAVOUR

It's all very well providing you with recipes that already offer flavour combinations that work together, but we also want to inspire you to experiment with flavour yourself. If we've used pistachio, we want you to have the confidence to switch it out for walnut, or peanut, or almond... whichever sings to your own favourite flavours. To do that confidently, it helps to understand more about how flavour works, and why some flavours work together and some don't. Furthermore, knowing how the way you cook an ingredient can change its profile and how to serve it at its best are also important for optimising flavour.

Taste vs flavour

Though we may use the terms synonymously, taste and flavour are not the same thing. We discern taste on our tongue – it's what our taste buds tell us and is, more or less, limited to just five 'basic' tastes. These are sweet, salt, sour, bitter and umami (a savouriness that you'll find in, for example, meat, aged cheeses, anchovies, miso and anything with soy in it). The taste buds pick out these basic tastes for two important reasons: first, they help tell the brain whether or not the food is safe and nutritious to eat (a life-saving skill for our hunter-gatherer ancestors) and, then, they help prepare our body to metabolise the food in the right way (umami, for example, is thought to signal that protein-containing foods are likely on the way, triggering the production of enzymes that enable us to make good use of our food). All that might sound a bit dull for deciding how to make the tastiest layer cake for your friend's birthday, so thank goodness we've evolved to discern flavour.

Flavour is far more about your nose – it's what gives our food all its accents and nuances and it is largely a result of aroma. At the back of your throat and into your olfactory cavity are thousands of tiny receptors that, as you chew, pick up on the smell of your food. This, combined with the basic tastes, leads to what we know of as flavour. Astonishingly, some experts think that olfaction (our sense of smell) can account for up to 80 per cent of our flavour experience. As a rule of thumb, then, if something smells good together, the likelihood is that it will taste good together, too.

Building flavour

We don't necessarily suggest that you need to get down to the nitty gritty of flavour compounds in certain foods to decide whether or not they will work together in your bake (although that's exactly what some of our bakers do), but Nature does provide some answers as to why some foods work together particularly well. Take nutmeg and parsnips. Want to give a comforting cottage pie a twist? Try a mashed parsnip topping instead of mashed potato, and lace it with a little nutmeg. This combination tastes heavenly because both nutmeg and parsnip contain the compound myristicin, which contributes to the delicate, underlying anise flavour in each (myristicin is also in dill, fennel and parsley). Combining them encourages those flavour notes to sing together. The same is true for thousands of other ingredient pairings – shared flavour compounds bring harmony.

Which brings us on to the notion of flavour 'hints', the accents of flavour that complement or enrich a particular ingredient in a bake.

Let's start with cake. In a cake, more often than not, the sponge is the backdrop. A hint of lemon or vanilla in your sponge is largely there to bring out the citrus or vanilla notes in the fillings or toppings. The citrus can balance the sweetness in a fruit syrup or add berry notes that complement layers of sponge lavished with raspberries, blackberries and strawberries. The same goes for pastry: a pastry case laced with tahini (a paste made from sesame seeds) in a caramel and chocolate tart (see page 227) brings a bitter nuttiness that takes the edge off the intense sweetness in the caramel, but also enhances the vanilla notes in the chocolate.

Of course, it's not as simple as saying apples do this and lemons do that. Varieties of the same ingredient can bring accents of flavour that really change the way a bake tastes. The part of the ingredient you use can make a difference, too. The juice or flesh of a blood orange brings a sweeter berry flavour to a bake than that of a navel orange, whose sharp citrus tang is almost lip-puckering. Grate in the zest, and the tartness gives way to bitterness, which is perfect for balancing out the sugar in a sweet bake. Interestingly, as an aside, lemon and white chocolate are a natural pairing (and a favourite in the *Bake Off* tent), and that's because white chocolate (which is made with cocoa butter, the fat extracted from the beans that make milk and dark chocolate) has its own lemony notes.

Next, think about how you treat your ingredients as you incorporate them into your bakes and how that might change their flavour nuances. Nuts and seeds make a good example. Raw nuts, chopped or ground and added as they are, often have a creamy, fresh, grassy flavour. However, as soon as they are toasted in a hot pan or roasted in the oven, the flavour profile is 'switched on' and they bring something far richer and deeper, and more... well, nutty. In fact, this effect is replicated in myriad protein-containing foods when we cook them and is called the 'Maillard reaction'. The reaction begins when a food reaches an internal temperature of about 140°C and begins to brown. As the temperature increases, the amino acids and sugars in the protein collide and combine, bringing deeper, sweeter and caramelised flavours to the food. It's worth noting, though, that the effect is optimised at an internal temperature of about 160°C, after which food will begin to burn and turn bitter – so always keep an eagle eye on nuts when you're toasting them.

Finally, consider the temperature of your bakes when you serve them. For flavour to sing, it needs usually to be somewhere between room temperature and warm/hot but not scorching. Chilling dumbs down flavour (sweetness in particular, which is why ice cream is made with a *lot* of sugar, but isn't necessarily that sweet on the tongue) and anyone who has ever made the mistake of launching into their pizza straight from the oven will know that the flavour of the tangy sourdough crust and melty, salty cheese topping is entirely lost to a tongue screaming in pain. So, when a recipe encourages you to serve warm or at room temperature, or to remove a chilled tart from the fridge for 20 minutes before plating, don't be tempted to ignore the advice – it's the best way to get the best flavour out of all the hard work that got you there in the first place.

OUR WHEEL OF FAVOURITE FLAVOURS

This wheel picks out the main favourite flavours that appear in the recipes in this book, all grouped according to our chapters and their predominant flavour profile. Of course, though, a banana is sweet and sticky, but arguably it's also rich and creamy, or fruity; dill is aromatic, but it's also earthy; rhubarb is fruity, but it's also tart and tangy – and so on. Use the wheel as a starting point to explore ingredients and flavour, and think about how one flavour might evolve into the next in a continuous wheel of baking deliciousness.

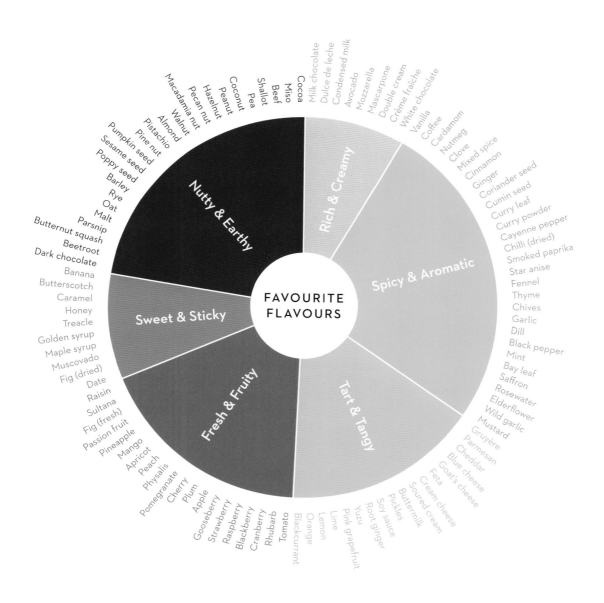

Abdul, 29
London
Electronics Engineer

Carole, 59
Dorset
Supermarket Cashier

Dawn, 60
Bedfordshire
IT Manager

Raised in Saudi Arabia to Pakistani parents, Abdul is the middle of three children – and the one who got into trouble for pulling apart the electronic devices around the house! All's well that ends well, though, and he is now an electronics engineer, dividing his time between London and Cambridge. A keen salsa dancer, and a self-confessed space nerd, his interest in baking began when he and his graduate colleagues baked for each other to brighten up their daily coffee breaks. He applies his precision thinking to the chemistry of creating bakes. Among his favourite flavours is matcha.

Born and bred in the West Country, Carole lives on a Dorset hillside with her husband, Michael. Her segment on a local radio show is called 'Compost Carole' – during which she shares her gardening know-how with listeners. Carole brings the artistry that she uses in her garden to her baking – creating colourful and eclectic bakes that are inspired by her passion for horticulture. She began her dedicated baking journey with a first birthday cake for her eldest granddaughter, Maisie. Since then, she has refined her skills, using YouTube to teach herself the finer techniques of decoration. Her favourite flavours are fruity and punchy.

The eldest of three children, Dawn lives with her partner, Trevor (the self-styled person who tidies up the kitchen after her!) and is mother to three, step-mother to two, and gran or step-gran to four. Describing herself as an artist in and out of the kitchen, Dawn loves the challenge of an illusion cake (the more impossible-sounding, the better), favouring whacky and intricate designs that allow her to express her creative talent. She prides herself on her steady hand and attention to detail, especially when it comes to the intricacy required for lace patterns on biscuits. Her favourite flavours are lemon, salted caramel and anything nutty.

James, 25
Cumbria
Nuclear Scientist

Proud kilt-wearer James grew up near Glasgow and moved to England after university. He is a self-proclaimed board-game geek and loves horror films from the 70s and 80s. An avid music fan, he has taught himself to play the piano. James believes that his love of science and art combine in his baking – which is now significantly better than it was during his childhood when he was burning pancakes in his mother's kitchen! He enjoys the technical side of baking, but is in his element when he makes his bakes his own, with his signature 'child-friendly horror' style and adorable decoration. His favourite flavours are anything autumnal, such as mixed spice, apples and caramel.

Janusz, 34
East Sussex
Personal Assistant to Head Teacher

Janusz grew up in Poland and moved to the UK 10 years ago. He is now living on the southeast coast with his boyfriend, Simon, and their sausage dog, Nigel. Apart from baking, Janusz's passions include internet culture, watching drag (he even bought his boyfriend a statue of Ru Paul) and collecting movie props. He was inspired to bake by his mother, who always baked on a Saturday – a tradition Janusz continued when he moved away from home to go to university. He describes his baking style as 'cartoon-like, colourful and camp', and loves working Polish ingredients into British staples. His favourite flavours are ginger and chocolate.

Kevin, 33
Lanarkshire
Music Teacher

Surrounded by family and much-loved animals, Kevin is devoted to his nearest and dearest and spends as much time as possible with his wife, Rachel, and his sisters and their partners, laughing, eating and playing board games. A talented musician, who not only teaches but also performs, Kevin is principally a saxophonist, but is accomplished at the flute, the piano and the clarinet too. He began baking when he was 17. His ethos in the kitchen is to use the best, seasonal ingredients and to spend time refining technique – with these in hand, he believes the presentation will take care of itself. He loves interesting combinations of fruits, herbs, nuts and spices.

Maisam, 18
Greater Manchester
Student & Sales Assistant

Originally from Libya, Maisam has lived in the UK since she was nine. She speaks five languages (English, Arabic, Amazigh, Spanish and Turkish) and aims to make that seven by the time she turns 20. Maisam has a strong creative streak, spending her spare time photographing still-lifes and the world around her. She has been baking since she was about 13 years old, and she loves the science required to get a bake right – often trying something multiple times until it is perfect. Her favourite flavours are inspired by her Mediterranean heritage – she loves the tang of olives, the sweetness of dates and the nuttiness of sesame seeds.

Maxy, 29
London
Architectural Assistant

Swedish-born Maxy studied fine art and went on to achieve a Masters degree in Architecture, pausing her final qualifications to raise her two daughters, Tyra and Talia. She has DIY-ed every corner of her flat – from laying the flooring and resurfacing the balcony to painting the walls and hanging her own artwork. She began baking five years ago, with the arrival of her first daughter, and uses her strong artistic skills to create beautifully decorated celebration cakes. Her favourite flavours link to her Scandinavian upbringing – the sweet and delicate spice of cardamom and saffron buns and cinnamon rolls.

Rebs, 23
County Antrim
Masters Student

Rebs spent her childhood in the countryside in Northern Ireland and loves everything to do with Irish culture – she can Irish dance and play the tin whistle. Her earliest baking memory is of being a child, aged only three years old, helping her mum in the kitchen, and of eating her granny's renowned lemon meringue pies! More recently, she returned to baking as a way to unwind from the stress of a busy life in the tech world. Flavour is paramount for her, and she has more recently started to play around with Middle Eastern ingredients – in a nod to her boyfriend Jack's Turkish family heritage.

Sandro, 30
London
Nanny

Sandro was born in Angola, but fled the Angolan war with his mum when he was two, settling then in London. Passionate about fitness, Sandro is a keen boxer – with a background in ballet and breakdance! When Sandro was 21 his father passed away and he turned to baking as a form of therapy. Now, though, he lives and breathes it, and is often found rustling up bakes in a relaxed vibe with the telly on, or running virtual baking classes for children with autism. He likes to infuse his bakes with flavours from his Angolan heritage – the spice of paprika paired with tangy cheese, and sweet bakes smothered in sticky dulce de leche.

Syabira, 32
London
Cardiovascular
Research Associate

Malaysian-born Syabira is one of seven children. She moved to the UK in 2013 to study for her PhD and is now happily settled in London with her boyfriend, Bradley. She loves gaming and often spends evenings playing an online World-War-II simulation game, which she credits with teaching her about leadership in the real world. Syabira started baking relatively recently – in 2017 – with a red velvet cake, which reminded her of the treats she shared with her friends back home. She is all for giving Malaysian flavour twists to British classics – chicken rendang Cornish pasties are a particular favourite.

Will, 45
London
Charity Director

One of three children, Will grew up just outside Bristol, before leaving for university in Liverpool. Now he lives in London with his wife, three children and a cat called Tiggy. When he's not hanging out with his kids, Will loves DIY and carpentry, which indulges his background in architecture, and cooking up new and exciting dishes in the kitchen. His passion for baking began when he was two, when his mum would give him her pastry trimmings to turn into little jam tarts. Intrigued by the technical side of baking, he is a particular fan of using yeast – and not just in bread! His favourite flavours are salted caramel and paprika (but not at the same time).

A Baker's Kitchen

You don't need a lot to be able to bake. With an oven, scales, a bowl and a baking sheet you can bake bread, biscuits, scones... add a couple of cake tins and a wooden spoon and you can whip up a cake. So, although the following list seems long, please don't feel overwhelmed – build up your kitchen gradually, as you build up your skills.

Baking beans
An essential to keep the base of a pastry case flat and the side upright while you blind bake (that is, bake it without its filling). Ceramic baking beans intended for this purpose are handy and reusable, but uncooked dried beans, lentils or rice will work well multiple times, too. Just make sure you store them in a labelled jar afterwards as, once baked, they won't be suitable for eating.

Baking paper and liners
These help prevent sticking. Choose non-stick baking paper (sometimes called parchment). Greaseproof is less sturdy and has a waxy coating that doesn't stand up as well to the heat of the oven. Reusable silicone liners are more expensive, but are easy to use, can be cut to fit your tins and trays (or buy them ready-cut) and can be wiped clean. With proper care they can last for life.

Baking sheets and trays
A baking sheet is flat with only one raised edge for gripping, making it good for bakes (such as biscuits and pavlovas) that you might want to slide to another surface. A baking tray has a rim or shallow edge all the way around. Aim to have at least one heavy-duty baking sheet, and two or three trays or lightweight sheets.

Baking tins
Always use the baking tin that's specified in the recipe as the quantities and baking time have been calculated accordingly. (See the 'You Will Need' lists at the end of each set of ingredients.) A really solid, good-quality tin will withstand repeated baking without scorching or losing its shape. Clean and dry your tins thoroughly after you've used them. Occasionally, a recipe will call for a specialist tin or mould, but in general the following will see you through nicely:

Loaf tins are essential for neat, brick-shaped breads and cakes. They're available in a variety of sizes, but the most-used sizes are 450g (measuring about 19 x 12.5 x 7.5cm and also sold as 1lb loaf tins) and 900g (measuring about 26 x 12.5 x 7.5cm, and also sold as 2lb loaf tins). Heavy-duty loaf tins won't dent or warp and will give you a better crust than equivalent silicone versions.

Muffin or cupcake tins are what you need for small bakes. They are usually 6- or 12-hole. Non-stick and silicone versions will produce equally good results, so choose what suits you best.

Pudding moulds (mini ones) are a bit of a luxury, but handy for making individual dessert bakes, such as individual chocolate fondants and sponge puddings.

Sandwich (or sponge) tins are essential. Aim to own two 20cm-diameter sandwich or round cake tins, each 4–5cm deep. A third tin is useful for baking American-style layer cakes.

Springform (or springclip) tins are deep metal tins with a spring release. Use them for cakes, tortes, pies, cheesecakes and pull-apart bread rolls because they won't damage the side of a fragile bake as you remove it. *Swiss roll tins* are rectangular (usually 20 x 30cm or 23 x 33cm) and about 2cm deep.

Tart and tartlet tins, available with fluted and straight sides, give the most professional results when made from sturdy metal, such as anodised aluminium. Choose non-stick, loose-bottomed versions for the best results.

Traybake tins are square or rectangular and about 4cm deep, and are used for brownies, shortbread and all traybakes. Buy loose-bottomed tins to help free your bakes easily.

Bowls

For versatility, sturdiness and durability, heatproof glass and stainless steel bowls are good choices for mixing and whisking, and glass or ceramic are best for melting ingredients over hot water, although plastic bowls are cheaper. (Note, too, that ceramic bowls look pretty but can be heavy.) A very large bowl with a snap-on lid is useful for mixing and rising bread doughs. Incidentally, make your bowls non-slip by resting them on a damp cloth as you mix.

Cake-decorating turntable

A cake-decorating turntable makes easy work of smoothing out buttercreams or ganache around the sides of a cake. It's especially handy if you're going for a semi-naked effect (such as in the Raspberry & Rose Drip Cake on page 33) or perhaps an ombre effect.

Cooling/wire racks

A large wire rack with legs allows air to circulate around and underneath a bake as it cools, avoiding any sogginess. A clean wire grill-pan rack makes a good improvisation, if necessary.

Dough scraper

One of the cheapest and most useful pieces of equipment, the dough scraper helps to scoop, scrape and divide bread dough, and makes easy work of cleaning bowls and worktops.

Electric stand mixers, processors and whisks

Lots of the recipes in the book call for a helping hand from an electric gadget, such as a stand mixer. Although these can make life easier, if you're new to baking, don't feel you have to rush out and buy one. Most of the recipes in the book can be made with muscle power – just remember to keep going (with a hand whisk, a wooden spoon, or your bare hands), until you reach the consistency described in the method.

A large-capacity stand mixer is a good investment if you do a lot of baking. Use the whisk attachment for meringues, buttercreams and light sponge mixtures; the paddle or beater attachment for heavier mixtures, such as richer cakes, choux pastry, and savarin-type enriched doughs; and the dough hook for mixing, then kneading bread doughs. A spare bowl will help with multi-element sponges.

An electric hand whisk is a good, versatile choice if you want to make whisked mixtures, creamed sponges, meringues, buttercreams or batter, or mixtures whisked over heat.

A hand-held stick blender (often with a whisk attachment, too) is good for smoothing out fruit sauces and crème pâtissière.

A food processor makes light work of blending fat and flour to make pastry. Use the 'pulse' button to avoid any overworking. It's also good for finely chopping nuts and herbs (try a mini version for small quantities).

Hand or balloon whisk
A wire hand whisk can be balloon-shaped or flat; a hand-held rotary whisk consists of a pair of beaters in a metal frame. Any of these is essential, even if you have an electric version.

Knives
The better the knife, the better your knife skills. Stainless steel knives are easy to keep clean, but need to be sharpened regularly; carbon-steel knives are more expensive, but easier to keep sharp. Gather a medium knife, about 20cm long; a small knife (useful for pastry work, trimming edges, and making decorations); and a good-quality serrated bread knife (for sawing through crusts).

Lame
A lame is useful for scoring bread – it's like a double-sided razor blade on a handle.

Measuring equipment
Baking is a science and, for perfect results, precision is essential. The following pieces of measuring equipment are must-haves for guaranteed success.
Digital scales are particularly useful. As well as weighing tiny ingredients and switching easily between units, you can 'zero' ingredients you've already weighed, then add further ingredients to the same bowl, weighing each as you go.
Measuring jugs, even if you have digital scales, are a must. Pick a heat-resistant and microwave-safe jug that starts at 50ml (ideally) or 100ml, and goes up to 2 litres.
Measuring spoons do a far better job than everyday spoons (teaspoons, dessert spoons,

tablespoons), which will give inconsistent results. Spoon measures in this book are level, not heaped or rounded, unless specified.

Metal spoon
A large, long metal spoon is invaluable for folding wet ingredients into dry.

Oven thermometer
Built-in oven thermostats can be inconsistent between brands and will become less efficient with age, so an oven thermometer is a good way to make sure your oven reaches the right temperature before you bake, as well as to identify the hot and cool spots to avoid uneven bakes. If you don't have a thermometer, get to know your oven, then increase or decrease the temperature or baking time accordingly to get the right results.

Palette knife
An offset palette knife (with a kink near the handle) is useful for spreading icings and delicate mixtures where you need a smooth, precise result. A straight palette knife is good for lifting and moving bakes from one surface to another.

Pastry brush
Opt for a heat- and dishwasher-proof, medium pastry brush – essential both for glazing pastry and bread and for brushing down sugar crystals in a pan as you make caramel.

Pastry cutters
Pick a double-sided (plain on one side, fluted on the other) nest of metal cutters. A pizza wheel-cutter is handy for cutting straight lines. Shaped cutters are infinite and lovely, too.

Piping bags and nozzles

The recipes in this book use both reusable and paper piping bags in various sizes. Piping nozzles range from wide, round tips for piping choux pastry and meringue, to star-shaped for icings, to small writing tips for delicate work. Set the nozzle in the bag, stand it in a jug, tall glass or a mug for support, then fill. Twist the top before you pipe to stop the contents of the bag escaping the wrong way. To keep things simple, we use small, medium and large when referring to the size of piping nozzles. As a guide, a small piping nozzle is about 5mm in diameter (a size 1 or 2 writing nozzle); a medium nozzle, about 1cm; and a large nozzle, about 1.5cm. An open star nozzle gives less distinct peaks and troughs in the piping (as in an iced gem) than a closed star nozzle.

Proving bags

Although not strictly necessary (covering with oiled cling film will do), proving bags (ideally two) are reusable, which makes them kinder to the environment. Lightly oil the inside of the bag, then slide in your dough on a baking tray and inflate the bag a little to stop the dough sticking to it as it rises.

Rolling pin

A fairly heavy wooden pin about 6–7cm in diameter and without handles will make the easiest work of rolling out pastry.

Rubber spatula

A strong and flexible spatula is useful for mixing, folding and scraping with ease.

Sieve

Every baker needs a sieve – to combine flour with raising agents; remove lumps from icing and sugars; and for straining and puréeing. Go for a large metal sieve that will sit over your largest mixing bowl for sifting tasks, and a smaller, tea-strainer-sized one for dusting.

Sugar thermometer/Cooking thermometer

Essential for sugar work (and deep-frying), a sugar thermometer will ensure your sugar reaches the correct temperature if, for example, you're making caramel or nougat, or tempering chocolate – among other baking tasks. Pick one that's easy to read and can clip onto the side of the pan. A thermometer with a probe will help you to measure the internal temperatures of your bakes for doneness, too.

Timer

A digital kitchen timer with seconds as well as minutes (and a loud bell) is essential baking equipment – don't rely on just your oven timer. Set the timer for a minute or two less than the suggested time in your recipe (especially if you're uncertain of your oven) – you can always increase the time your bake is in the oven if it's not quite done yet.

Wooden spoon

Cheap, heat-resistant, and safe on non-stick pans, a wooden spoon mixes, beats, creams and stirs – the essentials of good baking. (You can even use the handle to shape brandy snaps and tuiles.) Store your savoury and sweet spoons separately, as wood can absorb strong flavours.

Zester

A long-handled zester is the best and quickest way to remove the zest from citrus fruits (use unwaxed citrus fruits for zesting). Pick one that's sturdy and easy to hold.

A Baker's Larder

Most of the bakes throughout this book use ingredients that are easy to find and store. Keep the following in your store cupboard and, whether you need to whip up something for a cake sale, find an activity for the kids for the afternoon, or create a dinner-party showstopper, you'll be ready to start baking. As a rule of thumb: the best-quality ingredients tend to give the best results.

Baking powder, bicarbonate of soda and cream of tartar

Chemical raising agents, all these ingredients increase the lightness and volume of cakes and small bakes, and some types of biscuit and pastry. Always use the amount given in the recipe – but check the date stamps before you start, as raising agents will lose their potency over time. If you've run out of baking powder, you can easily make your own: for 1 teaspoon of baking powder combine ½ teaspoon of cream of tartar with ¼ teaspoon of bicarbonate of soda. If you are making a gluten-free bake, bear in mind that baking powder should be gluten-free, but some manufacturers add filling agents that may contain gluten. Always check the label.

Butter and other fats

Most of the recipes in this book use unsalted butter, as it has a delicate flavour, adds a good, even colour (perhaps because it contains less whey than salted), and allows you to season your bake to taste yourself, as relevant. Store butter tightly wrapped in the fridge, well away from strong flavours. When relevant, a recipe will tell you whether to use butter chilled (from the fridge) or softened at room temperature (in that case, don't be tempted to soften it in the microwave – you're looking for a texture that yields easily when pressed with a finger, but holds the shape, not melted). Cubed butter enables you to add small amounts at a time and makes the butter easier to combine with the other ingredients. *Lard, from pigs,* gives a short, flaky texture to traditional hot-water-crust pastry so that it bakes to a crisp, golden finish. White solid vegetable fat is a good alternative.

Dairy-free spreads, made from vegetable and sunflower oils, make good substitutes in most recipes that require softened or room-temperature butter, but always check the label to make sure it's good for baking beforehand. Some are made specifically for baking and you can use them straight from the fridge. They give good results, but may lack that buttery flavour. Avoid spreads designed for use on bread/crackers – they contain too much water and not enough fat to make good baking ingredients.

Solid coconut oil is a good option for dairy-free and vegan recipes, but isn't a like-for-like butter substitute.

Suet, from cows in its non-vegetarian form, gives a light, soft pastry rather than a very crisp or flaky one. Suet is more solid than butter or lard and melts much more slowly, forming tiny pockets in the dough as it cooks. Most supermarkets sell vegetarian suet, too.

Oil often pops up in bakes these days. Vegetable oil is a good all-rounder, but in baking, sunflower oil gives the best results as it's especially light and mildly flavoured.

Chocolate

Chocolate is a must in baking – from shards and shavings to ganache and buttercream, it features in many of the recipes in this book. **Dark chocolate,** with around 54% cocoa solids, is the kind most used in these recipes as it gives a good balance of flavour. Some recipes recommend 70% dark, which is a little less sweet. Chocolate with a higher percentage (75% and above) may be too bitter and dry for general baking.

Milk chocolate has a much milder and sweeter flavour – choose a good-quality favourite, and expect the best results from milk chocolate with good amounts of cocoa solids.

White chocolate doesn't contain any cocoa solids, just cocoa butter. Look out for brands with 30% or more cocoa butter as a measure of quality. White chocolate sets less firmly than dark or milk chocolate owing to the higher fat content, and melts at a lower temperature, so take care as it easily scorches and becomes unusable.

Cocoa powder

A dark, unsweetened powder made from pure cocoa beans after they have been dried and had all the cocoa butter removed. Cocoa powder is very bitter, strongly flavoured and gives a powerful hit. Never substitute cocoa powder with drinking chocolate, which contains milk powder and sugar, as well as cocoa powder itself.

Cream

Chill cream thoroughly before whipping (in hot weather, also chill the bowl and whisk).

Buttermilk, sometimes labelled 'cultured buttermilk', is low-fat or non-fat milk plus a bacterial culture to give it an acidic tang. It is often used along with bicarbonate of soda to add lightness as well as flavour to scones and cakes.

Crème fraîche is a soured cream with a creamy, tangy flavour. It won't whip, but you can use it for fillings, toppings and serving.

Double cream contains at least 48% butterfat. It whips well and has a richer flavour than whipping cream. The extra-rich type of double cream available is designed for spooning, rather than for whipping or ganache. Lactose-free and soy-based dairy-free creams can give varied results, and are usually unsuitable for whipping.

Single cream contains 18% butterfat and is good for adding to sauces and fillings, for adding richness to rubbed-in mixtures, or for pouring over desserts and pastries.

Soured cream has only 18% butterfat. It is made by introducing a bacterial culture to cream, giving a naturally sour tang.

Whipping cream usually contains at least 36% butterfat and is designed to whip well without being overly rich.

Dried fruit

Store dried fruit out of direct sunlight and tightly sealed in containers. Vine fruit, such as raisins, sultanas and currants, have a long shelf-life, but will always be best bought when you need them. Soft-dried apricots, as well as dried figs, cranberries, blueberries, sour cherries, and dates, can replace vine fruits in many recipes. They add sweetness and moisture, which is useful if you want to reduce refined sugar.

Eggs

When it comes to eggs, size really does matter. Unless otherwise stated, all the recipes in this book use medium eggs. If the eggs are too small, a sponge may not rise properly and look thin or dry; too big and a pastry or bread dough may be too wet or soft to handle.

For baking, use eggs at room temperature, which means taking them out of the fridge 30–60 minutes before you start cooking. If you forget, pop them into a bowl of lukewarm water for a couple of minutes.

Spare egg whites will keep for 3–4 days in a sealed container or jar in the fridge, or for up to a month in the freezer (defrost overnight in the fridge before using; yolks can't be frozen).

Extracts and flavourings

Avoid synthetic flavourings as much as you can – they often have an aftertaste that will spoil your hard work balancing your flavours. Here's a guide to the best to use.

Almond extract may be pricey, but most recipes need only a few drops. Avoid anything marked 'flavouring'.

Ground spices are best when you use them fresh, but if you're storing them, do so in screw-topped jars, rather than open packets.

Vanilla is usually the most expensive flavouring used in baking, although you need only small amounts. Vanilla extract – labelled 'pure' or 'natural' – costs more than vanilla essence, which might contain artificial flavourings. Vanilla paste is made from the seeds of the pods and has a thicker texture and more concentrated flavour. Best of all, though, are vanilla pods, which you can split to scrape out the tiny seeds to flavour custards and fillings. Don't throw away the pods: rinse and dry them, then put them in a jar of caster sugar to make vanilla sugar.

Flour

Whether made from wheat or other grains, flour has to be the most valued ingredient in the baker's larder. Avoid poor-quality, out-of-date or stale flour, as this will affect the result and taste of the final bake. Always buy the best and freshest flour you can afford.

Cornflour is added to biscuits to give a delicate crumb, and used to thicken custard and crème pâtissière.

Gluten-free flours are wheat-free mixtures of several ingredients, including rice, potato, tapioca, maize, chickpea, broad bean, white sorghum or buckwheat – depending on the brand. Ready-mixed gluten-free flours sometimes suggest adding xanthan gum (a powder sold in small tubs) to improve the texture and crumb of your bake – check the packet and, if your flour mixture doesn't already include it, add 1 teaspoon of xanthan gum per 150g gluten-free flour. Some gluten-free flours need a little more liquid than wheat flour doughs, so you can't substitute them exactly, but it is well worth experimenting.

Plain flour is a type of wheat flour used for making pastry, pancakes and rich fruit cakes, for example, and has no added raising agents.

Rye flour has a deep, dark flavour that works well in breads, particularly sourdoughs. It's low in gluten, which makes it harder to knead than wheat flours, and the dough rises less well. Available as wholegrain and a finer 'light' rye, which has had some of the bran sifted out, it is useful for crackers and adding to wheat flour for savoury pastry recipes.

Self-raising flour has added baking powder and gives a light, risen texture to sponges. If you run out of self-raising flour you can make your own: add 4 teaspoons of baking powder to every 225g plain flour, sifting them together a couple of times. Sponge self-raising flour is more expensive than regular self-raising, but is slightly 'softer' and silkier.

Semolina flour is a slightly gritty, pale yellow flour made from durum wheat, and is often used for pasta and Italian-style breads (as well as semolina pudding).

Speciality wheat flours are created from wheat varieties that are specifically grown to make flour for baking ciabatta, pizza bases, and baguettes.

Spelt flour comes from the same family as wheat, but has a slightly different genetic make-up and a richer and more nutty flavour – it is good for most recipes that call for flour, except very delicate biscuits and sponges.

Stoneground flour means that the grain (wheat, rye, spelt and so on) is milled between large stones instead of steel rollers, giving a coarser texture and fuller flavour.

Strong bread flour is made from wheat with a higher ratio of protein to starch than the cake and pastry flours. This increased ratio is crucial to bread-making: as you knead the dough, the protein develops into strands of gluten that stretch as the gases produced by the yeast expand, enabling the dough to rise. Strong bread flour has about 12–16% protein, which is ideal for most breads. Extra-strong or Canadian strong flour has even more (15–17%) – good for bagels or larger loaves.

Wholemeal or wholegrain flours are made from the complete wheat kernel, making them far more nutritious than white flours (which are made using 75% of the cleaned wheat kernel, and have most of the wheat bran and wheatgerm removed). The small specks of bran in these flours mean that they give a dough that rises less well than one made with all white flour. Wholemeal plain flour has been milled to make it lighter and more suitable for making pastry and cakes.

Nuts

Buy nuts in small quantities to use up quickly (always before the use-by date) – the high oil content means that once opened, nuts can quickly turn rancid. If you're storing them, do so in an airtight container in a cool, dark place. Most nuts benefit from being lightly toasted before use, to impart a richer, nuttier flavour to the finished bake.

Almonds are incredibly versatile – ground, chopped, flaked (toasted and untoasted) and whole (blanched or unblanched). To blanch (remove the skins) yourself, put the nuts in a small pan, add water to cover and bring to the boil. Remove the pan from the heat and drain, then slip the nuts out of their casings. Dry on kitchen paper.

Hazelnuts are usually ready-blanched (without their brown papery skins) or ground.

Pistachios are easy to find shelled and unsalted, but they usually come with their papery skins attached. To reveal the deep-green colour of the nuts, carefully tip them into a pan of boiling water. Remove from the heat, leave for 1 minute, then drain. Transfer the nuts to a clean, dry tea towel and rub gently to loosen the skins, then peel if necessary. Ready-ground pistachios are also available these days.

Walnuts and pecans, usually halved or chopped, are interchangeable in most baking recipes as they share a similar texture and appearance (walnuts are slightly more bitter). Gently toasting walnuts and pecans in a medium-heat oven gives them a much deeper, richer flavour.

Sugar

Different sugars combine and interact with other ingredients in different ways, affecting the end results of the bake. Always use the sugar the recipe specifies. Sugar doesn't have a shelf-life and will keep indefinitely in an airtight container in a cool, dark place.

Caster sugar comes as both refined white and unrefined golden. White provides sweetness with a neutral colour and flavour that is, for example, perfect for white meringues or very pale sponges. Unrefined golden caster sugar has a slight caramel, rich flavour. Use it when having a warmer colour in your final bake is not an issue. The fine grains of caster sugar break down easily during beating or creaming with butter for sponges, melt quickly for lemon curd, and disappear in pastry mixtures.

Fondant icing sugar sets hard, so it's good for decorating as it doesn't smudge. It contains glucose syrup to give a smooth, glossy finish.

Granulated sugar, available as white or golden, has bigger grains that take longer to dissolve. Keep it for making sugar syrups and drizzles, and for sprinkling on top of bakes to give a satisfying crunch.

Icing sugar is also available as refined (white) and unrefined (golden). Again, the unrefined version has a pale caramel colour and flavour. Use white icing sugar for icings, fillings and frostings that need to be very pale or that are to be coloured with food colouring. Sift icing sugar before use to remove any lumps so that your icing is perfectly smooth.

Jam sugar contains added pectin to help jam set, making it good for making jams that use fruits without high natural levels of pectin – raspberries, strawberries, apricots and ripe cherries, among them.

Muscovado sugars come as light muscovado and dark muscovado. These add a stronger, warmer caramel or molasses flavour and darker colour to bakes, but they can make

them more moist and heavy. They are good in rich fruity cakes, gingerbreads, parkins, and spice cakes. Press out any lumps with the back of a spoon before using.

Syrup and treacle

Golden syrup and thick black treacle add a rich, toffee-ish flavour, as well as sweetness, to bakes. They can be difficult to measure if you're spooning out of a tin, so warm the measuring spoon in a mug of just-boiled water before scooping, or stand the syrup or treacle tin in a bowl of boiled water for a few minutes to loosen the stickiness. Easier is to use a squeezy bottle – many brands of golden syrup now come readily available this way (similarly, for honey). Maple syrup has a lighter texture than golden syrup, but a distinctive flavour that works particularly well with nuts, and, of course, over pancakes.

Yeast

Yeast is a living organism that makes bread doughs rise. It needs moisture, gentle warmth and flour (or sugar) to stimulate its growth and the production of carbon dioxide, which expands the dough. Some recipes use fast-action dried yeast, available in 7g sachets or in tubs as easy blend or instant dried yeast. Always weigh your yeast, unless it's the exact amount in a sachet, and add it to the flour, never to the liquid. If you add it with the salt, do so on opposite sides of the bowl, as salt (and too much sugar) retards its growth. (And hot water kills it.) If you use too much yeast, the dough will be lively, but the baked loaf may have a strong aftertaste and will go stale more quickly. If you use too little, the dough will take longer to rise and prove, but will have a deeper flavour and most likely keep better.

& MATIC

Raspberry & Rose Drip Cake

The raspberry and rose compôte in this cake hints at an English country garden, while the blend of almonds, coconut and rose has all the fragrant notes of Middle Eastern baking. A skim of vanilla buttercream and a chocolate, pink drip bring all the flavours together.

VEGAN
Serves: 10
Hands on: 50 mins + chilling
Bake: 30 mins

For the sponges
225g plain flour
¾ tsp baking powder
¾ tsp bicarbonate of soda
60g ground almonds
40g unsweetened
  desiccated coconut
200ml unsweetened
  almond milk
2 tbsp vegan
  coconut yogurt
1 tsp vanilla paste
1 tsp rosewater
juice of 1 lemon
60g unsalted vegan block
  butter, softened
125g caster sugar
25g light brown soft sugar

*For the raspberry
& rose compôte*
150g raspberries
100g caster sugar
½ tsp rosewater

For the vanilla frosting
400g icing sugar, sifted
125g vegan spread
1 tsp vanilla paste

Continues overleaf

1. Make the sponge. Heat the oven to 180°C/160°C fan/Gas 4. Sift the flour, baking powder, bicarbonate of soda, ground almonds and desiccated coconut into a large mixing bowl and stir to combine.

2. In a large jug, whisk together the almond milk, vegan coconut yogurt, vanilla, rosewater and lemon juice and leave to stand for 5 minutes, until curdled.

3. Beat the vegan butter and both sugars in a stand mixer fitted with the beater, on medium speed for 3–5 minutes, scraping down the inside of the bowl from time to time, until pale and creamy. With the mixer still running, gradually pour in the almond milk mixture, alternating with a spoonful of the flour mixture, and beat until everything is incorporated and smooth and creamy.

4. Divide the mixture equally between the prepared tins and spread level. Bake on the middle shelf for 30 minutes, until golden and risen, and a skewer inserted into the centre of each sponge comes out clean. Leave to cool completely in the tins.

5. Make the raspberry and rose compôte. While the sponges are baking, put the raspberries, caster sugar and rosewater in a saucepan over a medium–low heat and bring to a simmer, stirring gently. Simmer for 10 minutes, until the fruit breaks down and the juices become syrupy and reduce slightly. Leave to cool.

6. Make the vanilla frosting. Beat the icing sugar, vegan spread and vanilla in a stand mixer fitted with the beater, on medium speed for 2–3 minutes, until light and fluffy. Spoon the frosting into the medium piping bag fitted with a large plain nozzle.

7. Assemble the cake. Turn the sponges out of the tins. Secure one of the sponges on the cake board or plate with piped dots of frosting. Pipe a rim of frosting around the edge of the sponge and fill the centre with the compôte. Repeat with a second layer of sponge, frosting and compôte.

Continues overleaf

Raspberry & Rose Drip Cake *continued*

To decorate
100g vegan white chocolate, broken into pieces
drop of pink food-colouring gel
6 edible roses, stems removed
few raspberries
lavender buds (optional)

You will need
15cm round cake tins x 3, greased, then base-lined with baking paper
1 medium piping bag fitted with a large plain nozzle
15cm cake board or plate
cake scraper

8. Add the final layer of sponge and pipe a generous mound of frosting on top. Smooth the frosting with an offset spatula, spreading the surplus over the edge of the cake and down the sides until the sponge layers are covered. Scrape away the excess with a cake scraper to achieve a semi-naked finish. Chill the assembled cake for 30 minutes.

9. Make the decoration. While the cake is chilling, melt the vegan white chocolate in a heatproof bowl set over a pan of barely simmering water, stirring until smooth. Stir in a drop of pink colouring, then carefully remove the bowl from the pan and leave to cool slightly. Using a teaspoon, drizzle the pink melted chocolate around the top edge of the chilled cake, allowing it to drip down the side. Finally, gently place the roses on top, interspersed with a few raspberries (and lavender buds, if using), to decorate.

Paul's Spicy Beef Tacos

These give smokiness in the spiced beef, sharp heat from the pico de gallo, tangy creaminess in the refried beans, and butteriness in the guacamole – a flavour explosion in every bite. Make the tortillas ahead of time to allow for soaking.

GLUTEN-FREE

Makes: 8
Hands on: 1 hour 20 mins
   + overnight soaking
Cook: 40 mins

For the tortillas
100g yellow field corn
½ tsp food-safe
   calcium hydroxide
1 tsp salt
20g masa harina flour
OR: use 100g yellow
   masa flour instead of
   the yellow corn/calcium
   hydroxide/masa mixture

For the beef
1 tsp ancho chilli powder
½ tsp ground cumin
½ tsp smoked paprika
   powder
½ tsp cayenne pepper
1 tsp garlic powder
½ tsp dried oregano
½ tsp salt
1 tsp light brown soft sugar
2 bavette steaks
2 tbsp corn oil

For the pico de gallo
1 large ripe tomato,
   deseeded and finely diced
¼ small white onion,
   finely diced
½ jalapeño chilli, deseeded
   and finely chopped
juice of ½ lime
¼ tsp salt
1 tbsp finely chopped
   coriander leaves

Continues overleaf

1. Make the tortillas. Put the yellow field corn into a stainless steel or cast-iron pan, cover generously with water and stir in the calcium hydroxide until well mixed. Bring the mixture to the boil, then reduce the heat and simmer, stirring occasionally and adding more water as necessary to cover the corn, for 30 minutes, until the outer skin of the corn slips off easily, and the kernels are slightly cooked on the outside but remain dry and uncooked inside.

2. Remove the pan from the heat, cover with a lid and leave the corn to stand for at least 8 hours, or overnight. After soaking, drain the corn in a colander, then rinse it under cold running water, rubbing the kernels between your fingers to dislodge the skins, until the water runs clear. Leave to drain before use.

3. Tip the prepared corn into a food processor with the salt and 2 tablespoons of water and blitz for 3–5 minutes, scraping down the inside of the bowl from time to time, to a smooth, thick paste – it may still feel a little sandy, but not grainy.

4. Tip the corn paste onto the work surface and mix in the masa harina to form a dough that is neither sticky nor dry. Cover and leave to stand for 30 minutes. (If you're using just masa harina flour – instead of a combination of yellow field corn, calcium hydroxide and masa – put 100g masa flour in a mixing bowl with 140ml of water and the salt and stir until combined. Leave to stand for 20 minutes.)

5. Prepare the beef. While the corn mixture is resting, mix the dried spices, oregano, salt and sugar in a bowl. Rub the spice mixture all over the steaks, then marinate it at room temperature for 1 hour.

6. Make the pico de gallo. While the steaks are marinating, place the tomato, onion and chilli in a bowl. Stir in the lime juice and salt and leave the mixture to stand for at least 1 hour. Sir in the coriander.

Continues overleaf

For the refried beans
2 tsp corn oil
½ small white onion,
    finely chopped
1 garlic clove, crushed
¼ tsp chilli powder
¼ tsp ground cumin
¼ tsp salt
440g can of black
    beans, drained
juice of ½ lime

For the guacamole
1 tomato, deseeded
    and chopped
¼ red onion, finely
    chopped
½ serrano chilli, deseeded
    and finely chopped
juice of ½ lime
1 tbsp finely chopped
    coriander leaves
¼ tsp salt
2 ripe avocados, peeled,
    destoned and diced

To serve
25g queso fresco or feta
wedges of lime,
    for squeezing

You will need
heavy, flat casserole lid
    or tortilla press

7. Make the refried beans. Heat the oil in a pan over a medium heat, add the onion and cook, stirring occasionally, for 5 minutes, until softened. Add the garlic, chilli powder, cumin and salt and cook, stirring continuously, for 1 minute, until the cumin releases its aroma. Add the black beans and 4 tablespoons of water and bring the mixture to the boil. Reduce the heat slightly and simmer for 5 minutes, until heated through. Using a potato masher, mash half of the beans, then stir everything together and stir in the lime juice. Cover and set aside until ready you're to serve.

8. Make the guacamole. Place the tomato, onion, chilli, lime juice and coriander in a bowl and stir well to mix. Add the salt, then gently fold in the avocados. Taste and adjust the seasoning, if necessary.

9. Shape the tortillas. Divide the rested tortilla dough into 8 balls (about 30g each). Heat a dry, non-stick frying pan over a medium heat. On the work surface, place a ball of dough between two sheets of food-grade plastic or in a freezer bag large enough to accommodate the flattened tortilla. Using the flat lid of a casserole dish or tortilla press, press the dough flat into a thin 12cm disc.

10. Heat a dry frying pan over a medium heat. Peel off the plastic or take the tortilla out of the freezer bag and place it in the pan. Cook for 1–2 minutes, until the tortilla puffs up slightly. Flip the tortilla and cook the other side for another 2 minutes, until cooked through. Wrap the cooked tortilla in a clean tea towel to keep it warm while you press and cook the remainder to give 8 tortillas in total.

11. Cook the beef. Heat a large frying pan over a high heat and add the corn oil. Add the steaks and cook for 2–3 minutes on each side for medium rare. Remove the steaks from the pan and leave them to rest for 3 minutes, then thinly slice.

12. To serve, place the tortillas on a serving board and top each one with equal amounts of the refried beans and guacamole. Top with the sliced beef and pico de gallo, then crumble over the queso fresco or feta. Serve immediately with wedges of lime for squeezing.

Coffee & Ginger Layer Cake

Centuries ago, black coffee laced with ginger, cinnamon and cloves was a favourite in coffee houses; today, it might be reinvented as a ginger-spiced latte or in *qishr*, a Yemeni drink. This cake, then, gives a classic, well-loved pairing. Brush the top with some syrup from the ginger jar before adding the final frosting, for an extra hit.

Serves: 8–10
Hands on: 1 hour
Bake: 25 mins

For the sponges
225g unsalted butter,
    cubed and softened
100g golden caster sugar
100g light muscovado sugar
2 tbsp treacle
4 eggs, lightly beaten
225g plain flour
2 tsp baking powder
1 tsp bicarbonate of soda
1 tbsp ground ginger
1 tsp ground cinnamon
pinch of salt
2 tbsp whole milk
1 tbsp instant espresso
    powder, dissolved in
    1 tbsp boiling water
50g crystallised stem
    ginger, finely chopped,
    to decorate

For the buttercream
175g golden caster sugar
3 egg whites
200g unsalted butter,
    cubed and softened
1 tbsp instant espresso
    powder, dissolved in
    2 tsp boiling water
gold sprinkles, to decorate

You will need
20cm round cake tins x 3,
    greased, then base-lined
    with baking paper

1. Make the sponges. Heat the oven to 170°C/150°C fan/Gas 3. Beat the butter, both types of sugar and the treacle in a stand mixer fitted with the beater, on medium speed for 3–5 minutes, scraping down the inside of the bowl from time to time, until pale and creamy. Add the eggs, a little at a time, beating well between each addition.

2. Sift the flour, baking powder, bicarbonate of soda, spices and salt into the bowl and mix to just combine. Add the milk and coffee and mix again until smooth and thoroughly combined.

3. Divide the mixture equally between the lined tins and spread it level. Bake on the middle shelves for 20–25 minutes, until golden and risen, and a skewer inserted into the centres comes out clean. Leave the sponges to cool in the tins for 5 minutes, then carefully turn them out onto a wire rack to cool completely.

4. Make the buttercream. Using a balloon whisk, combine the caster sugar, egg whites and 2 tablespoons of water in large heatproof bowl. Set the bowl over a saucepan of simmering water and whisk continuously for 5 minutes, until the mixture is hot to the touch, thickened and leaves a ribbon trail when you lift the whisk. Scoop the mixture into the bowl of the stand mixer and whisk on medium speed for 5 minutes, scraping down the inside of the bowl from time to time, until stiff, glossy and cold.

5. Gradually add the butter, whisking well between each addition and scraping down the inside of the bowl from time to time. Add the coffee and mix again to combine.

6. Assemble the cake. Place 1 sponge on a serving plate and spread one third of the frosting over the top. Top with the second sponge and spread over half of the remaining frosting. Finish with the third sponge and the rest of the frosting, spreading it in decorative swirls. Decorate with the crystallised stem ginger and gold sprinkles.

Syabira's Swirled Curry Puffs

These popular Malaysian puffs are unusual in that they are made with two different types of dough, which are repeatedly rolled and folded so, when they are stuffed and deep-fried, they puff up beautifully. Coriander adds fragrance to my spiced, vegan filling – swap the potatoes for chicken or lamb if you prefer a meaty version. I make the puffs in a really big batch and store them in the freezer, so they're always ready to go when the mood strikes.

VEGAN
Makes: 40
Hands on: 2 hours + chilling
Cook: 50 mins

For the filling
4 garlic cloves, peeled and chopped
4 red onions (about 350g), roughly chopped
3.5cm piece of fresh ginger, peeled and roughly chopped
5 tbsp curry powder (mild, medium or hot)
1–3 tbsp chilli powder, depending on preferred level of spice
2g curry leaves
1 tsp salt
4 tbsp vegetable oil, plus extra for deep-frying
500g red-skinned potatoes, peeled and cut into 1cm cubes
½ handful of coriander, leaves roughly chopped

For dough A
280g plain flour
75g rice flour
30g vegetable spread
55ml vegetable oil
½ tsp salt
120–130ml chilled water

Continues overleaf

1. Make the filling. In a food processor, blend the garlic, onions, ginger, curry powder, chilli powder, curry leaves and salt into a paste.

2. Heat the vegetable oil in a saucepan on a medium heat and cook the curry paste until aromatic and the oil begins to split from the paste. Pour 500ml of water into the pan and bring it to the boil.

3. Add the potatoes, making sure they are submerged in the liquid, and boil for 10–15 minutes, until tender. Turn the heat to low and continue to cook for about 40 minutes, stirring occasionally, until the mixture has dried out and thickened. (The consistency of the spiced potato should be thick enough not to leak through the pastry when fried.) Remove the pan from the heat and stir in the coriander, then spoon the mixture into a bowl and set aside to cool completely while you make the two doughs.

4. Make dough A. Sift both types of flour into a heatproof mixing bowl and set aside. Heat the vegetable spread and oil in a small saucepan until the mixture comes to the boil, then carefully add the hot oil to the flour and mix with a wooden spoon to a crumbly consistency. Add the salt, then add enough of the chilled water to bring the mix together into a dough. Turn out the dough onto the work surface and knead it for 3–4 minutes, until smooth and soft. Cover and leave to rest in the fridge for 10 minutes.

5. Make dough B. Using a wooden spoon, mix the rice flour and vegetable spread together until combined and smooth. Shape the dough into a ball, cover and leave to rest in the fridge for 10 minutes.

Continues overleaf

Syabira's Swirled Curry Puffs *continued*

For dough B
155g rice flour
130g vegetable spread

You will need
**cooking thermometer
    or deep-fat fryer**

6. Shape the doughs. Once rested, remove dough A from the fridge and divide it into 8 equal portions. Roll each piece into a ball, place the balls on a baking tray and cover them with a damp tea towel to stop them drying out. Repeat with dough B, making 8 smaller balls.

7. Take a ball of dough A and, using your hands, flatten it out into a circle, about 10–12cm in diameter. Place a ball of dough B in the centre and wrap the outer dough around, pinching at the join to enclose the ball of dough B. Repeat with the rest of the dough B balls to make 8 parcels in total.

8. Lightly flour the work surface. Take one dough ball parcel and roll it out into a rectangle, about 15 x 8cm and 5mm thick. Starting from one short end, roll up the dough to form a tight cylinder. Rotate the dough cylinder 90 degrees and roll it out again to a thin strip, around 25–30 x 10cm. Roll the strip of dough up again from a short end to form a tight cylinder. Repeat for the remaining balls to give 8 dough cylinders. Transfer these to the freezer for 5 minutes to rest.

9. Assemble the puffs. Using a sharp knife, cut each cylinder of dough into 5 equal pieces, each about 2cm wide. Roll out each piece into an 8–10cm-diameter round, about 3mm thick. Put a heaped teaspoon of the cooled potato filling into the centre, then fold the dough over the filling into a half-moon shape and pleat the edges or press them down with a fork to seal in the filling. Repeat to make 40 puffs in total.

10. Deep-fry the puffs. Half fill a large saucepan with vegetable oil and heat it to 180°C on the cooking thermometer; or set your deep-fat fryer to heat the oil to 180°C. Deep-fry the puffs in batches of 3 or 4 at a time for 3–4 minutes, until each batch is golden brown and heated through.

11. Remove each batch with a slotted spoon and drain the puffs on a tray lined with kitchen paper to remove any excess oil. Make sure the oil comes up to temperature again before frying the next batch. Serve the puffs warm or at room temperature. They are especially delicious with chutney.

Sri Lankan Fruit Cake

The Sri Lankan equivalent of a British Christmas cake, this heavily spiced cake is fragrant with rose and citrus. It's usually made with Sri Lankan chow-chow, a fist-shaped squash that punches out its flavour when it's been preserved in sugar syrup. Here, we've used spicier preserved ginger in its place, but you can buy chow-chow online, if you prefer.

GLUTEN-FREE
Serves: 12+
Hands on: 1 hour + overnight soaking
Bake: 1½ hours

175g sultanas
175g raisins
100g glacé cherries, quartered
125g glacé pineapple, cut into small pieces
150g unsalted cashews, cut into small pieces
100g candied peel, finely chopped
100g stem ginger preserve
4 tbsp brandy
1 tbsp rosewater
2 tsp vanilla paste
finely grated zest and juice of ½ unwaxed orange
finely grated zest and juice of ½ unwaxed lemon
175g unsalted butter, cubed, at room temperature
75g light brown soft sugar
75g dark brown soft sugar
2 tbsp runny honey
6 eggs, separated
150g semolina
2 tsp ground cinnamon
1 tsp ground cardamom
¼ tsp ground nutmeg
¼ tsp ground cloves
pinch of salt
icing sugar, for dusting

You will need
1.75-litre bundt tin, brushed with butter and dusted with flour

1. Tip the sultanas, raisins, glacé cherries and pineapple, cashews and candied peel into a large mixing bowl. Add the ginger preserve, brandy, rosewater, vanilla, and orange and lemon zest and juice. Mix well to combine, cover and leave to soak overnight at room temperature.

2. When you're ready to bake, heat the oven to 150°C/130°C fan/Gas 2. Beat the butter, both types of sugar and the honey in a stand mixer fitted with the beater, on medium speed for 3–5 minutes, scraping down the inside of the bowl from time to time, until pale and creamy. One at a time, add the egg yolks, beating well between each addition. Fold in the dried fruit mixture until combined, then mix in the semolina and ground spices and salt.

3. In a separate bowl, whisk the egg whites and salt with an electric hand whisk until they form stiff peaks, then, one third at a time, fold the meringue into the cake mixture until just combined.

4. Spoon the mixture into the prepared tin and level it with a palette knife. Bake on the middle shelf for 1½ hours, until golden and risen, and a skewer inserted into the cake comes out clean. Leave the cake to rest in the tin for 2 minutes, then turn it out onto a wire rack to cool completely. Dust with icing sugar to serve.

Wild Garlic & Goat's Cheese Gözleme

Gözleme are a stuffed flat bread from Turkey, here filled with creamy, sharp goat's cheese, spicy chilli and aromatic wild garlic, all cut through with a lemon tang. The game-changer, though, is the za'atar, a mixture of woody, floral oregano, thyme and marjoram, balanced by the acidity of sumac.

Makes: 4
Hands on: 40 mins + rising
Bake: 12–24 mins

For the dough
250g plain flour
3g fast-action dried yeast
½ tsp salt
75g Greek-style plain yogurt
1 tbsp extra-virgin olive oil

For the filling
50g pine nuts
1 mild green chilli,
    deseeded and
    finely chopped
5 spring onions,
    finely sliced
1 small preserved lemon,
    rind only, finely sliced
200g soft mild goat's
    cheese, sliced
125g wild garlic leaves,
    washed and dried,
    roughly chopped
salt and freshly ground
    black pepper

To serve
extra-virgin olive oil
1 tbsp za'atar
wild garlic flowers,
    to garnish (optional)

1. Make the dough. Mix the flour with the yeast and salt in a stand mixer fitted with the dough hook until combined.

2. Make a well in the centre of the dry ingredients. Add the yogurt, olive oil and 100ml of cold water. Mix on low speed to combine, then knead on low speed for 5 minutes, until the dough is smooth and elastic. Tip out the dough onto a lightly floured work surface and shape it into a ball. Lightly oil the bowl, return the dough, cover and leave to rise at room temperature for 1 hour, until doubled in size.

3. Make the filling. While the dough is rising, toast the pine nuts in a dry frying pan over a low–medium heat for 2 minutes, until golden brown, shaking the pan from time to time so that they colour evenly. Tip the toasted nuts into a mixing bowl and leave them to cool.

4. Add the chilli, spring onions, preserved lemon rind, goat's cheese and wild garlic to the bowl of pine nuts. Season with salt and pepper and mix well with clean hands until thoroughly combined. Set aside.

5. Shape the dough. Lightly dust the work surface with flour and knead the dough briefly to knock it back. Divide it into 4 equal portions. Roll 1 portion into a 20–22cm-diameter round. Scoop a quarter of the filling onto one side of the dough and spread it out evenly to cover one half, leaving a 1cm border around the edge of the filling. Fold the dough over to cover the filling and make a half moon-shaped pasty, then crimp the edges together using your fingers to seal. Repeat to make 4 gözleme in total.

6. Cook the gözleme. Heat a large, dry frying pan over a low–medium heat and, one by one, cook the gözleme for 6 minutes each, turning once, until crisp and golden brown. (If your pan is large enough, you may be able to cook 2 at a time.) Transfer the cooked gözleme to a board, drizzle with extra-virgin olive oil and sprinkle over the za'atar. Cut the gözleme in half and serve hot, garnished with wild garlic flowers, if available.

Janusz's Ginger Biscuits

Every single time we have a family party, the thing everyone asks almost before I've even got through the door is, 'Have you baked your ginger biscuits for us?' My partner's nan absolutely loves them – almost peppery in flavour, they are perfect for her to dunk into her favourite cup of tea.

Makes: 60
Hands on: 25 mins + chilling
Bake: 12 mins

175g salted butter, cubed
    and softened
125g caster sugar
225g dark brown soft sugar
1 large egg
1 tsp vanilla extract
275g plain flour
1 tsp bicarbonate of soda
4 tbsp ground ginger
1½ tbsp ground cinnamon
½–1 tsp ground cloves,
    to taste

You will need
3 baking sheets, lined
    with baking paper

1. Beat the butter in a stand mixer fitted with the beater, on a medium speed for 1–2 minutes, until pale and creamy. Turn down the speed to medium-low, then, a spoonful at a time, add both types of sugar, and continue to beat for 3 minutes, scraping down the inside of the bowl from time to time, until combined. Add the egg and vanilla to the bowl and mix again to fully incorporate.

2. In a separate bowl, sift in the flour, bicarbonate of soda and ground spices, then stir until mixed together. Add the mixture to the wet ingredients and mix to a very slightly sticky dough.

3. Divide the dough into about 60 equal pieces (about 15g each), and roll each one into a ball between your hands. Place the balls onto the lined baking sheets, spaced well apart to allow them to spread during baking, then slightly flatten the top of each one. Chill for 20 minutes while you heat the oven to 190°C/170°C fan/Gas 5.

4. Bake for 12 minutes, until the biscuits have spread and started to crisp around the edges. Leave the biscuits on the baking sheets to cool completely and firm up before serving.

Chai-spiced Apple Chelsea Buns

Chai is the Indian word for tea and comes from the Chinese *cha*, from which we derive our colloquial 'char'. The flesh of a Braeburn apple contains hints of flavours reminiscent of cinnamon and nutmeg, so the spicy chai butter is a perfect match.

Makes: 9
Hands on: 1 hour + rising
Bake: 30 mins

For the apple filling
5 Braeburn apples, peeled, cored and chopped
50g golden caster sugar
25g unsalted butter, cubed
juice of ½ lemon
75g raisins or sultanas

For the dough
500g strong white bread flour
50g golden caster sugar, plus extra for sprinkling
7g fast-action dried yeast
1 tsp mixed spice
½ tsp salt
250ml whole milk, plus extra for glazing
75g unsalted butter, cubed and softened
1 large egg, lightly beaten
finely grated zest of ½ unwaxed lemon

For the chai-spiced butter
100g unsalted butter, cubed and softened
75g light muscovado sugar
ground seeds from 6 cardamom pods
1 tsp ground cinnamon
¼ tsp ground cloves
¼ tsp grated nutmeg

You will need
23cm square cake tin, greased, then lined with baking paper
oiled proving bag

1. Make the apple filling. Tip the apples into a pan with the caster sugar, butter and lemon juice. Cover with a lid and cook over a low–medium heat, stirring occasionally, for 20 minutes, until the apples are soft. Remove the lid, cook off any excess liquid, then take the pan off the heat and stir in the raisins or sultanas. Leave to cool.

2. Make the dough. Mix the flour, sugar, yeast, mixed spice and salt in a stand mixer fitted with the dough hook until combined.

3. Gently warm the milk in a small saucepan over a low heat. Add the butter and let it soften, then pour the mixture into the bowl with the dry ingredients. Add the egg and lemon zest. Mix on low speed until combined, then knead on low–medium speed for a further 6–8 minutes, until smooth and elastic.

4. Tip the dough out onto the work surface and form it into a ball with your hands. Place it back in the bowl, cover and leave it in a warm, draught-free place for 1–1½ hours, until doubled in size.

5. Make the chai-spiced butter. While the dough is rising, beat all the butter ingredients together with a wooden spoon until smooth, soft and spreadable. Set aside.

6. Shape the buns. Lightly flour the work surface and roll the dough into a neat rectangle of about 50 x 30cm, with one of the long sides closest to you. Spread the spiced butter over the dough, leaving a 1cm border all round. Spread the apple mixture evenly over the top.

7. Beginning with the edge closest to you, roll up the dough, keeping the roll even and firm. Trim the ends, cut the roll into 9 equal slices and place these, cut-side up, in the lined cake tin. Slide the tin into the oiled proving bag and leave the buns to prove in a warm place for 45 minutes, until nearly doubled in size.

8. Bake the buns. Heat the oven to 180°C/160°C fan/Gas 4. Brush the top of the buns with milk, scatter with caster sugar and bake for 30 minutes, until golden and risen. Leave to cool in the tin, then serve at room temperature.

Fennel Seed, Chilli & Parmesan Grissini

Bite into a fennel seed and you get a delicious aniseed flavour that couples beautifully with the heat of chilli flakes and the rich saltiness of parmesan. Twist some salty prosciutto around the breadsticks and serve them with a balancing cream-cheese dip.

Makes: 24
Hands on: 30 mins + rising
Bake: 12 mins

375g strong white
   bread flour
3g fast-action dried yeast
½ tsp salt
200ml lukewarm water
3 tbsp extra-virgin olive oil
2 tsp malt extract
2 tsp fennel seeds
½–1 tsp crushed dried
   chilli flakes
1 tsp dried oregano
4 tbsp finely grated
   parmesan

To serve (optional)
slices of prosciutto
cream cheese & herb dip

You will need
2 large baking sheets,
   lined with baking paper
2 oiled proving bags

1. Mix the flour, yeast, salt, lukewarm water, olive oil and malt extract in a stand mixer fitted with the dough hook on low speed until combined. Increase the speed slightly and knead for 6 minutes, until the dough is smooth and elastic.

2. Meanwhile, lightly crush the fennel seeds using a pestle and mortar. Add the crushed seeds to the dough, along with the chilli flakes, oregano and parmesan and mix to combine.

3. Turn out the dough onto the work surface and shape it into a ball. Lightly oil the bowl, return the dough to the bowl, cover it and leave it to rise at room temperature for 1 hour, until doubled in size.

4. Tip out the risen dough onto the work surface, knead it briefly to knock it back, then divide it into 24 equal portions, each weighing about 25g. Roll each portion into a rope about 30cm long and place the ropes onto the lined baking sheets, leaving space between each one to allow for spreading during baking.

5. Slide the baking sheets into the oil proving bags and leave the dough sticks to rest for 15 minutes while you heat the oven to 200°C/180°C fan/Gas 6.

6. Bake the grissini for 12 minutes, until crisp and golden, turning the baking sheets around after 8 minutes so that the grissini brown evenly. Leave the grissini to cool on a wire rack before serving.

Bay Leaf Panna Cotta with Coriander Biscotti

Bay leaves have a slightly bitter edge to their flavour, but that's exactly what you want to introduce to a creamy panna cotta to balance the richness. The floral, citrussy notes of ground coriander in the biscotti pick up the orange and lemon perfectly.

Serves: 6 (with 30 biscuits)
Hands on: 45 mins
+ overnight chilling
Bake: 35 mins

For the panna cotta
600ml double cream
100g caster sugar
3 strips of unwaxed
  lemon peel
2 strips of unwaxed
  orange peel
4 bay leaves
½ vanilla pod, split
  lengthways
2 platinum-grade gelatine
  leaves
200ml crème fraîche
few blackberries, to serve
  (optional)

For the biscotti
100g whole almonds,
  roughly chopped
275g plain flour
150g caster sugar
½ tsp baking powder
1 tsp ground coriander
pinch of salt
finely grated zest of
  ½ unwaxed orange
finely grated zest of
  ½ unwaxed lemon
2 large eggs
1 tbsp orange juice
1 tsp vanilla extract

You will need
150ml pudding moulds
  x 6, lightly oiled
large baking sheet, lined
  with baking paper

1. **Make the panna cotta.** Put the cream, sugar, lemon and orange peels, bay leaves and vanilla pod in a saucepan and slowly bring to the boil. Remove from the heat and leave for 30 minutes to infuse.

2. Meanwhile, soak the gelatine in a bowl of cold water for 5 minutes.

3. Place the pan with the infused cream back over a low heat, stir in the crème fraîche and bring to just below boiling point, then remove from the heat. Drain and squeeze out the gelatine, then whisk it into the hot cream to dissolve. Strain the mixture into a jug, leave to cool slightly, then carefully pour it into the moulds. Leave to cool to room temperature, then cover and chill for at least 4 hours, until set.

4. **Make the biscotti.** Heat the oven to 170°C/150°C fan/Gas 3. Tip the almonds into a large bowl. Sift in the flour, sugar, baking powder, ground coriander and salt, then add both zests and mix well. Make a well in the centre.

5. Beat together the eggs, orange juice and vanilla. Pour the mixture into the well and mix with a wooden spoon until combined, then bring the dough together with your hands into a smooth ball.

6. Lightly flour your hands, halve the dough and roll each half into a log, about 20cm long and 4–5cm in diameter. Place the logs on the lined baking sheet, spaced well apart. Bake for 25 minutes, until firm and light golden, turning the tray halfway through baking to ensure the logs colour evenly. Leave to cool for 30–45 minutes.

7. Heat the oven again to 150°C/130°C fan/Gas 2. Using a long serrated knife, slice the cooled biscotti logs diagonally, about 5mm thick to give 30 biscuits. Lay the slices in a single layer on the lined baking sheet and bake for 5 minutes. Turn the biscotti over and cook for a further 5 minutes, until crisp but not coloured. Leave to cool on the trays, then store the biscotti in an airtight tin until needed.

8. To serve, briefly dip each mould into a bowl of hot water to loosen the panna cotta. Invert each onto a serving plate. Serve with biscotti, and a few blackberries, too, if you wish.

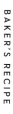

Dawn's Halloween Cupcakes

I always find myself last-minute baking for Halloween, so if it's in the cupboard, it goes in! These cupcakes are chocolate-flavoured with a little bit of aromatic coffee to enhance the chocolatiness. They would be equally delicious with the cocoa and a good zest of orange instead of coffee.

Makes: 12
Hands on: 1 hour
Bake: 20 mins

For the cupcakes
120ml whole milk
2 tsp lemon juice
150g plain flour
225g caster sugar
1 tsp coffee powder
40g cocoa powder
1 tsp baking powder
½ tsp bicarbonate of soda
¼ tsp salt
2 eggs
120ml vegetable oil
1 tsp vanilla extract

For the buttercream
150g unsalted butter,
    cubed and softened
300g icing sugar, sifted
1 tsp vanilla extract
few drops of bright green
    food-colouring gel

To decorate
50g ready-to-roll
    green fondant
400g ready-to-roll
    orange fondant
1 pot of edible gold dust

You will need
ice-cream scoop (optional)
12-hole cupcake tray,
    lined with 12 orange
    cupcake cases
8cm round cutter
fine cake-decorating
    paintbrush

1. Make the cupcakes. Heat the oven to 190°C/170°C fan/Gas 5. In a jug, mix the milk with the lemon juice, then set this aside to curdle and thicken slightly while you do the next step.

2. Sift the flour, caster sugar, coffee powder, cocoa powder, baking powder, bicarbonate of soda and salt into a large mixing bowl and stir to combine. Set aside.

3. Add the eggs, vegetable oil and vanilla to the jug containing the milk and lemon juice mixture, then whisk to combine.

4. Make a well in the centre of the dry ingredients and gradually pour in the wet ingredients, gently mixing with a balloon whisk until everything is combined and smooth.

5. Using an ice-cream scoop or dessert spoon, divide the mixture equally between the 12 cupcake cases – they should be about half full. Bake the cupcakes on the middle shelf for 20 minutes, until golden and risen, and a skewer inserted into the centre of each comes out clean. Leave the cupcakes to cool in the tray for 5 minutes, then transfer them to a wire rack to cool completely.

6. Make the buttercream. While the cakes are cooling, beat the butter in a stand mixer fitted with the beater, on medium speed for 5 minutes, scraping down the inside of the bowl from time to time, until pale and creamy.

7. With the mixer on low speed, add the icing sugar and beat until combined. Turn the speed to medium–high and beat for a further 3–4 minutes, scraping down the inside of the bowl from time to time, until light and fluffy. Add the vanilla and a few drops of the green food colouring. Continue to beat on medium–high for a further 1 minute, until you have an even green colour.

Continues overleaf

8. Prepare the decoration. Using your hands, divide the green fondant into 12 equal pieces, then shape each piece into a pumpkin-stalk shape with a flattened base.

9. Lightly dust the work surface with icing sugar and roll out the orange fondant to about 2mm thick. Use the 8cm cutter to cut out 12 orange fondant circles, then cover them to stop them drying out.

10. Assemble the cupcakes. Spoon a dollop of buttercream on top of one of the cupcakes and use a palette knife to smooth it into a dome shape. Carefully lay an orange fondant circle over the top of the dome of buttercream, then lightly press down around the edge so that there is no gap between the edge of the fondant and the paper case, sealing the buttercream inside.

11. Using the handle of a small wooden spoon, lightly press down into the fondant to create pumpkin-shaped sections, then brush each indentation with gold dust to highlight. Repeat steps 10 and 11 to make 12 covered cupcakes in total.

12. Put a small dab of water on the base of each green fondant stalk and press one onto the centre of each cupcake to complete the illusion of a pumpkin.

Aromatic Beef Slab Pie

This hearty beef pie is flavoured with warming cinnamon, star anise and Sichuan peppercorns. Make the filling the day (or at least a few hours) before you plan to bake and serve, to allow the flavours to mingle and mellow to the utmost deliciousness.

Serves: 6
Hands on: 3 hours + chilling
Bake: 40 mins

For the filling
1 tsp cumin seeds
1 tsp coriander seeds
1 tsp Sichuan peppercorns
2 large onions, halved and
  thinly sliced
3–4 tbsp olive oil
4 garlic cloves, crushed
5cm piece of fresh ginger,
  peeled and finely grated
  or chopped
2 cinnamon sticks
2 star anise
½ tsp Aleppo chilli flakes
2kg beef shin or chuck steak,
  cut into 3cm chunks
750ml beef stock
400g can of chopped
  tomatoes
1 tbsp tomato purée
2 tsp light brown soft sugar
15g plain flour
15g butter, softened
salt and freshly ground
  black pepper

For the pastry
400g plain flour
250g unsalted butter,
  cubed and chilled
1 large egg yolk
5 tbsp chilled water
1 tsp white wine vinegar
  or cider vinegar
1 egg, lightly beaten,
  to glaze

Continues overleaf

1. Make the beef filling. Toast the cumin seeds, coriander seeds and Sichuan peppercorns in a large, dry frying pan over a medium heat for 1 minute, until they smell aromatic. Tip the spices into a pestle and mortar or grinder and grind to a coarse powder.

2. Tip the onions into a casserole or saucepan with 2 tablespoons of the olive oil and cook over a low-medium heat, stirring often for about 10 minutes, until softened. Add the garlic, ginger, ground toasted spices, cinnamon, star anise and chilli flakes and cook for a further 1 minute. Remove from the heat.

3. Heat another 1 tablespoon of the oil in a large frying pan over a high heat and cook the beef in batches until browned all over, adding a little more oil when needed. Tip the beef into the casserole or pan with the onions.

4. Pour the beef stock into the frying pan, stirring well with a wooden spoon to incorporate any browned bits stuck on the bottom. Pour the stock into the casserole or pan along with the chopped tomatoes, tomato purée and brown sugar and mix well to combine. Season with salt and pepper, then bring to the boil. Cover the filling with a lid, reduce the heat to low and simmer for 2 hours, stirring occasionally, until the meat is tender.

5. Make the pastry. While the filling is cooking, tip the flour into a bowl and season with salt and pepper. Add the butter and, with a palette knife, cut the butter into the flour until the pieces are half their original size. Rub the butter into the flour with your fingertips until there are only very small flecks of butter remaining. Make a well in the centre, add the egg yolk, and the chilled water and the vinegar, then mix using the knife until the pastry starts to clump together, adding a little more water if needed. Gather the dough into a ball and very lightly knead it for 10 seconds, until smooth. Flatten the dough into a disc, wrap it and chill it for 1 hour.

Continues overleaf

You will need
large, heavy-based
    casserole or saucepan
    with a lid
30 x 20cm baking tin
    (about 4cm deep)
heavy baking sheet

6. Finish the filling. When the beef filling is cooked, strain it through a colander into a large bowl and pick out the star anise and cinnamon sticks. Return the liquid to the pan and bring it to the boil, then turn the heat down and simmer until reduced slightly. In a small bowl, mix the flour with the butter to a paste, add half to the pan and whisk to thicken the sauce. Add more of the butter and flour mixture, if needed, to thicken the sauce to a coating consistency. Taste the sauce and season with extra salt, pepper and a little sugar to balance the flavour. Return the beef to the pan, then remove it from the heat and leave to cool. Cover and chill until needed.

7. Assemble the pie. Divide the pastry into 2 unequal pieces of one third and two thirds. Lightly flour the work surface and roll out the larger piece into a neat rectangle large enough to line the base and sides of the baking tin. Using the rolling pin, lift the pastry into the tin, pressing it into the base and the sides and allowing any extra to hang over the edges. Spoon the beef filling into the pastry case and spread level.

8. Roll the second (smaller) piece of pastry into a neat rectangle slightly larger than the top of the pie. Brush the edges of the pastry lid with water, place it over the filling, then press the edges together to seal. Trim off any excess with a sharp knife, then crimp the edges decoratively. Any pastry offcuts can be re-rolled and cut into leaf shapes to decorate the top of the pie.

9. Chill the pie for 20 minutes while you heat the oven to 190°C/170°C fan/Gas 5. Place the heavy baking sheet on the middle shelf to heat up at the same time.

10. Brush the top of the pie with the beaten egg and bake on top of the hot baking sheet for 40 minutes, until the pastry is crisp and golden, and the pie filling is bubbling and hot. Cut into large squares to serve.

Tres Leches Splatter Cake

Two sponges – one flavoured with chilli and cinnamon, the other with chocolate, coffee and pecans – are soaked in three types of milk (literally, *tres leches*). Cherry compôte and cherry liqueur bring fruity booziness to this version of the Latin American classic. Don't be daunted by the recipe length – creating this bake is far simpler than it seems.

Serves: 30
Hands on: 3 hours + chilling
Bake: 1 hour

For the spiced chocolate sponges
375g plain flour
225g caster sugar
135g cocoa powder
2 tsp bicarbonate of soda
2 tsp baking powder
1½ tsp salt
1 tbsp ground cinnamon
2 tsp chilli flakes
3 large eggs
300ml buttermilk
260ml warm water
90ml vegetable oil
1 tbsp vanilla extract

For the spiced milk chocolate ganache
100ml double cream
150g milk chocolate, finely chopped
1 tsp ground cinnamon
¼ tsp chilli powder

For the cherry compôte
500g cherries, pitted and halved
3 tbsp granulated sugar
finely grated zest and juice of 1 large unwaxed orange
pinch of salt
1 tsp balsamic vinegar

Continues overleaf

1. Make the spiced chocolate sponges. Heat the oven to 180°C/160°C fan/Gas 4. Sift all of the dry ingredients into a large bowl and mix them together with a whisk. Separately, tip all of the wet ingredients into a large jug and whisk together to combine.

2. Make a well in the centre of the dry ingredients and gradually pour in the wet ingredients while mixing with a whisk, until you have a smooth batter.

3. Divide the mixture equally between the four 15cm cake tins and bake the sponges for about 30-35 minutes, or until a skewer inserted into the centre of each comes out clean. Leave the sponges in the tins to cool for 10 minutes, then turn them out onto a wire rack to cool completely.

4. Make the spiced milk chocolate ganache. Add the cream to a small saucepan over a low-medium heat and heat until it is almost boiling. Tip the chopped chocolate into a heatproof bowl.

5. Pour the hot cream over the chocolate and leave it to stand for 1 minute, then gently stir together with a whisk to bring together to a glossy ganache. Whisk in the cinnamon and chilli, then cover and set aside until ready to use.

6. Make the cherry compôte. Place the cherries, sugar, orange zest and juice, and salt into a medium saucepan and cook over a medium heat for about 8-10 minutes, until the fruit is soft and the juice has reduced until thickened and syrupy. Remove the pan from the heat and stir in the vinegar, then set aside until ready to use.

7. Make the chocolate, coffee and pecan sponge. Heat the oven to 180°C/160°C fan/Gas 4. Scatter the pecans in a single layer over a baking tray (you may need several trays) and toast for 5-8 minutes, until fragrant and beginning to brown, then set aside to cool (about 3-4 minutes).

Continues overleaf

Tres Leches Splatter Cake *continued*

For the chocolate, coffee & pecan sponge
200g pecans
6 tbsp coffee granules
400ml warm water
450ml buttermilk
5 large eggs
135ml vegetable oil
2 tbsp vanilla extract
570g plain flour
340g caster sugar
200g cocoa powder
1 tbsp bicarbonate of soda
1 tbsp baking powder
2 tsp salt
3 tbsp ground cinnamon
4 tsp chilli flakes

For the dulce de leche filling
50g granulated sugar
50g unsalted butter
80ml whole milk
1 x 397g can of condensed milk

For the cream-cheese frosting
300g full-fat cream cheese
300g mascarpone
100g icing sugar, sifted
½ tsp vanilla paste

For the cherry tres leches soak
150ml condensed milk
150ml evaporated milk
150ml whole milk
2 tbsp cherry brandy
½ tsp cherry flavouring

For the coffee tres leches soak
200ml condensed milk
200ml evaporated milk
200ml whole milk
1½ tbsp coffee
¾ tsp cinnamon
3 tbsp salted caramel Baileys

8. Roughly chop the toasted pecans into small pieces, then set aside. In a large jug, mix the coffee granules with the warm water to dissolve them, then whisk the rest of the wet ingredients into the jug and set aside.

9. In a large bowl, sift together all of the dry ingredients (except the nuts) and mix them with a whisk to evenly distribute them.

10. Make a well in the centre of the dry ingredients and gradually pour in the wet ingredients while mixing with a whisk, until you have a smooth batter. Mix in the chopped pecans.

11. Divide the mixture equally between the four 20cm cake tins and bake for about 30–35 minutes, or until a skewer inserted into the centre of each sponge comes out clean. Leave the sponges to cool in the tins for 10 minutes, then turn them out onto a wire rack to cool completely.

12. Make dulce de leche filling. In a large saucepan, melt the sugar over a medium heat for about 5 minutes, stirring until the sugar is completely melted and caramelised. Reduce the heat to low and add the butter a little at a time, mixing until fully incorporated. Gradually stir in the milk, followed by the condensed milk, then raise the heat to bring the mixture to the boil.

13. Boil the mixture for 4–5 minutes, stirring continuously to stop it from burning, then remove the pan from the heat and pour the dulce de leche into a shallow, wide container to allow it to cool. Cover and set aside until completely cool (about 1 hour).

14. Make the cream-cheese frosting. In the bowl of a stand mixer fitted with the beater attachment, beat together the cream cheese and the mascarpone on a medium speed for about 1 minute, until well combined. Add the icing sugar and vanilla paste and beat for a further 2–3 minutes, until well combined again, then transfer to the fridge until ready to use.

15. Make the tres leches soaking liquids. Take two large bowls or jugs. Whisk all of the ingredients for the cherry soak into one, and all of the ingredients for the coffee soak into the other. Place both jugs in the fridge until you're ready to use.

16. Make the buttercream frosting. You'll need to do this in two batches. In the bowl of a stand mixer fitted with the beater

*For the vanilla
buttercream*
1kg unsalted butter
2kg icing sugar, sifted
2 tbsp vanilla extract
50ml whole milk

*For the coloured
white chocolate
ganache decoration*
100ml double cream
200g white chocolate,
    finely chopped
red, yellow, green, blue,
    pink and purple food-
    colouring gels

You will need
15cm round cake tins x 4,
    greased, then base-lined
    with baking paper
20cm round cake tins x 4,
    greased, then base-lined
    with baking paper
4 lipped baking trays
large piping bag fitted
    with a large plain nozzle
25cm cake board or
    serving plate
cake-decorating turntable
18cm cake board
4 cake dowel rods
cake-decorating
    paintbrushes

attachment, beat half of the butter on a medium speed for
3–4 minutes until pale and fluffy, then add half of the sifted icing
sugar and mix on a low speed until just incorporated. Increase the
speed to medium–high and beat for another 3–4 minutes to a fluffy
buttercream. Mix in half of the vanilla and then while the mixer is
running, add just enough milk to achieve an easily spreadable but
sturdy buttercream. Transfer the buttercream to another bowl
and repeat with the remaining ingredients.

17. Soak the sponges. Place each of the 8 layers of sponge one
at a time onto a cake turntable and using a long, serrated knife,
slice off the domed tops to level. Lay out the cake layers onto lipped
baking trays, and pour the cherry soak over the 15cm layers and
the coffee soak over the 20cm layers. You may not need to use
all of the liquid, but the sponges should be well soaked.

18. Build the 20cm cake. First, ensure you have enough space in
your fridge or freezer to chill the tiers. Fill the large piping bag fitted
with the large plain nozzle with some of the vanilla buttercream.

19. Place the 25cm cake board or serving plate onto the turntable
and secure the first layer of 20cm sponge on top with a blob of
buttercream. Then, pipe a buttercream border around the top edge.
Fill the space inside the buttercream with a layer of cream-cheese
frosting and then swirl in some dulce de leche. Top with the next
layer of 20cm sponge and repeat the process with another two
layers of filling, topping with the fourth 20cm sponge layer. Use
a palette knife to spread a thin layer of buttercream over the top
and side of the cake to crumb coat, then place it in the freezer for
10 minutes to set (alternatively give it 30 minutes in the fridge).

20. Build the 15cm cake. Secure the base layer to the 18cm cake
board with a blob of buttercream, then pipe a buttercream border
around the top edge. Fill the space inside the buttercream with
a layer of spiced chocolate ganache and then top with cherry
compôte. Top with the next layer of 15cm sponge and repeat the
process with another two layers of filling, topping with the fourth
15cm sponge layer. Once you've built the cake, use a palette knife
to spread a thin layer of buttercream over the top and side of
the cake to crumb coat, then place the cake in the freezer for
10 minutes to set (alternatively give it 30 minutes in the fridge).

Continues overleaf

21. Once the 20cm cake is firm, remove it from the freezer (or fridge) and cover the top and sides with a thick layer of buttercream, using a palette knife to create a smooth finish, and ensuring that the top is as flat as possible to allow the other cake to sit on top when you stack them.

22. Place the cake back into the freezer (or fridge) to chill and firm up, and repeat this process with the smaller cake. Ensure both cakes are sufficiently chilled before stacking.

23. Make the white chocolate ganache. When you're ready to finish the cakes, add the cream to a small saucepan over a low–medium heat and heat the cream until almost boiling. While the cream is heating, place the chopped chocolate into a medium heatproof bowl. Pour the hot cream over the chocolate and leave it to stand for 1 minute, then gently stir it all together with a whisk to create a glossy, quite runny ganache. Divide the ganache into 6 small bowls and stir a drop of food-colouring gel to each bowl, to create 6 differently coloured ganaches.

24. Assemble and decorate the cake. Place the chilled 20cm tier on the turntable. Insert 4 cake dowels as if they are the 4 corners of a square, keeping them about 5cm apart so that the top tier will conceal them. They should reach down to the base board – trim them to sit flush with the top of the cake, if necessary.

25. Spread a thin layer of buttercream in the centre to stick the cakes together, then place the chilled 15cm tier, still on the cake board, on top. Using a cake-decorating paintbrush, splatter the surface of the stacked tiers with the coloured ganaches to decorate.

Prue's Lemon Meringue Pie

Beneath the puffy dome of soft meringue is a double hit of citrus – first, there's the lemon and then you get the sweet whammy of freshly squeezed orange juice, too. Chilling tempers flavour, so serve the pie warm to enjoy it at its best.

Serves: 12
Hands on: 40 mins + chilling
Bake: 40 mins

For the pastry
200g plain flour
pinch of salt
150g unsalted butter,
    cubed and chilled
25g icing sugar, sifted
1 egg, beaten

For the lemon filling
finely grated zest and juice
    of 6 unwaxed lemons
60g cornflour
150ml smooth orange juice
250g caster sugar
6 egg yolks

For the meringue
6 egg whites
½ tsp cream of tartar
300g caster sugar

You will need
23cm loose-bottomed
    fluted tart tin
baking beans or rice

1. Make the pastry. Tip the flour, salt and butter into a mixing bowl. Using your fingertips, rub the butter into the flour until the mixture resembles fine breadcrumbs. Add the icing sugar and egg, then mix to combine. Bring together to form a rough ball of dough.

2. Make the pastry case. Lightly flour the work surface and roll the pastry to a disc large enough to line the base and sides of the tin and about 3mm thick. (This is easier between 2 sheets of baking paper.) Lift the pastry into the tin, being careful not to stretch it as you press it into the base and sides. Trim the excess and chill it for 30 minutes, until firm. Heat the oven to 200°C/180°C fan/Gas 6.

3. Line the chilled pastry case with baking paper and baking beans or rice. Bake on the middle shelf for 15 minutes, until the top edge starts to turn crisp and golden. Remove the baking paper and beans or rice. Return the case to the oven and bake it for a further 5–10 minutes to dry out and cook the base. Leave to cool.

4. Make the filling. While the pastry case is cooling, mix the lemon zest and juice with the cornflour in a small bowl until smooth. Pour 150ml of water and the orange juice into a saucepan and bring it to the boil. Add the lemon mixture and simmer, stirring, until thick enough to coat the back of the spoon, then remove the pan from the heat.

5. In a large bowl, mix the caster sugar and egg yolks together, then pour in the hot lemon mixture, stirring continuously. Pour the mixture back into the pan and stir over a medium heat to a thick custard. Remove from the heat and leave to cool slightly, then pour the custard into the baked pastry case. Chill until set.

6. Make the meringue. Heat the oven to 150°C/130°C fan/Gas 3. Whisk the egg whites and cream of tartar in a stand mixer fitted with the whisk until soft peaks form. A spoonful at a time, add the caster sugar, whisking continuously until the meringue is stiff and glossy. Spoon the meringue in a large dome on top of the set lemon filling, creating swirls with the back of a spoon. Bake for 15 minutes, until the meringue is pale golden and crisp. Serve warm.

Seeded Sourdough Bread

As a sourdough starter bubbles away, it produces microorganisms that, along with the flour, give the dough its special sour taste and tangy flavour. Wholemeal flour and the seeded top offer complementary nuttiness; organic flour gives the best flavour of all. You'll need to forward plan to make sure your starter (see page 271) is active before you mix your dough. If you use and refresh your starter daily, give it a feed early in the morning and it will be active, doubled in volume, bubbly and ready to use 6–8 hours later.

VEGAN

Makes: 1 large loaf
Hands on: 30 mins (or 4 hours including resting) +overnight proving
Bake: 40 mins

125g active sourdough starter (see p.271)
325ml lukewarm water
450g strong white bread flour, plus 1 tbsp
50g strong wholemeal flour
25g pumpkin seeds
25g sunflower seeds
10g white sesame seeds
12g sea-salt flakes
10g poppy seeds
1 tbsp rice flour
10g black sesame seeds

You will need
1kg round banneton basket or a medium mixing bowl, lined with a clean tea towel
dough scraper
bench scraper
Dutch oven or cast-iron casserole or baking stone
oiled proving bag

1. Before you start, factor in that the sourdough takes at least 4 hours to make including resting, as well as overnight proving. The starter needs to be at its peak of activity with large air bubbles. To test if it is ready, drop a teaspoonful of the starter into a bowl of warm water – if it floats, then it is ready; if it sinks, you will need to give it more time, or feed it again and wait 6–8 hours.

2. Spoon the active starter into a large mixing bowl, preferably glass so you can see bubbles forming in the dough. Add the lukewarm water and mix to combine.

3. Add both types of flour and, with your hand or a spatula, mix to combine for about 2 minutes. There should be no dry flour in the bottom of the bowl, but the dough will not be smooth at this stage. Cover loosely with a clean, damp tea towel and set aside for 30 minutes at room temperature.

4. Meanwhile, toast the pumpkin and sunflower seeds in a dry frying pan over a low–medium heat for 2 minutes, stirring often, until crisp. Tip the pumpkin seeds into a bowl, then toast the white sesame seeds (not the black ones) for a similar length of time until starting to colour. Set aside until needed.

5. Grind the sea-salt flakes in a pestle and mortar and add this to the dough with 25ml of water. Using one hand, mix to combine, twisting and squelching the dough between your fingers. Continue to mix for about 1 minute, until smooth and the salt and water are thoroughly combined. Cover and rest for another 30 minutes.

6. Add all of the toasted pumpkin and sunflower seeds and half of the toasted sesame and half of the poppy seeds to the dough and mix to combine with a wet hand (to prevent the dough sticking).

Continues overleaf

7. The dough now needs to be stretched and folded in the bowl several times over a 2-hour period, each spaced 30 minutes apart. Using a wet hand, pick the top edge of the dough up, stretch it out slightly, then fold it down over the dough to meet the bottom edge. Turn the bowl 90 degrees clockwise and repeat this stretching and folding a further 3 times, turning the bowl between each fold. Cover and leave the dough to rest for 30 minutes.

8. Repeat this sequence of stretching and folding a further three times, each set 30 minutes apart, completing 4 sets of folds over a 2-hour period. Cover the bowl and leave the dough to ferment at room temperature for 2 hours, until risen by about 30 per cent.

9. Lightly flour the work surface and, using a dough scraper, turn the dough out of the bowl. Using a bench scraper, or with lightly floured hands, form the dough into a smooth, tight ball, cupping the dough under the bottom edge and swiftly turning it anti-clockwise in as few moves as possible. Lightly dust the top of the dough with flour and leave it to rest on the work surface for 15–20 minutes to let the gluten relax.

10. Meanwhile, mix the rice flour with 1 tablespoon of white flour and use this to dust the banneton or cloth-lined bowl. Tip the remaining toasted sesame seeds and poppy seeds with the black sesame seeds onto a dinner plate.

11. Using the bench scraper, flip the ball over so that the floured side is on the work surface. Lightly stretch out the edges of the dough – picture the dough as a clock face and, starting at 12 o'clock, pull the outside edge of the dough into the middle, turning the ball a quarter of a turn clockwise, then repeat 5 or 6 times until all the edges have been brought into the middle and the dough starts to form a ball. Gently flip the ball of dough over so that it is now smooth side up, cup your hands around the dough and gently pull it towards you on the work surface to tighten the top.

12. Using the bench scraper, quickly but gently flip the dough over into your hands and press the top into the seeds, then carefully place the dough into the prepared banneton or bowl, seed-side down. Place the banneton or bowl inside a proving bag and leave the dough to rest at room temperature for 30 minutes, then transfer it to the fridge to slowly prove for 10 hours, or overnight, until the loaf has risen almost to the top of the basket.

13. When you're ready to bake, heat the oven to 240°C/220°C fan/ Gas 9 or as hot as it will go and put a Dutch oven or cast-iron casserole in the oven at the same time to heat up for about 30 minutes.

14. Carefully remove the hot Dutch oven or casserole and take off the lid. Remove the basket or bowl from the proving bag and lay a disc of baking paper on top of the dough. Place a baking sheet on top and very gently flip the dough out of the basket or bowl and onto the paper. Using a very sharp knife, lame or razor, make 4 slashes around the top of the loaf, cutting about 1cm deep and at a 45-degree angle. Gently lift or slide the dough on the baking paper into the Dutch oven or casserole, quickly cover with the lid and bake for 35 minutes, until well risen and starting to turn golden.

15. Reduce the oven temperature to 200°C/180°C fan/Gas 6, remove the lid, if needed, and bake for a further 10–15 minutes, until golden brown and crisp. Turn out the bread, if needed, and leave to cool on a wire rack.

Pink Grapefruit & Olive Oil Cake

This brilliantly simple cake is a perfect balance of sweet and savoury. Peppery olive oil provides tartness, which is emphasised by bittersweet pink grapefruit with its herby, musky tones. Then there's an out-and-out sugary hit from the glacé icing.

Serves: 8
Hands on: 1 hour + overnight cooling + drying
Bake: 45 mins

For the candied grapefruit
1 pink grapefruit, washed and dried
150g caster sugar, plus 2 tbsp for scattering
1 star anise
1 bay leaf

For the sponge
3 large eggs
225g caster sugar
1 tsp vanilla paste
200ml olive oil
finely grated zest (washed and dried) and juice of 2 pink grapefruits
225g self-raising flour
1/2 tsp baking powder
1/4 tsp salt
50g ground almonds
2 tbsp soured cream

For the icing
about 2 tbsp pink grapefruit juice (reserved while making the candied peel)
175g icing sugar, sifted

You will need
900g loaf tin, greased, then lined (base and ends) with a strip of baking paper

1. Make the candied grapefruit. Do this a day ahead. Score the grapefruit into quarters, cutting through the skin only. Carefully peel off the skin quarters, leaving the fruit intact. Halve the fruit and squeeze the juice, covering and chilling it until needed. Cut the peel into 5mm strips and place them in a saucepan. Cover them with water, boil, then simmer for 1 minute. Drain and repeat twice more.

2. Return the peel to the pan and add the 150g of caster sugar, the star anise, bay leaf and 150ml of water. Boil, stirring, then simmer for 30 minutes, until the peel is soft, and the syrup has almost gone.

3. Lift the peel out of the pan. Discard the star anise and bay leaf, and place the peel in a single layer on a sheet of baking paper. Leave for 2 hours, until cold and starting to dry. Scatter the grapefruit peel with the 2 tablespoons of caster sugar to coat both sides, then arrange it on a wire rack to dry overnight, uncovered.

4. Make the sponge. Heat the oven to 180°C/160°C fan/Gas 4. Whisk the eggs, caster sugar and vanilla in a stand mixer, on medium–high speed for 4 minutes, until doubled, light and fluffy, and it holds a firm ribbon trail. On low speed, add the olive oil in a slow, continuous stream, scraping down the inside of the bowl from time to time. Add the zest and 5 tablespoons of juice. Whisk to combine.

5. Sift the flour, baking powder and salt into the bowl. Add the ground almonds and beat with a rubber spatula to combine. Add the soured cream and mix again until smooth. Pour the mixture into the lined tin and spread it level. Bake on the middle shelf for 45 minutes, until golden and risen, and a skewer inserted into the centre comes out clean. Leave to cool in the tin for 10 minutes, then carefully lift the cake out of the tin and leave it to cool completely on a wire rack.

6. Make the icing. Whisk the grapefruit juice with the icing sugar until smooth and spreadable. Spoon the icing over the top of the cake and leave it to set for 30 minutes before decorating it with candied grapefruit peel. Leave for another 30 minutes for the icing to dry completely, then cut into thick slices to serve.

Black Forest Pavlova

Never rush a pavlova – the base needs time to cool before you fill it, in this case with all the flavours of Black Forest Gâteau – two favourite desserts in one. Dark chocolate, cherries and cream are a winning flavour combination and a touch of vanilla and kirsch provides extra decadence. You can use frozen cherries if fresh are not in season.

GLUTEN-FREE

Serves: 8
Hands on: 45 mins + cooling
Bake: 1½ hours

For the meringue
6 large egg whites
pinch of cream of tartar
good pinch of salt
325g caster sugar
1 tsp vanilla paste
3 tsp cornflour
1 tsp cider vinegar or
    white wine vinegar

For the chocolate curls
100g 54% dark chocolate,
    broken into pieces

For the topping
400g pitted cherries, fresh
    or frozen and defrosted
juice of ½ lemon
50g caster sugar
2 tbsp kirsch (optional)
100g 54% dark chocolate,
    broken into pieces
400ml double cream
1 tbsp icing sugar, sifted
1 tsp vanilla paste
extra fresh cherries,
    to serve

You will need
large baking sheet
small baking tray with
    a smooth base
offset palette knife

1. Make the meringue. Heat the oven to 170°C/150°C fan/Gas 3. Draw a 20cm circle, using a cake tin or plate as a template, in the middle of a sheet of baking paper the same size as your large baking sheet. Lay the paper on the baking sheet, drawn-side down.

2. Whisk the egg whites, cream of tartar and salt in a stand mixer fitted with the whisk, on medium–high speed for 3–4 minutes, until the egg whites form stiff peaks but are not dry.

3. Add the caster sugar, 2–3 tablespoons at a time, whisking well between each addition and scraping down the inside of the bowl from time to time, until combined and the sugar dissolves into the egg whites. Once all the sugar has been incorporated, you should not be able to see or taste any crystals of sugar and the meringue will be very stiff and glossy. If there are still sugar crystals in the meringue, whisk it for 1 minute more, then check again.

4. Add the vanilla and whisk to combine. Add the cornflour and whisk again for 30 seconds to combine, then finally add the vinegar, whisking again for 30–60 seconds, until thoroughly incorporated.

5. Spoon the meringue into the middle of the circle on the baking paper and, using a palette knife, smooth the mixture into a 20cm cake shape with a flat top and straight sides. Drag the tip of the palette knife upwards around the sides of the meringue at regular intervals to give a ridged effect.

6. Slide the pavlova into the oven and immediately reduce the temperature to 100°C/80°C fan/Gas ¼. Bake for 1½ hours, until crisp and firm on the outside and soft and marshmallowy in the middle. Do not open the oven door during baking. Turn off the oven and leave the pavlova inside with the door closed to cool for 1 hour. Open the door and leave it slightly ajar until the meringue cools completely, or leave it like this overnight.

Continues overleaf

7. Make the chocolate curls. Melt the chocolate in a heatproof bowl set over a pan of barely simmering water. Stir until smooth and remove from the heat. Spoon the melted chocolate over the underside of the small baking tray and spread it level using a palette knife. Leave the chocolate at room temperature for about 1 hour, until set firm but not hard.

8. Using a kitchen knife held at a 45-degree angle to the tray, push the knife away from you across the top of the set chocolate to create curls. Transfer the curls to a plate and chill until needed.

9. Make the topping. Cook the cherries with the lemon juice, caster sugar and kirsch (if using) in a saucepan over a low–medium heat, stirring occasionally, for 5 minutes, until soft and juicy but the cherries still retain their shape. Tip the cherries into a sieve set over a bowl and leave the juices to drip through for 10 minutes. Leave the cherries in the sieve to cool to room temperature.

10. Return the cherry juice to the pan and reduce it over a medium heat for 1–2 minutes, until thickened and syrupy. The time will depend on how juicy the cherries are. Leave to cool to room temperature.

11. Melt the chocolate in a heatproof bowl set over a pan of gently simmering water. Stir until smooth. Remove the pan from the heat and leave the chocolate to cool for 10 minutes to room temperature.

12. Using a balloon whisk, whip the double cream with the icing sugar and vanilla in a large mixing bowl until soft and pillowy. Add 2 tablespoons of the cherry syrup, the cooled cherries and the melted chocolate and lightly fold them all together with a large spoon or rubber spatula.

13. Assemble the pavlova. Using a fish slice or cake lifter, carefully slide the pavlova off the paper onto a large serving plate or cake stand, then spoon the chocolate-cherry cream on top. Spoon the remaining cherry syrup over the pavlova and decorate with extra fresh cherries and the chocolate curls.

Ham & Pineapple Pizza

If ever there were a pizza to delight the taste buds it's this one: umami-rich mushrooms bring out the savouriness in the bacon, whose saltiness brilliantly offsets the sweetness of the pineapple (and vice versa). Top with some crisp, peppery watercress for a pleasantly bitter finish. It's a classic Hawaiian with a twist.

Makes: two 33cm pizzas
Hands on: 35 mins + rising
Bake: 13–15 mins

For the pizza bases
300ml room-temperature water
14g fast-action dried yeast
pinch of caster sugar
430g strong white bread flour
70g spelt flour
pinch of salt
semolina flour, for dusting

For the sauce
1 x 400g can of whole plum tomatoes (ideally San Marzano)
3 garlic cloves
1–3 tsp caster sugar
salt and freshly ground black pepper

For the toppings
150g pancetta, cut into 5mm dice
100g oyster or button mushrooms, torn into bite-sized pieces
2 garlic cloves, thinly sliced
200g thick-cut unsmoked bacon, cut into 2.5cm strips
½ ripe pineapple (about 300g), peeled, cored and chopped into 2.5cm pieces (about 1cm thick)

Continues overleaf

1. Begin the pizza base. Pour the water into a jug, then add the yeast and sugar. Whisk to combine, then set aside.

2. Tip both flours and the salt into a stand mixer fitted with the dough hook. Make a well in the centre, pour in the yeast mixture and mix on a medium speed for 10–12 minutes, until you have an elastic dough that springs back when you press it with a finger. Shape the dough into a smooth ball and place it into a clean, oiled bowl. Cover with a tea towel and leave it to rise for at least 1 hour, or until doubled in size.

3. Make the tomato sauce. While the dough is rising, empty the can of tomatoes into a sieve to drain off any excess liquid, then place the pulp into a food processor along with the garlic. Season with salt and pepper, then blitz to a smooth sauce. Taste the sauce – if it is too acidic, add the sugar, a little at a time until you're happy with the flavour. Set the sauce aside while you prepare the toppings.

4. Make the toppings. Add the pancetta to a cold frying pan, turn the heat to medium-high and cook for about 5 minutes, until it is brown and crispy. Remove the pancetta from the pan using a slotted spoon or spatula and set aside, retaining the fat in the pan.

5. Add the mushrooms to the pan and cook over a medium heat for about 3–4 minutes, until they start to brown. Add the garlic, season with salt and black pepper and cook for a further 1–2 minutes, until the garlic is fragrant. Tip the mixture into a bowl and set aside.

6. Wipe down the pan and add the strips of bacon. Cook over a medium heat for about 5 minutes, until browned, then empty the bacon into a bowl and set aside.

7. Add the pineapple pieces to the pan and cook over a medium heat for about 5 minutes, flipping occasionally until both sides turn golden. Remove the pineapple pieces from the heat and set aside.

Continues overleaf

200g low-moisture
   mozzarella
olive oil, for brushing
20g watercress, to garnish

You will need
pizza stones x 2 (or make
   1 pizza at a time)
pizza peels or large thin
   baking sheets x 2
   (or make one pizza
   at a time)

8. Drain the mozzarella by wrapping it in a clean tea towel and gently squeezing to remove any excess liquid, slice it, then set it aside. Place the pizza stones (or stone if you're making 1 pizza at a time) into the oven and turn the oven on to its maximum temperature.

9. **Finish the pizza bases.** Once the dough has doubled in size, tip it out onto the work surface and knead it briefly to knock out the air. Divide the dough into 2 equal pieces and shape each piece into a ball. Cover the balls with a clean tea towel and leave them to rest for 5–10 minutes.

10. Dust the work surface with semolina flour and, working with one dough ball at a time, tease each ball of dough out into a 33cm disc with your hands, pressing out from the centre and rotating the dough. If you don't have a pizza peel, do this part on a square of baking paper so that you can transfer each pizza to the oven. (If you have only one pizza stone and one peel, shape and top the first pizza and repeat for the second while the first is baking.)

11. **Add the toppings.** Move the dough discs each onto a pizza peel or slide the paper squares onto a thin baking sheet and add half the sauce to each base, spreading the sauce out with the back of a spoon, but leaving a 2.5cm border for the crust.

12. Add the mozzarella slices and toppings to each pizza, making sure the toppings are evenly distributed, and brush the crusts with olive oil to help them crisp up in the oven.

13. **Bake the pizzas.** Slide the pizzas from the peel (or slide the paper) onto the pizza stones and cook the pizzas for about 13–14 minutes, until browned and crisp. Garnish with the watercress, and serve immediately.

Will's Chorizo Tear & Share Buns

I came up with this recipe because one of my kids likes savoury breads more than sweet. We like to go out for lunch on a Sunday, so I make the dough for the buns before we leave, then it's ready to go into the oven when we get home. I love the way smoky chorizo and salty mature cheddar work together.

Makes: 12
Hands on: 50 mins + rising
Bake: 25 mins

For the dough
500g strong white
    bread flour
40g caster sugar
7g fast-action dried yeast
10g salt
1 large egg
200ml whole milk,
    plus extra if needed
50g unsalted butter,
    melted and cooled

For the filling
2 garlic cloves,
    finely grated
2 tsp smoked
    sweet paprika
1½ tbsp olive oil
pinch of salt
100g mature cheddar
    cheese, coarsely grated
80g ready-to-eat diced
    chorizo sausage
1 egg, beaten
5g sesame seeds
freshly ground
    black pepper

You will need
30 x 20cm baking tin,
    greased, then lined
    (base and sides)
    with baking paper
oiled proving bag

1. Make the dough. Mix the flour, caster sugar, yeast and salt in a stand mixer fitted with the dough hook until combined. Add the egg, milk and melted butter and mix on low speed until it all forms a soft dough. If it looks dry, add a little more milk. Turn the speed to medium–high and knead for 15 minutes, until smooth and elastic. Tip out the dough onto the work surface and shape it into a ball. Lightly oil the bowl, return the dough, cover it and leave it to rise for 2 hours, or overnight in the fridge, until doubled in size.

2. Prepare the filling. Put the garlic, paprika, olive oil and salt in a small bowl and season with pepper, then mix to form a light paste. In a separate bowl, mix the cheddar with the chorizo. Set both aside.

3. Shape the dough. Lightly flour the work surface and knead the risen dough gently to knock it back. Using your hands, loosely form the dough into a rectangle, then roll it out to a rectangle of about 48 x 35cm. This may take a few minutes as the dough stretches and relaxes, so roll it a little, rest it for a little, then roll again.

4. With a long edge closest to you, spread the garlic-paprika paste over the dough, leaving a 2cm border at the top, then sprinkle the cheese-chorizo mixture over the paste. Starting at the long edge closest to you, roll up the dough into a tight cylinder. Brush the strip at the top with a little beaten egg to stick down the edge.

5. With a sharp knife, cut the cylinder into 12 equal pieces, each about 4cm wide. Arrange the pieces in the lined tin, swirl upwards, in 3 rows of 4 buns. Slide the tin into the proving bag and leave the buns to prove for 45 minutes, until doubled in size. Heat the oven to 180°C/160°C fan/Gas 4.

6. Bake the buns. Brush the top of each bun with the remaining beaten egg and sprinkle with the sesame seeds. Bake for 25 minutes, until golden and risen. Transfer the buns to a wire rack to cool slightly, then serve them just warm or at room temperature.

Carole's Lemon Cake

Everyone has a favourite recipe for lemon cake and this is most definitely mine. The recipe is very rich: I don't stop at soaking the sponge with lemon juice, but sandwich it with freshly made lemon curd and whipped cream, then pour over sugary glacé icing. Enjoy!

Serves: 10
Hands on: 45 mins
Bake: 45 mins

For the sponge
250g unsalted butter,
    cubed and softened
250g caster sugar
finely grated zest of
    2 unwaxed lemons
4 eggs
250g self-raising flour
2 tbsp whole milk

For the soaking syrup
60g caster sugar
juice of 2 lemons

For the lemon curd
75g caster sugar
finely grated zest of
    1 unwaxed lemon
1 egg
1 egg yolk
75ml lemon juice
40g unsalted butter,
    cubed

For the cream filling
300ml double cream
1 tbsp icing sugar, sifted

For the drizzle icing
200g icing sugar, sifted
2 tbsp lemon juice, plus
    zest to decorate

You will need
900g loaf tin, greased,
    then lined (base and
    sides) with baking paper

1. Make the sponge. Heat the oven to 180°C/160°C fan/Gas 4. Beat the butter, caster sugar and lemon zest in a stand mixer fitted with the beater, on a medium speed for 3–5 minutes, scraping down the inside of the bowl from time to time, until pale and creamy. Turn the speed to low and, one at a time, add the eggs, beating well between each addition, stopping to scrape the bowl occasionally. Sift in half of the flour and mix to just combine. Add the milk, then sift in the remaining flour and mix again briefly until fully combined.

2. Spoon the mixture into the lined loaf tin and level it with a palette knife. Bake on the middle shelf for 45 minutes, until golden and risen, and a skewer inserted into the centre comes out clean.

3. Make the soaking syrup. While the sponge is baking, beat the caster sugar, lemon juice and 4 tablespoons of water in a small saucepan over a low heat until the sugar dissolves and the syrup just reaches the boil, then set aside.

4. Flavour the sponge. Remove the sponge from the oven and place it in the tin on a wire rack. Using a skewer, pierce holes all over the top of the cake, then slowly pour the syrup over the top, allowing it to soak in. Leave it to cool completely in the tin.

5. Make the lemon curd. While the sponge is cooling, put the caster sugar and lemon zest in a bowl and rub them together with your fingertips to release the oils from the zest. Whisk in the whole egg and egg yolk, followed by the lemon juice, then transfer the mixture to a small pan. Cook it over a low heat, stirring continuously to ensure the mixture doesn't catch on the bottom of the pan, until thickened enough to coat the back of the spoon. Turn off the heat and leave the mixture to cool slightly for 5 minutes. Using a balloon whisk, whisk in the butter, one piece at a time, until fully incorporated. Pass the curd through a sieve into a clean shallow container, then cover with a lid and chill for 1 hour, until thickened.

Continues overleaf

6. Prepare the cream filling. Once the lemon curd has cooled, in a large bowl, whip the double cream with the icing sugar until it holds soft peaks, then set aside.

7. Make the drizzle icing. Whisk the icing sugar and lemon juice in a bowl to a thick but pourable icing, then set aside.

8. Assemble the cake. Carefully remove the sponge from the tin (it will be very delicate as it is soaked in syrup). Using a serrated knife, slice the cake horizontally into 3 even layers. Place the bottom layer on a serving plate and spread it with half of the lemon curd, then half of the whipped cream. Carefully place the middle layer of sponge on top, then repeat with the rest of the lemon curd and cream. Finally, add the top layer of sponge and pour the drizzle icing over the top, spreading it evenly with a palette knife so that it just begins to drip over the edges. Sprinkle with lemon zest to serve.

Blackcurrant Millefeuille

Blackcurrants can be sharp and tangy, but with a little sugar and lemon they cook to a delicious jammy slump that is perfect with buttery pastry (that's so much more delicious when it's made at home) and rich, creamy, sweetened mascarpone. Garnish these delicate pastries with fresh black or white currants when in season.

Makes: 8
Hands on: 1 hour + chilling
Bake: 30 mins

─────────────

For the puff pastry
250g unsalted butter, chilled
150g plain flour
100g strong white bread flour
pinch of salt
100ml chilled water
1 tsp lemon juice
50g flaked almonds
2 tbsp icing sugar, sifted

For the blackcurrant filling
250g blackcurrants, fresh, or frozen and defrosted, plus optional fresh to decorate
100g caster sugar
juice of ½ lemon

For the cream filling
500g mascarpone
50g icing sugar, sifted, plus extra for dusting
2 tsp vanilla paste
finely grated zest and juice of ½ unwaxed lemon

You will need
4 baking sheets lined with baking paper
20cm square baking tin, lined (base and sides) with baking paper
medium piping bag fitted with a medium closed star nozzle

1. Make the puff pastry. Cut 50g of the chilled butter into cubes and tip it into a mixing bowl with both types of flour and the salt. Rub in the butter with your fingertips until the mixture resembles breadcrumbs. Make a well in the centre, add the chilled water and lemon juice and mix with a palette knife to roughly bring the mixture together, then gather the dough into a ball with your hands. Flatten into a neat rectangle, cover it and chill it for 30–45 minutes.

2. Lightly flour the work surface, then roll out the dough to a rectangle about 45 x 15cm and 4–5mm thick, with one of the short ends closest to you. Cut the remaining 200g of chilled butter into 2cm slices and lay the slices flat between two sheets of baking paper. Using a rolling pin, flatten the butter into a neat square slightly smaller than one third of the dough rectangle (about 14cm square). Place the butter on the middle section of the dough and fold the bottom third up over it, brush off any excess flour, and fold the top third down to completely encase the butter. Gently press together the edges of the dough around the butter to seal it in.

3. Brush any excess flour off the dough and turn the square 90 degrees clockwise, then roll it out again into a rectangle of about 45 x 15cm. Try to keep the pastry edges as neat as possible. Fold the bottom third of the rectangle up over the middle third and the top third down, brushing off any excess flour each time. Lightly press the edges of the dough together, turn the square 90 degrees clockwise, wrap and chill for 45 minutes. Repeat rolling and folding the dough into neat thirds once more, then wrap and chill it for 45 minutes.

4. For the final stage, roll the dough into a neat rectangle of about 45 x 15cm. This time fold the top edge down to the middle and the bottom edge up to the middle to meet it. Turn the dough 90 degrees clockwise, then fold it in half like closing a book. Cover and chill the dough for 2 hours before using.

Continues overleaf

5. Make the blackcurrant filling. While the pastry is chilling, cook the blackcurrants with the caster sugar and lemon juice in a small saucepan over a low heat, stirring often until the blackcurrants break down and become very soft and jammy (they contain lots of pectin so will thicken further once cold). Leave them to cool, then cover and chill them until you're ready to use.

6. Make the pastry sheets. Cut the pastry into 3 equal pieces. Lightly flour the work surface and roll each piece into a 25cm square (about 3mm thick). Slide the squares onto sheets of baking paper, then stack them on top of one another and chill them for 30 minutes. Heat the oven to 200°C/180°C fan/Gas 6.

7. Bake the pastry squares in batches (if you have 4 baking sheets you can cook 2 sheets of pastry at the same time). Lift 1 pastry square, on its paper, onto a baking sheet, prick it with a fork, scatter with one third of the flaked almonds and dust with icing sugar. Cover with a second piece of baking paper and place another baking sheet on top to keep the pastry flat. Bake for 25 minutes, until golden and starting to crisp. Remove the baking sheet and paper from the top of the pastry square and cook for a further 5 minutes, until the pastry is golden brown, flaky and crisp. Repeat to bake the remaining pastry squares, letting the trays cool down between each bake. Leave the pastry to cool completely on the paper.

8. Make the cream filling. While the pastry is cooling, in a large mixing bowl, beat together the mascarpone, icing sugar, vanilla and lemon zest and juice until smooth and thoroughly combined. Spoon 8 tablespoons of the mixture into the medium piping bag fitted with a medium star nozzle and chill until needed.

9. Assemble the millefeuille. Using the baking tin as a guide, trim each baked pastry sheet into a neat 20cm square. Place 1 pastry square in the bottom of the lined tin and spread it evenly with the remaining mascarpone mixture. Place another pastry square on top and press them gently together. Spread this with the blackcurrant mixture and top with the third pastry square, pressing gently together. Cover and chill for 15 minutes.

10. Using the lining paper to lift, remove the pastry from the tin and with a serrated knife cut the millefeuille into 8 rectangular portions. Pipe the reserved mascarpone on top and decorate with fresh blackcurrants when in season. Dust with icing sugar and serve.

Kevin's Sourdough Crackers

I've always thought what a waste it was to just bin the bits of sourdough starter I wasn't using each time I was refreshing it – enter my sourdough crackers! In this recipe, I've flavoured them with just a sprinkling of salt, but herbs, spices, even different flours, all work, too.

VEGAN

Makes: about 30
Hands on: 45 mins
Bake: 10 mins

———————————

200g sourdough
    starter discard
100g plain flour, plus
    extra if needed
50ml extra-virgin olive oil
½ tsp salt
rock salt, for grinding

You will need
3 baking sheets, lined
    with baking paper

1. Heat the oven to 200°C/180°C fan/Gas 6.

2. Using your hands, mix all the ingredients in a mixing bowl until they come together in a ball. Sourdough starters can vary widely depending on what and when you feed them and what stage they are at, so you may find that you need to add a little more flour if the dough is too loose.

3. Divide the dough into 3 equal pieces to make it easier to roll. Roll out 1 piece at a time between two sheets of baking paper until 2mm thick, keeping the rest of the dough covered with a clean, damp tea towel to stop it drying out. Once you have rolled out the first piece, use a sharp knife to cut out leaf shapes, each measuring about 8 x 4cm.

4. To decorate the leaves, score a line down the centre of each leaf shape, taking care not to cut all the way through the dough, and feather the edges by cutting small notches every few millimetres around the outside of the leaf. Using the tip of a sharp knife, make incisions in between the central line and the feathered edges to represent the veins. Re-roll any offcuts to cut out more crackers. Repeat with the rest of the dough pieces.

5. Gently lift the crackers onto the lined baking sheets, grind over some salt and bake them for 10 minutes, until lightly golden and firm. Leave to cool and crisp up on the baking sheets.

Lemon & Coconut Crackle Cookies

Coconut and lemon have always been the best of friends, and in these cookies milky coconut cream and the pronounced nuttiness of dried coconut enjoy a tangy citrus zip. We love the sweet burst you get from the icing-sugar crackle, too.

VEGAN

Makes: 25
Hands on: 20 mins + chilling
Bake: 15 mins

For the cookies
180g plain flour
1 tsp baking powder
¼ tsp bicarbonate of soda
40g unsweetened
    desiccated coconut
50g vegan unsalted block
    butter, softened
185g icing sugar, sifted
finely grated zest and juice
    of 1 unwaxed lemon
1½ tsp coconut extract

For the crackle coating
100g icing sugar, sifted

You will need
2 baking sheets, lined
    with baking paper

1. Make the cookies. Sift the flour, baking powder and bicarbonate of soda into a large mixing bowl. Stir in the desiccated coconut.

2. Beat the butter, icing sugar and lemon zest in a stand mixer fitted with the beater, on medium speed for 3–5 minutes, scraping down the inside of the bowl from time to time, until pale and creamy. With the mixer still running, beat in the coconut extract.

3. Turn the speed down to its lowest setting, add the dry ingredients and mix to make a stiff, dry dough. A teaspoon at a time, add the lemon juice, stopping as soon as the cookie dough becomes firm, smooth and pliable. Using your hands, form the dough into a ball, then wrap and chill it for at least 2 hours, or preferably overnight.

4. When you're ready to bake, heat the oven to 180°C/160°C fan/ Gas 4.

5. Add the crackle coating. Tip the icing sugar into a bowl. Using your hands, shape the dough into walnut-sized balls (about 25 in total). Tip each ball of dough into the icing sugar and roll to coat it all over, shaking off any excess. Now, roll the balls in the icing sugar again until thickly covered.

6. Place the sugar-coated dough balls on the lined baking sheets, spaced well apart to allow them to spread during baking. Bake for 13–15 minutes, until the edges start to turn golden and crisp. Leave the cookies to cool on the baking sheets for 10 minutes, then transfer them to a wire rack to cool completely.

Prue's Spring Rolls

Complex flavours are beautifully balanced in this filling: sweet, raw vegetables give way to salty oyster and soy sauces, spicy chilli, and earthy, umami mushrooms. Drying then rehydrating mushrooms only increases their umami-ness. Fun fact: the Japanese word *shii* means 'chestnut' – the tree under which shiitake mushrooms grow.

Makes: 8
Hands on: 40 mins + resting
Bake: 10 mins

For the wrappers
150g strong white
  bread flour
25g cornflour, plus extra
  for sprinkling
1 tsp salt
1 tbsp sesame oil
2 tbsp vegetable oil
1 egg, beaten
vegetable oil, for frying

For the filling
15g dried wood ear or
  shiitake mushrooms
25g vermicelli noodles
boiling water, to cover
1 tbsp chilli oil
1 garlic clove, peeled
  and finely chopped
3cm piece of fresh
  ginger, peeled and
  finely chopped
3 spring onions,
  finely chopped
75g shimeji mushrooms
75g carrots, peeled and
  cut into fine matchsticks
50g Chinese cabbage, cut
  into fine matchsticks
50g mange touts, cut
  into fine matchsticks
1 tsp cornflour

Continues overleaf

1. Begin the wrappers. Sift the flour, cornflour and salt into a large bowl. Make a well in the centre and add the sesame oil, vegetable oil and 5 tablespoons of water. Use your fingers to mix the ingredients to a stiff dough, adding a little more water if necessary. Turn out the dough onto the work surface and knead it until smooth, then wrap it and leave it to rest for 30 minutes.

2. Make the filling. While the dough is resting, place the dried mushrooms and the noodles in a bowl and cover them with the boiling water. Leave them to soak for 15 minutes, until soft, then drain them and squeeze out any excess liquid from the mushrooms. Slice the mushrooms into thin slices and the noodles into about 5cm lengths.

3. Heat a wok or large frying pan over a high heat until it is hot. Add the chilli oil and, when it's very hot, add the garlic, ginger and spring onions and stir-fry for 10 seconds. Add the soaked and fresh mushrooms, along with the carrots, cabbage and mange touts and continue to stir-fry for 1–2 minutes.

4. Mix the cornflour and soy sauce together, then add the mixture to the pan along with the bean sprouts and oyster sauce and stir-fry for 1–2 minutes, mixing well. Finally, stir in the sesame oil, then remove the pan from the heat and leave the filling to cool.

5. Finish the wrappers. Lightly knead the chilled dough for 2 minutes, then divide it into 8 equal pieces. On a lightly floured surface, roll out 1 piece of dough to an 8cm disc. Repeat with another piece of dough so you have two 8cm discs. Sprinkle the top of one of the discs with cornflour, then place the other disc on top. Roll out the stacked discs to a rough 20cm circle.

Continues overleaf

1 tbsp soy sauce
50g bean sprouts
1 tbsp oyster sauce
½ tsp sesame oil

For the dipping sauce
2 tbsp soy sauce
1 tbsp rice vinegar
1 tsp fish sauce
juice of ½ lime
1 tsp palm sugar, grated
½ tsp sesame oil

You will need
deep-fat fryer

6. Heat a non-stick frying pan over a low heat. Place the rolled circle of dough in the pan and cook it for about 30 seconds, until the dough begins to bubble slightly. Immediately turn the disc over and cook it for another 30 seconds, then remove it from the pan. Very carefully peel the dough layers away from each other so you have 2 transparent wrappers. Set them aside and cover them with a damp tea towel or kitchen paper to prevent them from drying out.

7. Repeat the process until you have 8 wrappers, stacking them on top of each other as you go. When you're ready to assemble the spring rolls, trim each wrapper into a square.

8. Assemble the spring rolls. Place about 3 tablespoons of filling 5cm in from a corner of each wrapper. Roll from the corner over the filling once, then fold in each side and then continue the roll until you have completely rolled up the filling inside the wrapper in a neat cylinder. Brush the loose edge with beaten egg to seal. Repeat for all the wrappers.

9. Fry the spring rolls. Heat a deep-fat fryer to 180°C, then in batches of about 2 or 3 rolls at a time, use tongs to gently lower the spring rolls into the oil. Fry for 3–4 minutes, turning from time to time, until the spring rolls are golden brown on the outside and cooked through inside. Remove the spring rolls with a slotted spoon and set them aside to drain on kitchen paper. Leave the oil to come back to temperature before frying the next batch.

10. Make the dipping sauce. Mix all the dipping sauce ingredients together in a jug, then pour them into a serving bowl. Serve alongside the rolls, for dipping.

Buttermilk Layer Cake with Gooseberry Curd

Raw gooseberries have a lip-puckering tartness – but introduce them to sugar and they become gently floral and creamy with just a slight tang that is perfect with freshly picked, perfumed elderflowers. In this bake a smooth gooseberry curd is sandwiched between a rich buttermilk cake and whipped elderflower cordial cream.

Serves: 10
Hands on: 1 hour + chilling
Bake: 20 mins

For the gooseberry curd
500g gooseberries
125g caster sugar
50g unsalted butter
2 eggs
2 egg yolks

For the sponges
175g unsalted butter,
    cubed and softened
225g caster sugar
4 eggs, beaten
1 tsp vanilla paste
275g plain flour
2 tsp baking powder
½ tsp bicarbonate of soda
pinch of salt
125ml buttermilk, at
    room temperature

For the cream filling
400ml double cream
3 tbsp elderflower cordial
2 tsp vanilla paste
fresh elderflowers,
    to decorate

You will need
18cm round cake tins x 3,
    greased, then base-lined
    with baking paper

1. Make the gooseberry curd. Do this ahead of time to allow at least 4 hours for it to chill and set. Add the gooseberries to a saucepan with 2 tablespoons of water and cook over a low–medium heat, half-covered with a lid and stirring occasionally, until mushy.

2. Press the cooked gooseberries through a fine nylon sieve set over a clean pan to remove any pips and skin. Place the pan over a low heat and cook the purée for 4 minutes, until thickened to a soft jam consistency. Add the caster sugar and butter and stir to melt the butter and dissolve the sugar.

3. Whisk together the whole egg and yolks and add them to the pan, stirring continuously. Continue to cook the curd over a low heat until the mixture starts to bubble, and thickens enough to coat the back of a spoon – but do not boil or the eggs may scramble. Pass the curd through a sieve into a clean bowl, then cover the surface to prevent a skin forming and leave to cool. Once cooled, chill for 4 hours, until set or until needed. You'll need only two thirds of this quantity for the cake – separate out one third and store it in a separate sealed jar in the fridge for up to 1 week – it's delicious on toast.

4. Make the sponges. Heat the oven to 180°C/160°C fan/Gas 4. Beat the butter and caster sugar in a stand mixer fitted with the beater, on medium speed for 3–5 minutes, scraping down the inside of the bowl from time to time, until pale and creamy. Add the eggs, a little at a time, beating well between each addition. Mix in the vanilla.

5. Sift the flour, baking powder, bicarbonate of soda and salt into a separate bowl. Add one third to the sponge mixture and mix to just combine. Add half of the buttermilk and mix again. Continue to add the dry ingredients and buttermilk alternately and mix until smooth.

Continues overleaf

6. Divide the mixture equally between the lined tins and spread it level. Bake the sponges on the middle shelves for 20 minutes, until golden and risen, and a skewer inserted into the centre of each comes out clean. Leave the sponges to cool in the tins for 5 minutes, then turn them out onto a wire rack to cool completely.

7. **Make the cream filling.** In a large bowl, whisk the double cream with the elderflower cordial and vanilla until it holds soft peaks.

8. **Assemble the cake.** Place 1 sponge layer on a serving plate and spread one third of the gooseberry curd over the top. Spoon over one third of the whipped cream and top with the second sponge. Spread with another third each of the curd and cream and top with the third sponge layer.

9. Loosely fold the remaining curd into the rest of the whipped cream and spoon the mixture on top of the cake in voluptuous clouds. Decorate with fresh elderflowers to serve.

& RUITY

Raspberry, Lemon, Pistachio & Rose Cake

We all know that feasting begins with the eyes, and this cake is as pretty as a picture. Lemon zest adds zip to the moist sponges, while ripe raspberries have sweet and floral notes that lend themselves to a truly aromatic jam – adding rosewater intensifies that profile. Pistachio and rosewater is a well-loved pairing, making the pistachio-flavoured buttercream the perfect filling to complement the jam.

Serves: 10+
Hands on: 2 hours + cooling
Bake: 25 mins

---

*For the raspberry
& rose jam*
100g raspberries
125g jam sugar
2 tsp rosewater

*For the pistachio
& lemon sponges*
125g unsalted butter,
 cubed and softened
350g caster sugar
125ml sunflower oil
4 eggs, lightly beaten
3 egg yolks
250g plain flour
75g ground pistachios
1 tbsp baking powder
pinch of salt
150ml whole milk, at
 room temperature
finely grated zest of
 3 unwaxed lemons
300g raspberries

*For the crystallised
rose petals*
1 egg white, lightly beaten
50g caster sugar
10 small pale pink
 rose petals

Continues overleaf

1. Make the jam. Do this ahead to allow time for it to cool and set. Put the raspberries and jam sugar in a small saucepan over a low heat. Leave to melt and collapse and then come to the boil. Then, once the sugar has completely melted, increase the heat and boil for another 5 minutes, until the temperature on a sugar thermometer reaches 105°C. Remove the pan from the heat, add the rosewater and leave the jam to cool for 1 hour, until set. Chill until needed.

2. Make the sponges. Heat the oven to 180°C/160°C fan/Gas 4. Beat the butter and caster sugar in a stand mixer fitted with the beater, on medium speed for 3–5 minutes, scraping down the inside of the bowl from time to time, until pale and creamy. Add the sunflower oil and continue to mix for 3 minutes, until pale, light and fluffy.

3. A little at a time, add the beaten eggs, beating well between each addition, then scrape down the inside of the bowl. One at a time add the egg yolks, again beating well between each addition.

4. Sift the flour, ground pistachios, baking powder and salt into the bowl. Add half of the milk and mix on low speed to combine. Add the remaining milk and mix again until silky smooth. Fold the lemon zest and raspberries through the batter using a large metal spoon, being careful not to crush the raspberries.

5. Divide the mixture equally between the prepared tins and spread level. Bake the sponges on the middle shelves for 22–25 minutes, until golden and risen, and a skewer inserted into the centres comes out clean. Leave to cool in the tins for 10 minutes, then carefully turn out the sponges onto a wire rack to cool completely.

6. Make the crystallised rose petals. While the sponges are baking, tip the egg white and caster sugar into two shallow bowls. Using your fingertips or tweezers, carefully dip the rose petals into the

Continues overleaf

For the buttercream
5 egg whites
275g caster sugar
pinch of salt
450g unsalted butter,
    cubed and softened
2 tsp vanilla paste
1 tsp pistachio extract

To decorate
200g raspberries
75g slivered pistachios
icing sugar, for dusting

You will need
sugar thermometer
20cm round cake tins x 3,
    greased, then base-lined
    with baking paper
baking sheet, lined with
    baking paper
large piping bag fitted
    with a medium
    plain nozzle
cake-decorating turntable
    (optional)

egg white, turning to coat both sides before lightly tossing them in the caster sugar. Sprinkle on additional caster sugar to ensure an even coating. Gently shake the petals to remove any excess sugar, then place them on the lined baking sheet. Leave until dry and hardened (about 2 hours).

7. Make the buttercream. Using a balloon whisk, combine the egg whites, caster sugar, salt and 1 tablespoon of water in a large heatproof bowl. Set the bowl over a pan of gently simmering water and whisk continuously for 5 minutes, until the meringue is hot to the touch and leaves a ribbon trail when you lift the whisk. Scoop the meringue into the bowl of a stand mixer fitted with the whisk, and whisk on medium speed for 5 minutes, scraping down the inside of the bowl from time to time, until the meringue forms glossy, stiff peaks and cools.

8. Gradually, add the butter to the meringue mixture, whisking continuously and scraping down the inside of the bowl, until silky smooth and glossy. Add the vanilla paste and pistachio extract and mix again to combine. Spoon the buttercream into the large piping bag fitted with a medium plain nozzle.

9. Assemble the cake. Place 1 sponge layer on a serving plate (and then on a cake-decorating turntable, if using) and spread a thick layer (about 4 tablespoons) of the raspberry and rose jam over the sponge with a palette knife. Pipe a layer of buttercream on top of the jam and top with a second sponge. Repeat with another layer of the jam and buttercream filling. Top with the third sponge and gently press the layers together. Chill the cake for 30 minutes.

10. Remove the cake from the fridge and spread the remaining buttercream on top of the cake. Decorate with fresh raspberries, the crystallised rose petals and the slivered pistachios. Dust with icing sugar before serving.

Apple, Shallot & Blue Cheese Tarte Tatin

Braeburn apples have notes of cinnamon and nutmeg, and go perfectly with the almost spicy tang of blue cheese. Mild-mannered shallots take on a fruity sweetness when caramelised, and a drizzle of sweet, sticky balsamic vinegar is the perfect finish.

Serves: 4–6
Hands on: 1 hour + chilling
Bake: 30 mins

_____

For the rough puff pastry
200g plain flour
¼ tsp salt
175g unsalted butter,
  cubed and chilled
4 tbsp chilled water
1 tsp white wine vinegar
  or lemon juice

For the topping
40g unsalted butter
2 tbsp olive oil
400g banana shallots
  (about 12 small shallots),
  peeled and halved
  lengthways, root
  end intact
2 Braeburn apples, cored
  and cut into eighths
2 garlic cloves, crushed
1½ tbsp golden
  caster sugar
1 thyme sprig, leaves
  picked
150g blue cheese
  (such as St Agur or
  Stilton), crumbled
salt and freshly ground
  black pepper

To serve
2 tbsp balsamic vinegar
1 tbsp roughly chopped
  flat-leaf parsley

Continues overleaf

1. Make the rough puff pastry. Mix the flour and salt in a large mixing bowl. Lightly rub in the butter with your fingertips, just enough to knock the corners off the butter pieces – it should still be in rough dice. Pour in the chilled water and vinegar and quickly mix with a palette knife to bring the dough together into a ragged ball, adding more water if needed.

2. Lightly flour the work surface, tip the dough out of the bowl and flatten it into a square. Roll out the dough to a rectangle that is three times as long as it is wide – about 36 x 12cm, with one of the short ends closest to you. Fold the top third down to the middle and the bottom third up to cover it to create a three-layered square of dough. Wrap the dough and chill it for 1 hour.

3. Lightly flour the work surface and roll out the dough to a rectangle, this time about 45 x 15cm, with one of the short ends closest to you. Fold the top edge down to the middle and the bottom edge up to meet it in the middle. Turn the dough 90 degrees clockwise and fold the dough in half, much like closing a book. Wrap and chill for another 1 hour, or until you're ready to bake.

4. Make the topping. While the pastry is chilling, melt 15g of the butter with 1 tablespoon of the olive oil in a large frying pan over a medium heat. Add the shallots, cut-side down, and cook without stirring for 3–4 minutes, until golden. Turn the shallots over and cook the other side for 2 minutes, until lightly coloured. Using a fish slice or palette knife, remove the shallots to a large plate and season well with salt and pepper.

5. Heat another 15g of the butter and the remaining olive oil in the frying pan. Add the apples and cook each side for 2 minutes, until lightly caramelised. Add the garlic, season with salt and pepper and cook for another 1 minute. Remove the apples to a plate.

Continues overleaf

Apple, Shallot & Blue Cheese Tarte Tatin *continued*

You will need
ovenproof frying pan or
   skillet, with a 20cm base

6. Assemble the tatin. Spread the remaining butter over the base of the ovenproof pan or skillet and scatter with the caster sugar. Place the shallots and apples in the pan (they don't have to be neatly arranged) and scatter with the thyme and half of the blue cheese.

7. Lightly flour the work surface. Roll out the pastry and cut it into a 28–30cm disc (about 3mm thick). Lay the pastry over the shallots and apples and tuck the edges down the inside of the pan. Chill for 20 minutes while you heat the oven to 200°C/180°C fan/Gas 6.

8. Cut a steam hole in the top of the pastry and place the pan over a medium heat for 2 minutes, until the edges of the pastry start to sizzle and bubble. Then, transfer the pan to the oven and bake for 30 minutes, until the pastry is crisp and golden all over.

9. Meanwhile, bring the balsamic vinegar to the boil in a small saucepan over a medium heat until reduced by half. Remove from the heat and leave to cool.

10. Leave the baked tart to rest in the tin for 2 minutes, then place a board or serving plate on top of the pan and carefully flip the pan over to turn out the tart. Drizzle with the reduced balsamic vinegar and scatter with the remaining blue cheese and the parsley, to serve.

Prue's Garibaldi Biscuits

Named to honour Italian General Giuseppe Garibaldi, who visited England in the 1850s, these are a dried-fruit pastry sandwich, here using sweet currants and tart cranberries plumped up with tangy orange juice. Ours have the bonus of being half-dipped in rich chocolate.

Makes: 12
Hands on: 1 hour + chilling
Bake: 15 mins

150g currants,
    roughly chopped
50g dried cranberries,
    roughly chopped
150ml orange juice
125g self-raising flour
pinch of salt
75g unsalted butter,
    cubed and chilled
25g caster sugar
1 large egg, separated

To decorate
200g 54% dark chocolate,
    broken into pieces
100g white chocolate,
    broken into pieces

You will need
baking tray, lined
    with baking paper
small piping bag
    fitted with a small
    writing nozzle
cocktail stick

1. Make the biscuits. Heat the oven to 180°C/160°C fan/Gas 4. Place the currants and cranberries in a small pan with the orange juice and bring to the boil over a medium heat. Reduce the heat slightly, then simmer for 5 minutes, until the fruit has softened. Remove the pan from the heat, then drain the fruit, discarding the orange juice. Spread the fruit out on a plate lined with kitchen paper to cool and remove any excess moisture.

2. Sift the flour and salt into a mixing bowl. Add the butter and rub it into the flour with your fingertips until the mixture resembles fine breadcrumbs. Mix in the caster sugar until combined.

3. Add the egg yolk and 1 tablespoon of water and mix with a table knife until the mixture comes together to form a firm dough. Knead the dough very gently into a ball, then flatten it into a disc. Wrap the disc and chill it for 20 minutes.

4. Lightly dust the work surface with flour, cut the dough in half and roll out each piece to a 20 x 15cm rectangle (about 3mm thick).

5. Lightly brush one of the rectangles with beaten egg white, then scatter the soaked currants and cranberries evenly over the top. Lay the second rectangle of pastry directly on top to cover.

6. Dust the work surface with a little more flour, then evenly roll out the layered pastry and fruit into a 25 x 20cm rectangle. Trim the edges neatly, then cut the rectangle lengthways in half. Cut each new rectangle of pastry crossways into 6 equal biscuits (each about 9cm long x 3.5cm wide), to make 12 biscuits in total. Prick the dough all over with a fork and brush with the remaining beaten egg white.

7. Place the biscuits on the lined baking tray, spacing them out evenly. Bake for 12–15 minutes, until light golden brown. Remove the biscuits from the oven and leave them to cool on the tray for 5 minutes, then transfer them to a wire rack to cool completely.

Continues overleaf

8. Decorate the biscuits. While the biscuits are cooling, melt the dark chocolate in a heatproof bowl set over a pan of gently simmering water, stirring until smooth. Pour the melted chocolate into a wide, shallow bowl or large ramekin. At the same time, melt the white chocolate in a separate heatproof bowl in the same way, then spoon it into the small piping bag fitted with a small writing nozzle.

9. Dip one long side of one biscuit into the melted dark chocolate until it is half coated. Scrape the bottom of the biscuit along the edge of the bowl to remove any excess chocolate on the base, then place it on a wire rack. Pipe 3 thin lines of white chocolate lengthways down the dark chocolate coating. Using the cocktail stick, drag the lines of white chocolate first one way towards the centre of the biscuit, then in the opposite direction towards the edge of the biscuit, repeating to make a feather pattern across the coated half of the biscuit.

10. Repeat Step 9 with the remaining biscuits. Once you have decorated all of the biscuits, chill them for 5 minutes, until set, before serving.

Passion Fruit Trifle

Fresh mango, peaches and passion fruit bring zesty fruitiness to this centrepiece pud, while crisp savoiardi biscuits are a wonderful texture contrast to the creamy custard. You won't need all of the biscuits for this trifle, but any leftovers will keep well in an airtight tin and can be used to make tiramisú or served as a treat with tea or coffee.

Serves: 8
Hands on: 1½ hours
   + chilling
Bake: 9 mins

For the savoiardi biscuits
3 eggs, separated
pinch of salt
100g caster sugar, plus
   extra for sprinkling
1 tsp vanilla extract
100g plain flour
25g flaked almonds,
   crushed

For the fruit jelly layer
2 platinum-grade
   gelatine leaves
200ml ready-made
   strained passion-fruit
   pulp (from about 8
   large passion fruit)
50g caster sugar
1 large mango, peeled,
   destoned and sliced
2 peaches, halved,
   destoned and sliced

For the custard
300ml whole milk
3 egg yolks
75g caster sugar
1½ tbsp cornflour
1 tsp vanilla paste

Continues overleaf

1. Make the savoiardi biscuits. Heat the oven to 180°C/160°C fan/ Gas 4. Whisk the egg whites with the salt in a stand mixer fitted with the whisk until they form stiff peaks. Add 50g of the caster sugar and continue to whisk to a glossy, smooth meringue, and until the sugar dissolves. Using a large metal spoon or rubber spatula, scoop the meringue into a clean bowl.

2. In the same mixer bowl (no need to wash it), whisk the egg yolks, vanilla and the remaining sugar until doubled in volume, thick and mousse-like, and the mixture holds a ribbon trail when you lift the whisk. Using a large metal spoon, fold the meringue, half at a time, into the egg-yolk mixture. Sift the flour into the bowl and fold in until thoroughly combined.

3. Scoop the mixture into the large piping bag fitted with a medium plain nozzle and pipe about 24 neat, long biscuits, about 7cm in length, on the lined baking sheets. Scatter with crushed flaked almonds, sprinkle with caster sugar and bake for 9 minutes, until golden. Leave the biscuits to cool and crisp up on the baking sheets.

4. Make the fruit jelly layer. While the biscuits are cooling, soak the gelatine in a bowl of cold water for 5 minutes, until floppy. Combine the strained passion-fruit pulp, caster sugar and 60ml of water in a jug and whisk to combine and dissolve the sugar. Pour half of the mixture into a small saucepan, place the pan over a low heat and bring the liquid to just below boiling. Then, remove the pan from the heat. Drain the gelatine, squeeze out any excess water, and add the leaves to the hot passion-fruit pulp. Whisk until the gelatine dissolves, then whisk in the remaining cold passion-fruit mixture until combined. Leave to cool to room temperature.

5. Arrange half of the mango slices and half of the peach slices in the bottom of a large trifle dish and pour over the jelly mixture. Cover and chill for about 2 hours, until set.

Continues overleaf

Passion Fruit Trifle *continued*

To assemble & serve
3 tbsp rum
3 tbsp passion-fruit syrup
300ml double cream
3 tbsp icing sugar, sifted
1 tsp vanilla paste
4 passion fruit, halved
  and pulp scooped out

You will need
large piping bag fitted with
  a medium plain nozzle
2 baking sheets, each lined
  with baking paper

6. Make the custard. While the jelly layer is setting, pour the milk into a saucepan, place it over a low–medium heat and bring it to the boil. Whisk the egg yolks, caster sugar, cornflour and vanilla in a mixing bowl until smooth and thoroughly combined. Slowly pour half of the hot milk into the bowl, whisking continuously until combined. Pour the mixture back into the pan containing the rest of the milk and cook over a low heat until it just comes to the boil, whisking continuously for 1–2 minutes, until the custard thickly coats the back of a spoon, and you can no longer taste the cornflour. Strain the custard into a clean bowl and cover the surface with baking paper to prevent a skin forming. Leave to cool, then chill until needed.

7. Assemble the trifle. Mix the rum with the passion-fruit syrup in a jug. Arrange a layer of savoiardi on top of the set jelly layer and sprinkle with the rum and passion-fruit syrup. (You won't need all the biscuits.) Whip the double cream with the icing sugar and vanilla until it holds stiff peaks, then fold one third into the cold custard. Spoon the custard on top of the biscuits and return the trifle to the fridge for 30 minutes, until set.

8. Arrange the remaining mango and peaches on top of the custard layer and spoon over half of the passion-fruit pulp. Spoon over the remaining whipped cream, then cover and chill the trifle for 2 hours to allow the layers to set and the biscuits to soften.

9. To serve, scatter with 4 or 5 crumbled savoiardi and the remaining passion-fruit pulp.

Plum Skillet Cake

Stone fruit are so good with almonds, which have a mild and sweet nutty flavour. If you like, add some slightly more bitter almond extract to the cake mixture to accentuate the nutty notes. Serve this cake warm, straight from the pan with as much cream as you like.

Serves: 6
Hands on: 30 mins
Bake: 40 mins

110g unsalted butter, cubed and softened
125g golden caster sugar, plus 1 tbsp
1 tsp vanilla extract
2 eggs, lightly beaten
100g plain flour
50g ground almonds
1 tsp baking powder
pinch of salt
75ml buttermilk
6 large ripe, purple-skinned plums, halved, stone removed and each half cut into 4-5 wedges
50g flaked almonds
vanilla ice cream, crème fraîche or softly whipped double cream, to serve

You will need
20cm (at the base) ovenproof skillet or cast-iron pan, greased (base and sides)

1. Heat the oven to 180°C/160°C fan/Gas 4.

2. Beat 100g of the butter, the 125g of caster sugar and the vanilla in a stand mixer fitted with the beater, on medium speed for 3-5 minutes, scraping down the inside of the bowl from time to time, until pale and creamy. Add the eggs, a little at a time, beating well between each addition.

3. Sift the flour, ground almonds, baking powder and salt into the bowl and mix again to combine. Finally, add the buttermilk and mix until smooth. Spoon the mixture into the greased skillet or pan and spread it level.

4. Arrange the plums in tightly packed concentric circles on top of the cake mixture. Dot with the remaining 10g of butter and scatter with the flaked almonds and the 1 tablespoon of caster sugar.

5. Bake the cake on the middle shelf for 40 minutes, until it is golden and risen, and the plums are juicy and caramelised at the edges. Leave the cake to cool for 2 minutes, then serve in hearty spoonfuls with scoops of vanilla ice cream, or spoonfuls of crème fraîche or softly whipped double cream.

Tropical Fruit Gâteau

Mango and passion fruit are both uniquely creamy and floral in their fruitiness – introduce them to some freshly squeezed, slightly astringent lime juice and the flavour will sing. More mango and sweet-tart physalis make the perfect flavour-filled decoration. You can prepare the layers a day ahead and then partly assemble them a few hours before serving to allow all the flavours to mingle, if you wish.

Serves: 12
Hands on: 1½ hours
  + chilling
Bake: 25 mins

___

For the sponges
6 eggs, separated
100ml sunflower oil
100ml buttermilk
50g unsalted butter, melted
250g caster sugar
finely grated zest and juice
  of 1 unwaxed lime
pinch of cream of tartar
2 pinches of salt
175g plain flour
1 tsp baking powder
¼ tsp bicarbonate of soda
50g unsweetened
  desiccated coconut

For the rum & lime syrup
1 lime
100g caster sugar
3 tbsp white or dark rum

For the mango cream
250g ripe mango chunks
400ml double cream
2 tbsp icing sugar, sifted
2 passion fruit, halved and
  pulp scooped out

Continues overleaf

1. Make the sponges. Heat the oven to 180°C/160°C fan/Gas 4. Whisk the egg yolks with the oil, buttermilk and melted butter in a large mixing bowl until combined. Add half of the caster sugar and the lime zest and juice and whisk again to combine.

2. Whisk the egg whites with the cream of tartar and a pinch of the salt in a stand mixer fitted with the whisk, on medium speed until the egg whites form soft peaks. Add the remaining caster sugar a tablespoon at a time, and continue to whisk until you have a stiff, glossy meringue.

3. Sift the flour, baking powder, bicarbonate of soda and remaining pinch of salt into the egg-yolk mixture. Add the desiccated coconut and whisk to combine.

4. Using a large metal spoon, fold one third of the meringue mixture into the flour mixture to loosen, then gently fold in the remaining meringue until combined.

5. Divide the mixture equally between the prepared tins and gently spread it level. Bake the sponges for 22–25 minutes, until well risen and springy, and a skewer inserted into the centre of each comes out clean. Invert the cakes still in their tins onto a wire rack and leave to cool (with the tins still in place) for 30 minutes, then carefully remove the tins and leave the cakes to cool completely.

6. Make the rum and lime syrup. Finely grate the zest from the lime and set it aside, covered, to use in the mango cream. Squeeze the lime juice into a small saucepan and add the caster sugar and 2 tablespoons of water. Set the pan over a medium heat, stir to dissolve the sugar, then bring the liquid to the boil. Reduce the heat a little and simmer for 1 minute, until slightly syrupy, then remove the pan from the heat and stir in the rum. Leave to cool.

Continues overleaf

To decorate
75g unsweetened
    desiccated coconut
400ml double cream
2 tbsp icing sugar, sifted
1 large ripe mango, peeled,
    destoned and cut into
    long slices
2 kiwi fruit, peeled and
    sliced into rounds
seeds from
    ¼ pomegranate
6–8 physalis

You will need
23cm springform cake
    tins x 2, base greased,
    then lined with baking
    paper (do not grease
    the sides of the tins)

7. Make the mango cream. Purée the mango chunks in a blender until smooth. Whip the cream with the icing sugar until it holds stiff peaks. Add the mango purée, passion fruit pulp and the reserved lime zest and fold them in to combine.

8. Assemble the gâteau. Line the base of one of the springform tins with a disc of baking paper. Cut each sponge in half horizontally to make 4 even layers. Place one sponge in the tin, cut-side up, and brush the top with a third of the rum and lime syrup. Spoon over one third of the mango cream and spread it level with an offset palette knife. Top with a second sponge, brush with more lime syrup and spread with another third of the mango cream. Repeat this layering, ending with the fourth sponge layer, placing it cut side down. Gently press the layers together, cover, and chill the gâteau for 2 hours to allow the layers to set and the flavours to mingle.

9. Decorate the gâteau. Toast the desiccated coconut in a dry frying pan over a medium heat, stirring for 1 minute, until golden. Tip the toasted coconut onto a plate and leave it to cool. Whip the double cream with the icing sugar until it just holds stiff peaks.

10. Release the gâteau from the tin and transfer it to a serving plate. Cover the top and sides with the whipped cream, spreading it evenly with a palette knife. Coat the sides with the toasted coconut. Arrange the mango and kiwi fruit on top of the cake. Scatter with the pomegranate seeds and physalis, then slice to serve.

Victoria Sandwich Traybake

The leafy, floral raspberries and intensely perfumed jam are the stars of these elegant traybake slices. Raspberries, like strawberries, have hints of milk in them, making them a perfect pairing for cream. You could try stirring a little chopped fresh basil into the cream, if you like, to up the ante and add a spicy freshness.

Makes: 16
Hands on: 40 mins + chilling
Bake: 20 mins

For the sponge
225g unsalted butter, cubed and softened
225g caster sugar
4 large eggs, lightly beaten
1 tsp vanilla paste
175g plain flour
50g cornflour
2 tsp baking powder
pinch of salt
3 tbsp whole milk

For the filling
300ml double cream
2 tbsp icing sugar, sifted, plus extra for dusting
1 tsp vanilla paste
4 tbsp homemade raspberry jam (see p.270)
300g raspberries

You will need
20cm square cake tins x 2, greased, then base-lined with baking paper
baking sheet, lined with baking paper

1. Make the sponges. Heat the oven to 180°C/160°C fan/Gas 4. Beat the butter and sugar in a stand mixer fitted with the beater, on medium speed for 3–5 minutes, scraping down the inside of the bowl from time to time, until pale and creamy. Add the eggs, a little at a time, beating well between each addition. Add 1 tablespoon of the flour if the mixture starts to curdle at any stage. Add the vanilla.

2. Sift the flour, cornflour, baking powder and salt into the bowl and mix until just combined. Add the milk and mix again until smooth.

3. Divide the mixture equally between the lined tins and level with a palette knife. Bake on the middle shelf for 20 minutes, until golden and risen, and a skewer inserted into the centres comes out clean. Leave to cool in the tins for 5 minutes, then turn out the sponges onto a wire rack to cool completely.

4. Make the filling. Whip the cream, icing sugar and vanilla in a bowl using an electric hand whisk until it holds firm peaks.

5. Assemble the cakes. Place one of the sponges on the lined baking sheet and spread it with the raspberry jam. Arrange the raspberries on top and cover with an even layer of whipped cream. Gently press the second sponge on top. Cover the cake and chill it for 1 hour to make cutting easier.

6. Dust the top of the cake with icing sugar. Using a long, serrated knife, cut the cake in half, then cut each half into 8 equal slices. Remove the slices from the tin to serve.

Piña Colada Cake

If you like slightly spicy, fruity and almost alcoholic-tasting-when-ripe pineapple, then you're going to love this cake. Beautiful pineapple flowers, flambéed boozy pineapple slices and a tangy pineapple curd are all deliciously sandwiched between coconut- and rum-flavoured sponges.

Serves: 14
Hands on: 2¼ hours
Bake: 1½ hours

---

*For the coconut
& vanilla sponges*
200g salted butter
200g margarine
370g caster sugar
7 eggs
2½ tsp vanilla extract
350g self-raising flour
½ tsp baking powder
130g desiccated coconut
25ml semi-skimmed milk
20ml white rum

*For the dried
pineapple flowers*
1 ripe pineapple

*For the flambéed
pineapple filling*
75ml white rum
75ml coconut rum
9 canned pineapple slices

For the pineapple curd
1 x 280g can of pineapple
   slices, juice and fruit
125g frozen pineapple
1 tbsp lemon juice
90g caster sugar
40g salted butter
1 egg
2 egg yolks
20g cornflour

Continues overleaf

1. Make the sponges. Heat the oven to 180°C/160°C fan/Gas 4. Cream the butter, margarine and sugar in the bowl of a stand mixer fitted with the beater, on a medium speed for about 3–4 minutes, scraping down the inside of the bowl from time to time, until pale and fluffy.

2. In a jug, whisk together the eggs and vanilla extract. Reduce the speed of the stand mixer to medium–low and gradually pour the egg mixture into the butter and sugar and mix until fully combined.

3. Sift together the flour and baking powder, then fold this into the mixture using a metal spoon, followed by the desiccated coconut. Finally, mix through the milk and rum to loosen. Divide the mixture equally between the prepared tins and bake for 25–30 minutes, until golden and risen and a skewer inserted into the centre of each sponge comes out clean. Leave the sponges to cool in the tins for 10 minutes, then turn them out onto a wire rack to cool completely.

4. Make the dried pineapple flowers. Heat the oven to 100°C/80°C fan/Gas ½. Cut the top and bottom from the pineapple, then use a large, sharp knife to remove the skin. Using the sharp knife or a mandoline, slice the pineapple into very thin slices. Pat the slices dry with kitchen paper, then place them onto the lined baking sheets and bake for about 1 hour, turning them over after 30 minutes, or until completely dried out on both sides and just starting to colour at the edges. This may take a little longer if the slices are thicker.

5. Once the pineapple slices are dried out, remove them from the sheets and, while they are still warm, place each slice into a hole in the muffin tin, pressing them down so that each slice forms a flower shape. Set aside in the tin until you're ready to decorate.

Continues overleaf

*For the coconut
buttercream*
165g salted butter
80ml canned
    coconut cream
1kg icing sugar, sifted
40ml white coconut rum
25ml white rum

To decorate
60ml white rum
200g desiccated coconut

You will need
20cm round cake tins x 4,
    greased, then base-lined
    with baking paper
mandoline
2 baking sheets, lined
    with baking paper
12-hole muffin tin
cooking thermometer
25cm cake board or plate
cake-decorating turntable
large piping bag fitted
    with a medium
    plain nozzle
bristle pastry brush

6. Begin the flambéed pineapple filling. Add the white rum and coconut rum to a wide shallow container, then lay the pineapple slices in the liquid and leave them to soak while you make the curd.

7. Make the pineapple curd. Add the tinned pineapple, frozen pineapple and 50ml of water to a large saucepan and bring the mixture to the boil. Boil for 3–4 minutes to soften the fruit, then remove from the heat and, using a hand-held stick blender, blitz the pineapple to a purée. Pass the purée through a sieve, reserving both the liquid and the pulp. Return the liquid to the pan and bring it back to the boil. Reduce the heat and simmer until you have about 125ml of liquid left. Then, add the lemon juice, caster sugar and butter to the pan and continue to heat until the sugar has dissolved and the butter has melted.

8. In a medium bowl, whisk together the whole egg, egg yolks and cornflour, then gradually pour the hot pineapple mixture over the egg mixture, whisking continuously, until they are fully combined.

9. Pour the mixture back into the saucepan and return the pan to a low–medium heat. Stir continuously with a whisk until the mixture starts to thicken and reaches 84°C on the cooking thermometer. Remove the curd from the heat and pass it through a sieve into a clean bowl. Whisk the reserved pulp back into the mixture, cover and set it aside to cool.

10. Finish the flambéed pineapple filling. Place a large frying pan over a high heat and add the rum-soaked pineapple slices. Cook for 3–4 minutes on each side, until they begin to caramelise. Add a splash of the soaking rum and set the rum alight to flambé. Once the liquid has burned off, place the pineapple rings in a bowl and set them aside to cool.

11. Make the buttercream. In the bowl of a stand mixer fitted with the beater, beat together the butter and coconut cream on medium speed for 2–3 minutes, until combined and pale. Add half of the icing sugar and mix on a low speed to incorporate, then add the other half and continue to mix on a low speed until the mixture is combined. Add the rums, then beat on medium speed for 3–4 minutes, until pale and fluffy, then beat on low for about 8–10 minutes to a smooth buttercream. Transfer half of the buttercream to the large piping bag.

12. Assemble the cake. Place a cake board or serving plate on the turntable. Pipe a small blob of buttercream on the board and use it to secure the first layer of sponge. Then, brush the sponge with a third of the white rum and pipe a buttercream border around the top edge. Fill the space inside the buttercream with a thin layer of pineapple curd, then slice the flambéed pineapple rings in half and use 6 halves to create a layer of pineapple slices, in a fan radiating from the centre of the curd around the cake. Top with the next layer of sponge and repeat the process. Top with the third layer and repeat for a third time, then finally top with the fourth and final sponge layer.

13. Use a palette knife to spread a thin layer of the remaining half of the buttercream over the top and side of the cake to crumb coat, then place the stacked cake in the fridge for 10 minutes to firm up.

14. Remove the cake from the fridge and place it on a large tray. Using a palette knife, evenly cover the top and side of the cake with the buttercream. While the buttercream is still sticky, use your hands to press the coconut all around the side and top of the cake – the tray will catch any falling coconut, making it easier to scoop up and re-use.

15. Once the cake is completely covered with coconut, use blobs of buttercream to stick the pineapple flowers in a swoop up one side of the cake, over the top edge, and down the other side.

Blackberry, Yuzu & Passion Fruit Cake

Yuzu is a citrus fruit from Asia with a tangy, floral flavour that pairs beautifully with sweet berries and passion fruit. This cake has three layers of buttery sponge filled with lip-smacking yuzu and passion fruit curd and coated in berry buttercream – the perfect combination of citrus, sweet and cream. Make the curd ahead to give it time to cool and set.

Serves: 10+
Hands on: 2 hours + cooling
Bake: 25 mins

For the yuzu &
passion fruit curd
5 egg yolks (use the whites
    for the buttercream)
150g caster sugar
60ml yuzu juice
1 large passion fruit, halved
    and pulp scooped out
100g unsalted butter, cubed

For the blackberry purée
450g blackberries
50g caster sugar
1 tbsp yuzu juice

For the sponges
125g unsalted butter,
    cubed and softened
350g caster sugar
125ml sunflower oil
2 tsp vanilla extract
4 eggs, lightly beaten
3 egg yolks
325g plain flour
3 tsp baking powder
pinch of salt
150ml whole milk

For the buttercream
5 egg whites
275g caster sugar
pinch of salt
450g unsalted butter,
    cubed and softened
2 tsp vanilla extract

Continues overleaf

1. Make the yuzu and passion fruit curd. Whisk together the egg yolks and sugar with a balloon whisk in a heatproof bowl. Add the yuzu juice and passion-fruit pulp and whisk to combine. Set the bowl over a pan of gently simmering water, add the butter and stir until melted. Continue to cook the curd, whisking occasionally, for 15 minutes, until it thickly coats the back of a spoon. Pass the curd through a sieve into a clean bowl, discarding the passion fruit seeds, cover the surface with baking paper to prevent a skin forming and leave to cool for 4 hours, until set. Chill until needed.

2. Make the blackberry purée. While the curd is chilling, cook the blackberries, caster sugar and yuzu juice in a small saucepan over a low heat, stirring frequently, for 5 minutes, until the berries burst and release their juice. Simmer for a further 4–5 minutes, until the berries break down into a soft, jammy mixture and most of the excess juice has been cooked off. Remove the pan from the heat, then press the berries through a fine-mesh sieve to remove the skin and pips. The purée should be a thick jam consistency, but if it is still juicy, return it to the pan and simmer over a low heat for another minute to thicken. Leave to cool, then cover and chill until needed.

3. Make the sponges. Heat the oven to 180°C/160°C fan/Gas 4. Beat the butter and caster sugar in a stand mixer fitted with the beater, on medium speed for 3–5 minutes, scraping down the inside of the bowl from time to time, until pale and creamy. Add the oil and vanilla and continue to mix for 3 minutes, until pale, light and fluffy.

4. Add the beaten eggs, a little at a time, beating well between each addition. Scrape down the inside of the bowl and add the egg yolks, one at a time, beating well between each addition.

5. Sift the flour, baking powder and salt into the bowl, add half of the milk and mix on low speed to combine. Add the remaining milk and mix again until silky smooth.

Continues overleaf

Blackberry, Yuzu & Passion Fruit Cake *continued*

To decorate
edible flowers
handful of blackberries
   (optional)

You will need
20cm round cake tins x 3,
   greased, then base-lined
   with baking paper
4 medium piping bags,
   each fitted with a
   medium plain nozzle
cake-decorating turntable
   (optional)
cake smoother or bench
   scraper (optional)
2 small piping bags

6. Divide the mixture equally between the lined tins and spread it level with a palette knife. Bake on the middle shelves for 22–25 minutes, until golden and risen, and a skewer inserted into the centres comes out clean. Leave the sponges to cool in the tins for 10 minutes, then carefully turn them out onto a wire rack to cool completely.

7. Make the buttercream. While the sponges are cooling, using a balloon whisk, combine the egg whites, caster sugar, salt and 1 tablespoon of water in a large heatproof bowl. Set the bowl over a saucepan of gently simmering water and whisk continuously for 5 minutes, until the meringue is hot to the touch and leaves a ribbon trail when you lift the whisk. Scoop the meringue into the bowl of a stand mixer and whisk on medium speed for 5 minutes, scraping down the inside of the bowl from time to time, until it forms stiff peaks and cools.

8. Gradually, add the butter to the meringue mixture, whisking continuously and scraping down the inside of the bowl, until silky smooth and glossy. Add the vanilla and mix again to combine. Spoon about one fifth of the buttercream into one of the medium piping bags fitted with a medium plain nozzle.

9. Assemble the cake. Place 1 sponge layer on a serving plate and pipe a ring of buttercream around the top edge. Fill the middle of the buttercream ring with about 4 tablespoons of the yuzu curd and spread it level with a palette knife. Pipe a thin layer of buttercream on top of the curd and spread it with a palette knife to cover. Top with a second sponge and repeat with the buttercream and curd. Cover and chill any leftover curd.

10. Top the stacked sponges with the third sponge layer and gently press the layers together. Cover the sides with a thin crumb coat of buttercream and the top with a neat, smooth, slightly thicker layer. Chill the cake for 30 minutes.

11. Divide the remaining buttercream between 4 bowls and leave 1 bowl plain. Add 1 tablespoon of the blackberry purée to the second bowl and mix to combine. Add 2 tablespoons of the purée to the third bowl and 3 tablespoons to the fourth. The buttercream should range in colour from creamy white to very pale purple through to dark purple, so adjust the colours accordingly and save any leftover purée to decorate the finished cake. Spoon each coloured buttercream into a separate piping bag fitted with a medium plain nozzle. You can use the bowl of plain buttercream to top up the piping bag containing the buttercream you've already used to fill the cake.

12. Place the cake on the turntable, if using. Starting at the base of the cake, pipe 2 rows of the darkest purple buttercream around the side. The rows should cover one quarter of the height of the cake. Repeat with the slightly lighter purple buttercream and so on, ending with the plain buttercream at the top.

13. Using a palette knife, roughly blend the different layers of buttercream together, then, using a large palette knife, bench scraper or cake smoother held at a 45-degree angle to the side of the cake, turn the turntable (if using) and smooth the sides to ombre the buttercream – merging the colours at the edges. For best results, try to do this in one continuous sweep.

14. Pipe different coloured buttercream kisses decoratively over the top of the cake using any remaining buttercream in the piping bags. Spoon any leftover blackberry purée into one of the small piping bags and the curd into the other. Snip off the end of each piping bag to a 2–3mm point, then pipe dots of both over the top of the cake around the piped buttercream kisses. Decorate the cake with edible flowers, and fresh blackberries if you wish.

Savoury Fruit Loaf

Over time, an aged cheddar, for example, develops notes of fruit and nuts – the very same ingredients in this loaf, and the reason why it is a perfect accompaniment to cheese. Try sour cherries instead of cranberries for an alternative hit of fruitiness.

Serves: 6–8
Hands on: 30 mins
  + soaking + rising
Bake: 30 mins

For the soaked fruit
1 tea bag, such as builder's
75ml just-boiled water
50g currants
50g sultanas or raisins
50g dried cranberries
75g soft dried figs or
  apricots, roughly
  chopped

For the loaf
300g strong white
  bread flour
50g wholemeal spelt flour
5g fast-action dried yeast
½ tsp salt
175ml lukewarm water
2 tbsp rapeseed or olive oil
1 egg, lightly beaten
1 tbsp dark agave syrup
  or runny honey
soaked dried fruit
  (see above)
100g hazelnuts,
  roughly chopped

You will need
large baking sheet, lined
  with baking paper
oiled proving bag

1. Soak the fruit. Place the tea bag in a mixing bowl, pour over the just-boiled water and leave the tea to brew for 5 minutes. Squeeze out the bag and discard. Add the currants, the sultanas or raisins, the cranberries and the figs or apricots to the bowl. Stir the fruit and leave it to soak for 1 hour.

2. Make the loaf. Mix both types of flour, the yeast and salt in a stand mixer fitted with the dough hook until combined. Make a well in the centre of the dry ingredients, add the lukewarm water, rapeseed or olive oil, egg and agave syrup or honey. Mix on low speed until combined, then increase the speed slightly and knead for a further 5 minutes, until the dough is smooth and elastic. Add the soaked dried fruit and any leftover liquid in the bowl and the hazelnuts, then continue to mix until combined.

3. Tip out the dough onto a lightly floured work surface and shape it into a ball. Lightly oil the bowl, return the dough, cover with a clean tea towel and leave to rise at room temperature for 1 hour, until doubled in size.

4. Lightly flour the work surface and knead the dough gently for 20 seconds to knock it back. Shape the dough into a neat, tight ball and place it on the lined baking sheet with the seam on the underside. Dust the top with flour. Slide the baking sheet into the proving bag and leave the loaf to prove at room temperature for 45 minutes, until nearly doubled in size. Heat the oven to 200°C/180°C fan/Gas 6.

5. Using a sharp knife or lame, cut a cross into the top of the proved loaf. Bake for 20 minutes, until golden and risen. Reduce the oven temperature to 180°C/160°C fan/Gas 4 and bake the loaf for a further 10 minutes, until deep golden brown, and the loaf sounds hollow when tapped on the underside. Leave to cool completely on a wire rack, before serving sliced with salted butter, cheese and pickles.

Strawberry Mousse with Hazelnut Dacquoise Biscuits

Bright and breezy, this fresh strawberry mousse goes for the classic pairing of strawberry and mint – tangy, spicy mint, along with the lemon juice in the mousse really ramp up the fruits' sweetness on the taste buds. The creaminess in the nutty biscuits provides balance. This is a great make-ahead dessert for a summer party.

Serves: 8
Hands on: 45 mins + chilling
Bake: 15 min

For the strawberry mousse
5 platinum-grade
  gelatine leaves
350g strawberries,
  hulled and halved
  or quartered if large
1 tbsp lemon juice
65g caster sugar
60g pasteurised egg whites
200ml whipping cream
1 tsp vanilla extract

For the dacquoise biscuits
50g roasted hazelnuts,
  finely chopped
50g icing sugar, sifted,
  plus extra for dusting
small pinch of salt
1 large egg white,
  at room temperature
1 tbsp caster sugar
2 drops of almond extract

To decorate
150ml whipping cream
½ tsp vanilla paste
8 strawberries, halved
  or quartered
few mint leaves

Continues overleaf

1. Make the mousse. Soak the gelatine leaves in a bowl of cold water while you prepare the strawberries.

2. Place the strawberries into the bowl of a food processor with the lemon juice and ½ tablespoon of the caster sugar. Blitz until smooth, then pass the purée through a fine sieve into a large bowl to remove the seeds.

3. Add 100ml of the strawberry purée to a small saucepan and gently warm it over a low heat – do not let it boil. When the purée is warm and beginning to steam, remove the pan from the heat, squeeze out the gelatine and add it to the pan. Mix until the gelatine has melted, then stir the warmed mixture back into the rest of the strawberry purée and set aside.

4. In the bowl of a stand mixer fitted with a whisk attachment, whisk the egg whites on a high speed until foamy, then gradually add the remaining sugar, whisking until soft peaks form.

5. In a separate bowl, using a hand-held electric whisk, whisk the cream and vanilla extract together until it forms medium peaks.

6. Fold the egg whites into the strawberry purée, then fold in the softly whipped cream until fully combined.

7. Divide the mousse equally between the serving glasses and place them in the fridge for at least 2 hours for the mousse to set.

8. Make the dacquoise biscuits. While the mousse is chilling, heat the oven to 180°C/160°C fan/Gas 4. Tip the hazelnuts, icing sugar and salt into the bowl of food processor and blitz to a fine powder. Set aside.

Continues overleaf

You will need
8 serving glasses
large piping bag fitted
   with a medium
   plain nozzle
baking sheet, lined
   with baking paper
medium piping bag
   fitted with a medium
   petal nozzle

9. In a bowl using a hand-held electric whisk or a balloon whisk, whisk the egg white to soft peaks. Gradually add the caster sugar, a little at a time, whisking continuously until stiff peaks form. Add the almond extract and whisk for a couple of seconds to combine.

10. Using a large metal spoon, fold the hazelnut powder into the egg white until fully combined. Spoon the mixture into the piping bag fitted with a medium plain nozzle and pipe about thirty 4cm-diameter rounds onto the lined baking sheet, spacing them well apart to allow for spreading. Bake the biscuits for 15 minutes, until crisp and light golden. Leave to cool completely on the baking sheet, then dust with icing sugar to finish.

11. Decorate the mousses. When you're ready to serve, whisk the whipping cream and vanilla paste together until the cream forms stiff peaks and can hold its shape when piped. Transfer the whipped cream to the piping bag fitted with the petal nozzle, and pipe a zig-zag or swirl of cream on top of each mousse. Finish each portion with some strawberry halves or quarters and mint leaves to decorate. Serve with the dacquoise biscuits.

Apple & Almond Cake

Apples are blessed with both creamy and spicy flavour notes, which is why the cream-cheese frosting and the cinnamon and star anise (in the apple poaching liquid) work so well in this cake. We've used tart Braeburns, but a mixture of sour Bramleys, crisp Granny Smiths and sweet Galas would really ramp up the complexity of the apple flavours.

Serves: 16
Hands on: 1½ hours
Bake: 45 mins

For the streusel topping
120g plain flour
120g light muscovado sugar
120g ground almonds
120g unsalted butter,
  cubed, at room
  temperature
80g flaked almonds

*For the apple
& almond sponges*
160g unsalted butter,
  at room temperature
270g light muscovado
  sugar
3 large eggs,
  lightly beaten
1½ tsp almond extract
1½ tsp vanilla paste
370g self-raising flour
½ tsp salt
160ml whole milk,
  at room temperature
2 Braeburn apples, peeled,
  cored and each cut
  into 16 thin slices

For the Bourbon drizzle
50g unsalted butter
50g runny honey
50ml Bourbon liqueur

Continues overleaf

1. Make the streusel topping. Combine the flour, sugar and ground almonds in a medium bowl, then add the butter and rub it in with your fingertips until everything comes together. Use a butter knife to break it up into smaller pieces, then stir through the flaked almonds until evenly distributed. Set aside.

2. Make the sponges. Heat the oven to 190°C/170°C fan/Gas 5. Cream the butter and sugar together in a stand mixer fitted with the beater on a medium speed for 3–4 minutes, until pale and fluffy.

3. In a jug, lightly beat together the eggs, almond extract and vanilla. Gradually add this mixture to the butter and sugar, mixing on a low speed until fully combined.

4. In a separate bowl, sift together the flour and salt. Add half into the butter mixture and mix on a low speed until almost combined, then pour in half of the milk and mix until well incorporated. Repeat with the other half of the flour and the remaining milk.

5. Divide the batter equally between the prepared cake tins and spread it level, leaving the batter slightly higher around the edges. Lay the apple slices concentrically on top of the cake batter and then scatter the streusel topping over the apples. Bake for 45 minutes, or until a skewer inserted into the centre of each sponge comes out clean.

6. Make the Bourbon drizzle. While the sponges are baking, combine all of the drizzle ingredients in a small saucepan and place it over a low heat until the butter has just melted. Set aside.

7. Once the sponges are ready, remove them from the oven and use a skewer to poke holes in the top of each. Pour over the drizzle, then leave the sponges to cool in their tins for 10 minutes, before turning them out onto a wire rack to cool completely.

Continues overleaf

For the poached apples
2 Braeburn apples,
    peeled, cored and
    cut into eighths
1 cinnamon stick
2 star anise
300ml apple cider

For the cream-cheese frosting
300g icing sugar, sifted
335g full-fat cream cheese
165ml double cream

For the almond brittle
25g flaked almonds
65g caster sugar

You will need
23cm springform cake
    tins x 2, greased,
    then base-lined
    with baking paper
wooden skewer
2 silicone baking mats
    (optional)

8. Prepare the poached apples. While the sponges are cooling, place the apples into a medium saucepan. Add the spices and pour in the cider. Place a small plate or paper cartouche on top to stop the apples rising above the surface of the liquid and place the pan over a medium heat. Bring the liquid to the boil, then simmer for 20 minutes, or until a sharp knife slips easily into the apple flesh. Remove the apples from the poaching liquid and leave them to cool completely. Discard the liquid.

9. Make the cream-cheese frosting. Cream together the icing sugar and cream cheese in the clean bowl of a stand mixer fitted with the beater, on low–medium speed for 2–3 minutes, until just combined, taking care not to incorporate too much air.

10. In a separate bowl, use an electric hand whisk to whisk the double cream to stiff peaks. Add the cream-cheese mixture to the bowl with the whipped cream, and beat them together with the electric hand whisk to combine, then chill until needed.

11. Make the almond brittle. In a large saucepan set over a medium heat, toast the almonds for about 5 minutes, until they begin to colour and smell fragrant. Add the caster sugar and continue to heat gently, stirring, until the sugar has melted into a rich amber caramel. Pour out the caramel onto a sheet of baking paper or a silicone mat, cover with another sheet of baking paper or silicone mat, and roll it with a rolling pin to about 2–4mm thick. Leave the brittle to cool and harden.

12. Assemble the cake. Take a cooled sponge and top it with just under half of the cream-cheese frosting. Place the second sponge on top and top with the remaining frosting, spreading it towards the edges with a palette knife. Place the poached apple wedges on top of the cake and then break the almond brittle into triangular shards, placing the shards around and in between the apples to decorate.

Paul's Pain aux Raisins

The fruity raisins in these crisp, puff-pastry swirls filled also with vanilla crème pâtissière become sweeter still with baking. The woody, citrus notes in the cinnamon pick up the citrus of the orange zest, too.

Makes: 12
Hands on: 1 hour
  +chilling + rising
Bake: 20 mins

For the dough
350g strong white
   bread flour
250g unsalted
   butter, chilled
30g golden caster sugar
7g fast-action dried yeast
1 tsp salt
125ml whole milk
50ml warm water
1 large egg, plus 1 beaten
   egg to glaze

For the crème pâtissière
50g caster sugar
2 large egg yolks
20g cornflour
250ml whole milk
½ vanilla pod, split and
   seeds scraped out

For the filling
100g raisins
¼ tsp ground cinnamon
finely grated zest of
   1 unwaxed orange

For the icing
200g icing sugar, sifted
juice of 1 orange

You will need
dough scraper
2 sheets of baking paper
2 large baking trays, lined
   with baking paper
2 oiled proving bags

1. Make the dough. Put the flour in a mixing bowl. Cut 25g of the butter into cubes, add these to the bowl and rub in the butter with your fingertips until the mixture resembles breadcrumbs. Add the caster sugar, yeast and salt and stir to combine.

2. Beat the milk, warm water and egg together in a separate bowl and pour the wet mixture into the flour mixture. Mix with a wooden spoon to bring the ingredients together, then turn out the mixture onto the work surface and knead it with a dough scraper for 5 minutes, until you have a slightly sticky dough. Wrap the dough and chill it for 1 hour.

3. Place the remaining block of chilled butter between 2 sheets of baking paper and flatten it out with a rolling pin to a rectangle measuring about 33 x 19cm.

4. Lightly flour the work surface and roll out the chilled dough to a rectangle about 1cm thick and measuring 50 x 20cm. With a short end of the dough closest to you, lay the butter on top of the dough, so that it covers the bottom two thirds. Make sure that it is positioned neatly and almost reaches the sides.

5. Fold the exposed dough at the top (without the butter) down to cover half of the butter. Fold the bottom third of the dough (with butter) up over the dough – you will now have a sandwich of 2 layers of butter and 3 layers of dough. Pinch together the edges of the dough lightly to seal in the butter and turn the dough/butter parcel 90 degrees, so the long seam is on the left-hand side. Wrap the dough and chill it for 20 minutes to harden the butter.

6. With the seam still on the left, roll out the dough on a lightly floured work surface to a rectangle, about 1cm thick and 50 x 20cm, as before. With a short end of the dough closest to you, fold the bottom one third of the dough up and then fold the top third down on top. Put the dough back in the fridge for 20 minutes.

Continues overleaf

7. Make the crème pâtissière. While the dough is in the fridge, in a medium bowl and using a balloon whisk, whisk the caster sugar with the egg yolks, cornflour and 1 tablespoon of the milk until pale and combined.

8. Gently heat the remaining milk with the vanilla seeds in a small saucepan until it just comes to the boil. Pour the hot milk into the egg mixture and whisk until well combined. Return the mixture to the pan and heat it gently, whisking continuously, until the mixture thickens to a custard consistency. Pour the crème pâtissière into a bowl, cover the surface and leave it to cool. Then, chill it until set.

9. Finish the pain aux raisins. Remove the dough from the freezer, unwrap it and roll it out on a lightly floured work surface to a rectangle about 1cm thick and 50 x 20cm, as before. With one of the short edges closest to you, fold the bottom one third of the dough up and then fold the top third down on top. Roll out the dough to a 30cm square.

10. Spread the crème pâtissière over the dough, leaving a 2cm border on the side furthest from you.

11. Sprinkle the raisins, cinnamon and orange zest over the crème pâtissière, then starting from the edge furthest from you, roll the dough towards you into a spiralled sausage shape, keeping it as tight as possible – give the dough a gentle tug each time you roll to tighten it up and give it a little tension. When you reach the end, roll the sausage back and forth a few times to seal the join.

12. Cut the roll into 12 equal slices, each about 2.5–3cm wide. Lay the slices, cut-side up and spaced apart to allow for rising, on the lined baking trays. Put each tray inside a proving bag and leave the dough to prove for 1 hour, until it has at least doubled in size.

13. Heat the oven to 220°C/ 200°C fan/Gas 7. Brush the risen dough with beaten egg and bake the pains for 15–20 minutes, until golden brown and risen. If they look like they are over-browning, cover them with foil for the last 5 minutes of baking. Remove the pains from the oven and leave them to cool.

14. Make the icing. Mix the icing sugar and 2 tablespoons of the orange juice to make a stiff but pourable icing. Drizzle the orange icing over the cooled pain aux raisins, then leave them for a few minutes for the icing to set before serving.

Rhubarb & Strawberry Crumble Cake

Sweet, delicate, early forced rhubarb makes for a gorgeous burst of flavour and splash of colour in this twist on a classic pud (if you can't find forced, the aromatic, candied notes of later rhubarb are just as delicious). Here, strawberries add a burst of sweetness, and the textures of cream, crumble and soft sponge are an adventure for the tongue as well as the taste buds.

VEGAN
Serves: 16–18
Hands on: 1 hour + cooling
Bake: 30 mins

For the crumble layer
130g plain flour
100g ground almonds
125g vegan block butter, cubed and chilled
50g demerara sugar
pinch of salt

For the sponges
450g plain flour
1½ tsp baking powder
1½ tsp bicarbonate of soda
150g ground almonds
400ml unsweetened almond milk
80g coconut yogurt
2 tsp vanilla paste
juice of 2 lemons
100g coconut oil, softened
250g golden caster sugar
50g light brown soft sugar
100g rhubarb, cut into 1cm dice
100g strawberries, hulled and chopped into 1cm dice

Continues overleaf

1. Make the crumble layer. Heat the oven to 180°C/160°C fan/ Gas 4. Mix the flour and ground almonds together, then rub in the butter with your fingertips until the mixture resembles coarse breadcrumbs. Add the sugar and salt and continue to mix with a table knife until the crumble starts to clump together. Spread the crumble mixture onto the lined baking tray and bake for 15–20 minutes, until golden and crisp. Leave to cool.

2. Make the sponges. While the crumble is baking, sift the flour, baking powder, bicarbonate of soda and ground almonds into a large mixing bowl and stir to combine.

3. In a large jug, whisk together the almond milk, coconut yogurt, vanilla and lemon juice to make a vegan buttermilk, then leave to stand for 5 minutes.

4. Beat the coconut oil and both types of sugar in a stand mixer fitted with the beater, on medium speed for 3–5 minutes, scraping down the inside of the bowl from time to time, until pale and creamy. With the mixer on, gradually pour in the buttermilk mixture, alternating with spoonfuls of the flour mixture until everything is smooth and creamy.

5. Divide the mixture equally between the lined tins and spread it level with a palette knife. Scatter a third each of the rhubarb and strawberries over the top of each sponge, lightly pressing them into the mixture. Bake on the middle shelves for 30 minutes, until golden and risen and a skewer inserted into the centres comes out clean. Leave to cool completely in the tins.

6. Make the strawberry and rhubarb compôte. While the cakes are baking, put the rhubarb, strawberries, caster sugar and vanilla in a saucepan, stir until combined and leave to stand for 10 minutes

Continues overleaf

*For the rhubarb &
strawberry compôte*
150g rhubarb, cut into
    2–3cm pieces
150g strawberries,
    hulled and chopped
150g caster sugar
1 tsp vanilla paste

For the vanilla frosting
400g icing sugar, sifted
125g vegan spread
1 tsp vanilla paste

To decorate
200g strawberries,
    halved if large
few thyme flowers
    (optional)

You will need
baking tray, lined
    with baking paper
20cm round cake tins x 3,
    greased, then base-lined
    with baking paper
medium piping bag fitted
    with a large plain nozzle
20cm cake board or plate

to allow the fruit to release some liquid. Bring to the boil, then reduce the heat slightly and simmer, stirring occasionally, for 10 minutes, or until softened. Remove the pan from the heat and leave the compôte to cool.

7. Make the vanilla frosting. Beat the icing sugar, vegan spread and vanilla in a stand mixer fitted with the beater, on medium speed for 2–3 minutes, scraping down the inside of the bowl from time to time, until pale and creamy. Spoon the frosting into the medium piping bag fitted with a large plain nozzle.

8. Assemble the cake. Turn the sponges out of the tins. Secure one of the sponges on the cake board or plate with piped dots of frosting. Pipe one third of the frosting evenly over the top. Spoon half the compôte on top, spreading it out evenly, and top with one third of the crumble. Place the second sponge on top and repeat with the frosting, compôte and crumble. Finish with the final sponge and pipe the remaining frosting over the top. Decorate with strawberries and thyme flowers (if using) and the rest of the crumble.

Raspberry & Custard Tart

This is a tart to celebrate the green, sugary acidity of fresh raspberries. Vanilla (in the pastry) brings out their sweetness, as does the final flourish of fresh mint, while lemon picks up their tart tones.

Serves: 10
Hands on: 1½ hours
+ chilling
Bake: 25 mins

For the pastry
150g unsalted butter,
  cubed and at room
  temperature
75g icing sugar, sifted
seeds from ½ vanilla pod
2 egg yolks
finely grated zest of
  ½ unwaxed lemon
200g plain flour
pinch of salt
1 tbsp double cream

*For the crème
diplomat filling*
500ml whole milk
seeds from ½ vanilla pod
pared rind of ½ unwaxed
  lemon
2 platinum-grade
  gelatine leaves
5 egg yolks
100g caster sugar
40g cornflour
pinch of salt
150ml double cream
2 tbsp icing sugar, sifted

To decorate
450g raspberries
few mint leaves

You will need
23cm loose-bottomed
  fluted tart tin
baking beans or rice

1. Make the pastry. Beat the butter, icing sugar and vanilla seeds in a stand mixer fitted with the beater, on medium speed for 2–3 minutes, scraping down the inside of the bowl from time to time, until pale and creamy. One at a time, add the egg yolks, beating well between each addition. Add the lemon zest and mix again until combined.

2. Sift the flour and salt into the bowl, add the double cream and mix again briefly until the dough starts to clump together, taking care not to overwork it. Add a little more double cream, if needed, to bring the dough together. Tip the dough out onto a work surface and lightly knead it to bring it together into a neat ball. Flatten the dough into a disc, wrap it and chill it for at least 1 hour, until firm.

3. Begin the crème diplomat filling. While the pastry is chilling, pour the milk into a saucepan and add the vanilla seeds and pared lemon rind. Place the pan over a low heat and slowly bring the milk to the boil. Remove from the heat and leave to infuse for 20 minutes.

4. Soak the gelatine leaves in a bowl of cold water for 5 minutes, until soft.

5. Using a balloon whisk, whisk the egg yolks, caster sugar, cornflour and salt in a large mixing bowl for 1 minute, until pale.

6. Bring the milk back to the boil. Remove the pared lemon, then pour one quarter of the hot milk into the egg mixture, whisking continuously until thoroughly combined. Gradually add the remaining milk, whisking continuously until smooth.

7. Return the egg mixture to the pan, then place the pan over a low–medium heat. Cook for 2 minutes, whisking continuously, until the custard thickens to the consistency of softly whipped cream, and you can no longer taste the cornflour.

Continues overleaf

8. Squeeze any excess water from the gelatine leaves and add the leaves to the custard. Whisk until melted and thoroughly combined, then pass the custard through a sieve into a clean bowl. Cover the surface with baking paper to prevent a skin forming and leave the custard to cool to room temperature, then chill it for at least 2 hours, until set.

9. Make the tart case. Roll out the pastry on a lightly floured work surface into a neat disc about 2mm thick and large enough to line the base and sides of the tart tin. Transfer the pastry to the tin, pressing it neatly into the base and the sides. Trim the excess from the top and chill the pastry case for at least 20 minutes. Meanwhile, heat the oven to 180°C/160°C fan/Gas 4.

10. Prick the base of the chilled tart case all over with a fork, line it with baking paper and fill it with baking beans or rice. Bake the tart case on the middle shelf for 20 minutes, until the top edge starts to turn crisp and golden. Remove the paper and beans or rice and return the tart case to the oven for a further 5 minutes, until the base is crisp. Leave to cool.

11. Finish the crème diplomat filling. Whip the cream with the icing sugar until it holds soft peaks. Whisk the cold custard until smooth, then fold in half of the whipped cream to loosen. Fold in the remaining cream until combined.

12. Assemble and decorate the tart. Place the pastry case on a serving plate, fill it with the crème diplomat and spread it level with a palette knife. Pile the raspberries on top of the custard to generously cover the tart. Chill the tart for 20 minutes, then dust the top with icing sugar and decorate with mint leaves to serve.

Banoffee Layer Cake

Oozing with caramel and inspired by legendary banoffee pie, this cake takes full advantage of the honeyed sweetness of ripe bananas. Grassy with a hint of pear drops when young, bananas take on notes of cloves, butterscotch and vanilla as they ripen.

VEGAN

Serves: 16–18
Hands on: 50 mins + cooling
Bake: 30 mins

For the sponges
400g self-raising flour
70g ground almonds
2 tsp baking powder
8 ripe bananas, mashed
100ml light olive oil
160g light brown soft sugar
2 tsp vanilla paste
100ml unsweetened
    almond milk
150g vegan dark chocolate,
    finely chopped

For the caramel sauce
3 tbsp canned coconut cream
75g light brown soft sugar
½ tbsp golden syrup
¼ tsp vanilla paste
½ tsp cornflour

For the vanilla frosting
400g icing sugar, sifted
125g vegan spread
1 tsp vanilla paste

To decorate
2 ripe bananas, sliced and
    tossed in lemon juice
20g vegan dark
    chocolate, grated

You will need
20cm round cake tins x 2,
    greased, then base-lined
    with baking paper
medium piping bag fitted
    with a large plain nozzle
20cm cake board or plate

1. Make the sponges. Heat the oven to 180°C/160°C fan/Gas 4. Sift the flour, ground almonds and baking powder into a large mixing bowl and stir to combine. Whisk the bananas, oil, sugar, vanilla and almond milk in a stand mixer fitted with the whisk, on medium speed for 2 minutes, until combined. Using a metal spoon, gently fold in the flour mixture and dark chocolate to make a thick batter. Do not over-mix. Divide the mixture equally between the lined tins and spread it level. Bake the sponges on the middle shelves for 30 minutes, until golden and risen, and a skewer inserted into the centres comes out clean. Leave to cool in the tins.

2. Make the caramel sauce. Place 2 teaspoons of the coconut cream in a small bowl, then place the remainder in a small saucepan. Add the sugar, golden syrup and vanilla to the pan and warm over a low heat, stirring until the sugar dissolves. Mix the cornflour into the reserved coconut cream, then whisk it into the warm sauce to combine. Bring to the boil, then reduce the heat slightly and simmer for 5 minutes, until the sauce is thick and syrupy. Leave to cool.

3. Make the vanilla frosting. Beat the icing sugar, vegan spread and vanilla in a stand mixer fitted with the beater, on medium speed for 2–3 minutes, scraping down the inside of the bowl from time to time, until light and fluffy. Spoon the frosting into the medium piping bag fitted with a large plain nozzle.

4. Assemble the cake. Turn out the sponges and carefully slice each sponge in half horizontally to give 4 layers. Secure one of the layers on the cake board or plate with piped dots of frosting. Pipe 1 quarter of the frosting evenly over the top of the sponge, then drizzle with a quarter of the caramel sauce and scatter over a quarter of the sliced banana. Repeat twice more with the second and third layers of sponge, and a quarter each of the frosting, caramel sauce and banana. Top with the last sponge and pipe a final layer of frosting on top. Scatter with the remaining slices of banana, drizzle with caramel sauce and finish with the grated chocolate.

Ginger Treacle Tart

The sweet heat of stem ginger calms the bitter notes of the treacle and marmalade in this tart, and there's a spritz of lemon in both the pastry and the filling to bring out the ginger's own lemoniness. Serve a slice or two with something creamy for balance.

Serves: 8
Hands on: 30 mins + chilling
Bake: 1 hour

For the pastry
175g plain flour
25g icing sugar, sifted
good pinch of salt
1 tsp ground ginger
100g unsalted butter,
    cubed and chilled
1 large egg, separated
1½ tbsp chilled water
1 tsp lemon juice

For the filling
250g day-old white
    breadcrumbs
finely grated zest of
    ½ unwaxed lemon
1 tsp ground ginger
300g golden syrup
50g treacle
50g ginger conserve
    or jam, or fine-shred
    marmalade
75ml double cream
2 large eggs, lightly beaten
1 large egg yolk
4 stem ginger balls in
    syrup, drained and
    finely sliced
large pinch of sea-salt flakes
thick double cream, crème
    fraîche or vanilla ice
    cream, to serve

You will need
22cm fluted tart tin
baking beans or rice

1. Make the pastry case. Combine the flour, icing sugar, salt and ground ginger in a large mixing bowl. Rub in the butter with your fingertips until the mixture resembles breadcrumbs. Make a well in the centre, add the egg yolk, chilled water and lemon juice and mix with a palette knife, then your hands to bring the dough together. Tip the dough onto the work surface and knead it very briefly to shape it into a ball. Flatten it into a disc, cover and chill it for 1 hour.

2. Roll out the pastry on a flour-dusted work surface to a disc about 2mm thick and large enough to line the base and sides of the tin. Transfer the pastry to the tin, pressing it neatly into the base and fluted sides. Trim the excess and chill the pastry case for 20 minutes. Meanwhile, heat the oven to 180°C/160°C fan/Gas 4. Place a baking sheet on the middle shelf of the oven to heat up at the same time.

3. Bake the pastry case. Prick the base of the chilled tart case with a fork, line it with baking paper and fill it with baking beans or rice. Place the tart on top of the hot baking sheet and bake it for 15 minutes, until the top edge starts to turn crisp and golden. Remove the paper and baking beans or rice and return the case to the oven for a further 5 minutes to dry out the base. Lightly beat the reserved egg white until foamy and brush a thin layer over the bottom of the pastry case. Return the pastry case to the oven for 2 minutes, until it is dry and sealed.

4. Make the filling. While the pastry case is baking, tip the breadcrumbs into a bowl, add the lemon zest, ground ginger, golden syrup, treacle, ginger conserve or jam or marmalade, double cream, beaten eggs, egg yolk and salt and mix well to combine.

5. Arrange the stem ginger in the bottom of the baked pastry case and spoon the filling on top, spreading it out evenly. Bake for 20 minutes, then reduce the oven to 150°C/130°C fan/Gas 2 and bake for a further 15–20 minutes, until the filling is set. Leave to cool to warm or room temperature, sprinkle with the salt flakes, then serve with thick double cream, crème fraîche or vanilla ice cream.

Sticky Toffee Cakes

Dried figs are rich with nutty sugariness and notes of honey and black treacle. Date syrup, maple syrup or honey flavours the little pillow of cream cheese that decorates the cakes – whichever you choose will reinforce the dried fruits' natural, earthy sweetness.

GLUTEN-FREE
Makes: 12
Hands on: 40 mins + chilling
Bake: 20 mins

For the cakes
125g pitted Medjool dates, roughly chopped
75g soft dried figs, roughly chopped
½ tsp bicarbonate of soda
75g shelled pecans or walnut halves
100g unsalted butter, cubed and softened
75g light brown soft sugar
50g dark brown soft sugar
2 eggs, lightly beaten
1 tsp vanilla extract
150g gluten-free self-raising flour, sifted
pinch of salt
2 tbsp whole milk

For the toffee sauce
50g light brown soft sugar
30g dark brown soft sugar
30g unsalted butter, cubed
100ml double cream
½ tsp sea-salt flakes

To decorate
200g full-fat cream cheese
1 tbsp date syrup, maple syrup or runny honey
1 tsp vanilla extract
4 fresh figs, each cut into 6

You will need
12-hole muffin tin, lined with paper cases

1. Make the cakes. Put the dates and figs in a saucepan with 125ml of water, then simmer them over a low heat for 3 minutes, until softened. Remove the pan from the heat, add the bicarbonate of soda and stir to combine – the mixture will foam up. Use a hand-held stick blender to blitz the mixture until nearly smooth, then leave it to cool to room temperature. Heat the oven to 170°C/150°C fan/Gas 3.

2. Spread the nuts on a baking tray and toast them in the oven for 5 minutes, until crisp. Roughly chop the toasted nuts and leave them to cool while you prepare the cake mixture.

3. Beat the butter and light and dark sugars in a stand mixer fitted with the beater, on medium speed for 3–5 minutes, scraping down the inside of the bowl from time to time, until paler and creamy. Add the eggs, a little at a time, beating well between each addition. Mix in the vanilla, then sift in the flour and salt and mix again. Fold in the cooled fig mixture, the milk and 50g of the toasted chopped nuts.

4. Divide the mixture equally between the paper cases in the muffin tin. Bake the cakes for 20 minutes, until golden and risen and a skewer inserted into the centres comes out clean. Leave the cakes to cool in the tin for 2 minutes, then carefully lift them out and place them on a wire rack to cool completely.

5. Make the toffee sauce. While the cakes are baking, put both sugars and the butter in a small saucepan over a low heat and stir to melt the butter and dissolve the sugar. Add the cream, bring the mixture to the boil, then simmer for 1 minute, until slightly thickened. Remove the pan from the heat, stir in the salt flakes, then leave the sauce to cool to room temperature. Chill for 1 hour to thicken.

6. Decorate the cakes. Beat the cream cheese with the syrup or honey and the vanilla until combined. Place a good spoonful of the cream-cheese mixture on top of each cake and make an indent in the middle using the back of a teaspoon. Fill each indent with a teaspoon of the toffee sauce and top with wedges of fig and the reserved nuts. Serve any remaining toffee sauce alongside.

James's Salted Pretzel Caramel Brownies

These are a bit indulgent, but that's because they have both a caramel and salty pretzel topping and a cake flavoured with coffee, cocoa, white and milk chocolates, and nutty malted milk. Sweet, salty, crunchy and fudgy – perfect.

Makes: 16
Hands on: 45 mins + cooling
Bake: 30 mins

For the brownies
150g 80% dark chocolate, broken into pieces
90g unsalted butter, cubed
60ml vegetable oil
1 tbsp instant coffee
60ml just-boiled water
25g 100% cocoa powder
100g caster sugar
100g light brown soft sugar
2 eggs
1 tsp vanilla extract
100g plain flour
25g malted milk powder
pinch of salt
100g white chocolate, roughly chopped
100g milk chocolate, roughly chopped

For the pretzel topping
150g salted mini pretzels, plus extra to decorate
40g butter, melted
40g caster sugar
40g malted milk powder

For the caramel
230g caster sugar
155ml double cream
80g unsalted butter

You will need
23cm square cake tin, greased, then lined with baking paper
baking sheet, lined with baking paper
sugar thermometer

1. Make the brownies. Heat the oven to 180°C /160°C fan/Gas 4. Melt the dark chocolate with the butter and oil in a large heatproof bowl set over a saucepan of gently simmering water. Stir until smooth, then set aside to cool.

2. In a separate small bowl, dissolve the coffee in the just-boiled water. Sift in the cocoa powder and mix to make a paste.

3. Whisk both sugars into the cooled melted chocolate mixture, followed by the eggs and vanilla, then whisk in the cocoa paste.

4. In a separate bowl, sift in the flour, malted milk powder and salt, then fold this into the wet ingredients until you have a smooth, glossy mixture. Gently fold in the chopped white and milk chocolate.

5. Pour the mixture into the lined cake tin and spread it level with a palette knife. Bake the brownie for 25–30 minutes, until the top forms a dry, shiny crust. Leave the brownie in the tin and place it on a wire rack to cool. Leave the oven on.

6. Make the pretzel topping. While the brownie is baking, slightly crush the pretzels with the end of a rolling pin and add them to a bowl with the melted butter, caster sugar and malted milk powder. Mix to combine, then spread the mixture out on the lined baking sheet and bake for 6–8 minutes, until browned. Set aside on a wire rack to cool and set, then crumble it into small pieces.

7. Make the caramel. While the topping is cooling and setting, pour enough of the caster sugar into a medium saucepan just so that it covers the base. Heat it over a low–medium heat until the sugar melts and starts to caramelise. Little by little, add the remaining sugar, waiting until each addition has melted before adding more. Stir occasionally to ensure that the sugar melts evenly. Once you have added all the sugar, cook to a golden caramel.

Continues overleaf

8. Turn off the heat and, using a balloon whisk, carefully whisk in the double cream, followed by the butter. Return the pan to a medium heat and continue to cook until the caramel reaches 110°C on the sugar thermometer.

9. Turn off the heat and carefully mix the crumbled pretzel mix into the caramel, then pour the caramel–pretzel mixture over the cooled brownie and spread it out evenly with a palette knife. Top with extra whole mini pretzels to decorate.

10. Leave the topped brownie in the tin for at least 30 minutes, until the caramel cools and sets, then chill it for 20 minutes to firm up. Once cool, cut the brownie into 16 equal squares to serve.

Daisy Macarons

Toffee and cream are the main flavours in these pretty, light-as-air macarons, sandwiched with salted caramel sauce and a creamy mascarpone filling. If you want to splash out on the decoration, add flecks of gold leaf to the finished macarons – it doesn't have a flavour, but it certainly adds a bit of glamour.

Makes: 20
Hands on: 2¾ hours
   + resting
Bake: 12 mins

For the salted caramel sauce
15g salted butter
40g light brown soft sugar
75ml double cream
pinch of salt

For the macaron shells
125g ground almonds
120g icing sugar
3 egg whites, weighed
   and divided into
   2 equal portions
125g granulated sugar
⅛ tsp cream of tartar

For the mascarpone cream filling
25g mascarpone
50g full-fat cream cheese
35g icing sugar, sifted
35ml double cream

For the royal icing
1 egg white
225g icing sugar, sifted
½ tsp lemon juice
yellow food-colouring gel

To finish (optional)
freeze-dried raspberry
   pieces
edible gold leaf

Continues overleaf

1. Make the salted caramel sauce. Tip the butter and sugar into a small saucepan set over a medium heat and cook until the sugar has dissolved. Gradually pour in the cream and whisk the mixture to combine, then raise the heat to bring the mixture to the boil and boil for 2 minutes, until thickened. Stir in the salt, then pour the caramel into a shallow container and set aside to cool.

2. Make the macaron shells. Using a food processor, blitz the ground almonds and icing sugar together, then sift them into a bowl. Add 1 portion of the egg whites and mix to form a paste, then cover the bowl and set the mixture aside. Place the remaining egg whites into the bowl of a stand mixer fitted with the whisk.

3. Set aside 25g of the granulated sugar. Tip the remaining 100g of sugar along with 30ml of water into a small saucepan. Place the pan over a high heat and when the syrup is just beginning to boil, turn the stand mixer to medium–high speed to begin whipping the egg whites. When they begin to form bubbles, add the cream of tartar then turn the mixer to high and gradually add the reserved 25g of sugar. Continue whisking until the whites form a meringue consistency.

4. When sugar syrup reaches 115°C on the sugar thermometer, immediately remove the pan from the heat and, with the mixer still running, carefully pour the syrup down the inside of the mixer bowl into the egg whites, taking care not to pour it directly onto the whisk. Continue whisking on high speed until the meringue forms stiff peaks, then stop the mixer and allow the meringue to cool.

5. Add one third of the cooled meringue into the almond paste and mix vigorously until combined, then, using a silicone spatula, gently fold the remaining meringue into the mixture. Keep folding until the mixture falls off the spatula in a thick ribbon that holds its shape for around 20 seconds before gradually blending into the batter.

Continues overleaf

Daisy Macarons *continued*

You will need
sugar thermometer
large piping bag fitted
   with a small plain nozzle
3 large baking sheets,
   lined with baking paper
medium piping bag
   fitted with a medium
   plain nozzle
medium piping bag fitted
   with a petal nozzle
small piping bag fitted
   with a grass nozzle

6. Transfer the mixture to the large piping bag fitted with a small plain nozzle. Pipe the mixture in flower shapes onto the prepared baking sheets – to create the shapes, each time pipe a wheel of five teardrops with the thin ends joining in the middle. After you have piped each tray (you should get about 40 flowers altogether), tap the trays on the work surface to remove any air bubbles, then leave the piped macarons to rest, uncovered, for about 30 minutes so that a skin forms on the surface of each petal. Meanwhile, heat the oven to 150°C/130°C fan/Gas 2.

7. Once the macarons have rested, transfer the trays to the centre of the oven and bake the macarons for 12–13 minutes, until crisp on top and risen with a 'foot' formed at the base. Remove the macarons from the oven and slide the baking paper from the baking trays to leave the macarons to cool.

8. **Make the mascarpone cream.** While the macarons are cooling, in a medium bowl combine the mascarpone, cream cheese and icing sugar together with a wooden spoon, then, using an electric hand whisk, whisk the mixture while gradually pouring in the double cream. Whisk until the mixture forms soft peaks. Transfer the mascarpone cream to the medium piping bag with a medium plain nozzle and refrigerate it until you're ready to use.

9. **Make the royal icing.** Whisk the egg white in a stand mixer fitted with the whisk, on medium speed until foamy, then a spoonful at a time add the icing sugar. Once you've incorporated all the icing sugar, add the lemon juice and increase the mixer speed to high. Continue to whisk until stiff peaks form. Spoon the icing into the medium piping bag fitted with the petal nozzle, and cover any leftover icing to stop it from drying out.

10. **Assemble the macarons.** Sort the shells into pairs, turning over one half of each pair to give you a top and a bottom. Pipe a ring of mascarpone cream onto the bottom shells, and fill the centre of each ring with salted caramel. Sprinkle over some freeze-dried raspberries, if you wish, and sandwich with the corresponding top.

11. Decorate each macaron, using the white royal icing to pipe petals on top to form a daisy. Once you have piped all of the petals, colour any remaining icing yellow and use this to fill the small piping bag fitted with a grass nozzle. Squeeze a blob of the yellow icing into the centre of the petals to complete the daisy. Finish with tiny flecks of gold leaf, if you wish.

Paul's S'Mores

In the 1920s in the USA, girl scouts on camp called for more melty, sandwiched marshmallow – 'Some more!' – and s'mores were born. These digestive biscuits are treacly with brown sugar and the marshmallows fragrant with vanilla.

Makes: 8
Hands on: 1 hour
  + chilling + setting
Bake: 20 mins

For the digestives
170g wholemeal flour
2 tbsp wheatgerm
110g unsalted butter,
  chilled and cubed
75g light brown soft sugar
½ tsp baking powder
1 tsp salt
about 4 tbsp whole milk
plain flour, for dusting

For the marshmallow
50g icing sugar
1 tbsp cornflour
vegetable oil, for greasing
4 platinum-grade
  gelatine leaves
3 egg whites
¾ tsp cream of tartar
125g caster sugar
175g corn syrup
2 tsp vanilla paste

For the chocolate ganache
100g 54% dark chocolate,
  finely chopped
100ml double cream

Continues overleaf

1. Make the digestives. Tip the flour and wheatgerm into a food processor and blitz to a fine flour. Add the butter, sugar, baking powder and salt and blitz until the mixture resembles fine breadcrumbs. Add the milk a little at a time and pulse to form a dough (you may not need all the milk). Turn out the dough onto the work surface and shape it into a flat disc. Wrap and chill the disc for 20 minutes.

2. Make the marshmallow. While the dough is chilling, in a small bowl, mix together the icing sugar and cornflour. Oil the baking paper in the prepared tin, then dust it with half of the icing-sugar mixture so that you coat the paper.

3. Soak the gelatine leaves in a bowl of cold water for 5 minutes, until soft. Place the egg whites and cream of tartar in the bowl of a stand mixer fitted with the whisk and whisk to stiff peaks.

4. Tip the sugar and corn syrup into a clean saucepan and place the pan over a medium–high heat. Bring the mixture to the boil and boil until the temperature on the sugar thermometer reaches 115°C. Immediately remove the pan from the heat and, with the whisk on low, pour the hot sugar down the inside of the bowl into the egg whites. Increase the speed to medium and whisk for 3 minutes to a thick, warm meringue.

5. Drain the gelatine, squeezing out any excess, then roughly chop it into small pieces. Add a few pieces at a time to the meringue, whisking between each addition, until all the gelatine has melted into the meringue and the marshmallow is stiff. Whisk in the vanilla, then scrape the marshmallow into the lined tin, level the surface and leave the marshmallow to set at room temperature for 1½ hours.

6. Make the chocolate ganache. While the marshmallow is setting, tip the chocolate into a small bowl. Heat the cream in a small saucepan over a low–medium heat until just simmering, then

Continues overleaf

Paul's S'Mores *continued*

You will need
sugar thermometer
20cm square cake tin,
  lined (base and sides)
  with baking paper
medium piping bag
  fitted with a medium
  plain nozzle
5cm plain round cutter
decorative biscuit stamp
  (optional)
baking sheet, lined
  with baking paper
kitchen blowtorch

immediately remove the pan from the heat and pour the cream over the chocolate. Leave to stand for 4 minutes, then stir to a smooth ganache. Leave the ganache to cool for about 45–60 minutes, depending on the temperature in your kitchen, until it reaches a piping consistency, then spoon the ganache into the piping bag fitted with the medium nozzle. Set aside at room temperature until you're ready to use.

7. Finish the digestive biscuits. Roll out the disc of chilled dough on a lightly floured surface to 3mm thick. Using the 5cm cutter, stamp out 16 discs re-rolling and stamping the trimmings as necessary. Lightly flour the biscuit stamp (if using) with plain flour, then stamp each disc to create a pattern. This will cause the discs to spread a little as you press down, so re-cut them using the cutter to neaten as necessary.

8. Place the 16 discs on the lined baking sheet and chill them for 20 minutes, while you heat the oven to 190°C/170°C fan/Gas 5. Bake the biscuits for 15–20 minutes, until the edges start to turn a dark golden colour. Leave the biscuits to cool on the baking sheets for 5 minutes, then transfer them to a wire rack to cool completely.

9. Assemble the s'mores. Turn all 16 biscuits so that the flat base (underside) is upwards. Pipe an even layer of the chocolate ganache onto each one.

10. Lay a sheet of baking paper on the work surface and sprinkle the remaining icing-sugar mixture over it. Turn out the marshmallow onto the paper and, using the 5cm plain cutter again, cut out 8 rounds of marshmallow (discard the trimmings). Place one round on top of the ganache layer on 8 of the biscuits, then sandwich the marshmallow using the remaining biscuits, ganache-side downwards.

11. Immediately before serving, use the kitchen blowtorch to toast the marshmallow edges until golden brown and a bit gooey.

Gulab Jamun

A popular treat at Indian festivals, these orbs of deep-fried milk dough soak up all the flavours of the scented syrup – in this case flavoured with sweet, musky rosewater that's tempered by the bitter hints of cinnamon and cardamom.

Makes: 20-24
Hands on: 1 hour
  + overnight soaking
Cook: 40 mins

---

*For the cardamom
& rose syrup*
350g caster sugar
6 cardamom pods, split
1 large cinnamon stick,
  broken in half
pinch of saffron threads
2 tsp rosewater

For the dough balls
1 litre sunflower oil,
  for deep-frying
200g dried whole
  milk powder
75g plain flour
⅛ tsp bicarbonate of soda
75ml whole milk, plus
  extra if needed
75g plain yogurt
2 tbsp ghee or clarified
  butter, melted

To serve
40g slivered pistachios
2 tsp edible dried rose
  petals (optional)

You will need
cooking thermometer
baking tray, lined with
  baking paper

1. **Make the cardamom and rose syrup.** Tip the sugar and 500ml of water into a large saucepan. Add the cardamom, cinnamon and saffron. Bring to the boil over a medium heat, then reduce the heat and simmer for 5 minutes, until the sugar dissolves and the liquid is syrupy. Remove from the heat and stir in the rosewater. Set aside.

2. **Make the dough balls.** Pour the sunflower oil into a large pan, wok or deep-fat fryer and heat it over a low heat until it reaches 160–170°C on the cooking thermometer.

3. While the oil is heating, sift the milk powder, flour and bicarbonate of soda into a large bowl. Make a well in the centre and add the milk, yogurt and 1 tablespoon of the ghee or clarified butter. Quickly mix until combined and smooth, adding a little extra milk if the mixture appears dry – the dough will be sticky, but the milk powder will absorb the liquid as you mix.

4. Lightly grease the palm of your hands with a little of the remaining ghee. Working quickly, pinch off a walnut-sized nugget of dough and roll it into a smooth ball between your palms. Place the ball on the lined baking tray and repeat until you have 20–24 equal balls. Loosely cover the tray with a slightly damp tea towel. Once the oil is to temperature, bring the syrup back to the boil, then remove it from the heat.

5. Carefully drop 4 or 5 balls into the hot oil, maintaining the heat, and fry for 3–4 minutes, turning once, until evenly golden brown and almost doubled in size. Using a slotted spoon, scoop out the balls, drain them briefly on kitchen paper, then drop them into the hot syrup. If the syrup cools down too much, gently reheat it over a low heat without boiling. Continue to fry, transferring each batch to the hot syrup, then leave the dough balls to soak overnight in the syrup.

6. The next day, scoop out the cardamom pods and cinnamon stick and transfer the gulab jamun and syrup to a large, shallow serving bowl. Serve with a spoonful of the syrup, scattered with pistachios and rose petals (if using).

Congo Bars

Somewhere between a chocolate-chip cookie, a blondie and a cake, congo bars get their gooey sweetness from two types of brown sugar, and the mouthfuls of chocolate-coated caramels that appear in every bite.

Serves: 12–16
Hands on: 30 mins
Bake: 25 mins

175g unsalted butter, cubed and softened
100g light brown soft sugar
100g dark brown soft sugar
2 tsp vanilla extract
2 large eggs, lightly beaten
225g plain flour
1 tsp baking powder
pinch of salt
100g walnuts, roughly chopped
120g dark chocolate chips
120g milk chocolate-coated caramels, halved or roughly chopped, depending on the brand

You will need
30 x 20cm brownie tin, greased, then lined (base and sides) with baking paper

1. Heat the oven to 180°C/160°C fan/Gas 4.

2. Beat the butter, both types of sugar and the vanilla in a stand mixer, on medium speed for 3–5 minutes, scraping down the inside of the bowl from time to time, until pale and creamy.

3. Add the eggs, a little at a time, beating well between each addition. Sift the flour, baking powder and salt into the bowl and mix again to combine.

4. Fold in the walnuts and dark chocolate chips until thoroughly combined, then spoon the mixture into the lined tin and spread it level. Press the milk chocolate-coated caramels into the mixture, making sure they are evenly spaced apart.

5. Bake the mixture for 25 minutes, until golden and risen, then leave the traybake to cool in the tin before cutting it into 12–16 bars or squares.

Alfajores

With origins in 8th-century, fruit-filled cookie sandwiches that made their way from the Middle East via Spain to South America, alfajores are now loved for their delicious, sticky dulce de leche interior. A final edging in desiccated coconut rounds off the sweetness.

Makes: 24
Hands on: 1 hour + chilling
Bake: 2¾ hours

For the dulce de leche
2 x 397g cans of
   condensed milk

For the biscuits
150g unsalted butter,
   cubed and softened
125g icing sugar, sifted
finely grated zest of
   ½ unwaxed lemon
1 tsp vanilla paste
1 tbsp brandy
1 egg, lightly beaten
1 egg yolk
225g plain flour
125g cornflour
½ tsp baking powder
good pinch of salt
50g unsweetened
   desiccated coconut

You will need
medium ovenproof gratin
   dish (about 20 x 14cm)
4.5cm round cutter
2 baking sheets, lined
   with baking paper
medium piping bag
   fitted with a medium
   plain nozzle

1. Make the dulce de leche. Heat the oven to 200°C/180°C fan/ Gas 6. Spoon the condensed milk into an ovenproof dish, cover tightly with foil and place in a roasting tin. Pour just-boiled water into the tin to come halfway up the sides of the dish. Bake for 45 minutes, remove the foil, stir the condensed milk and re-cover with foil. Top up the boiling water in the roasting tin, if necessary. Return the tin to the oven for a further 45 minutes, then stir the condensed milk again. Re-cover the dish with foil, add more just-boiled water to the tin, if needed, then cook for a further 45–60 minutes, until the condensed milk is thick and a rich, golden brown. Carefully remove the dish from the roasting tin and leave the dulce de leche to cool.

2. Make the biscuits. Beat the butter and icing sugar in a stand mixer fitted with the beater, on medium speed for 2–3 minutes, scraping down the inside of the bowl from time to time, until pale and creamy. Add the lemon zest, vanilla and brandy and mix again to combine. Add the whole egg and egg yolk and beat again until smooth.

3. Sift the flour, cornflour, baking powder and salt into the bowl and mix until smooth. Don't over-mix. Shape the dough into a ball, flatten it into a disc, then cover it and chill it for 2 hours, until firm.

4. Roll out the chilled dough on a lightly dusted work surface until about 4–5mm thick. Using the cutter, stamp out as many discs as possible and place them on the lined baking sheets. Gather the scraps, re-roll and stamp out more discs until you have 48. Chill the discs for 30 minutes. Heat the oven to 170°C/150°C fan/Gas 3.

5. Bake the biscuits on the middle shelf for 12–13 minutes, until firm but not coloured. Leave them on the sheets to cool and harden.

6. Fill and decorate the biscuits. Spoon the cold dulce de leche into the piping bag. Turn half of the biscuits flat-side up and pipe a generous layer of dulce de leche over the top of each. Sandwich with the other biscuits, flat-side down. Tip the desiccated coconut into a bowl and roll the sides of the biscuits in the coconut to coat the filling. They will store in an airtight tin for up to 24 hours.

Fig & Date Steamed Puddings

Steaming intensifies flavour. In this dessert, the natural caramel-like notes of the Medjool dates is deeply enticing and cleverly picked up in the caramel sauce. Add some rich, creamy custard perfumed with saffron, and fresh fig decorations for a stunning finish.

Serves: 8
Hands on: 1¼ hours
Bake: 40 mins

For the fig & date sponge
180g pitted Medjool dates, finely chopped
75g dried figs, finely chopped
¼ tsp bicarbonate of soda
180ml boiling water
150g self-raising flour
1 tsp ground cinnamon
½ tsp ground ginger
¼ tsp ground nutmeg
150g unsalted butter, softened
150g dark brown soft sugar
2 large eggs

For the vanilla custard
250ml whole milk
250ml single cream
2 tsp vanilla paste
1 tsp ground cardamom
6 egg yolks
100g caster sugar
10 saffron threads

For the caramel sauce
200g granulated sugar
175ml double cream
50g salted butter

To decorate
100g white chocolate, broken into pieces
4 figs, quartered
20g pistachio kernels, finely chopped
edible dried rose petals

Continues overleaf

1. Heat the oven to 180°C/160°C fan/Gas 4 and place the prepared pudding tins in the fridge.

2. **Make the sponge.** Place the chopped dates and figs into a medium heatproof bowl. Add the bicarbonate of soda and pour over the boiling water, then stir everything together and set the bowl aside to leave the fruit to soak until needed.

3. Sift the flour and spices into a medium bowl and set aside.

4. Add the butter and sugar into the bowl of a stand mixer fitted with the beater and beat on a medium speed for 3–4 minutes, until pale and fluffy. Add the eggs one at a time, beating well between each addition until incorporated.

5. Using a wooden spoon or spatula, gently fold in the sifted dry ingredients, followed by the soaked dates and figs, including the soaking liquid, until fully combined.

6. Divide the mixture equally between the 8 prepared pudding moulds – they should be about three quarters full. Place the tins into the deep roasting tray and pour some boiling water around them until it reaches halfway up the sides of the pudding tins. Cover the roasting tray with foil and carefully place it into the oven. Bake the puddings for about 40 minutes, or until springy on top and a skewer inserted into the centre of each pudding comes out clean. Carefully remove the puddings from the roasting tray and leave them to cool for 10 minutes in their tins.

7. **Make the vanilla custard.** While the puddings are baking, add the milk, cream, vanilla and ground cardamom to a medium saucepan and bring the mixture to a simmer over a low heat.

8. Meanwhile, add the egg yolks and sugar to a large bowl and whisk to combine. When the milk and cream mixture begins to bubble, slowly pour half of the liquid into the egg mixture and whisk together, then pour everything back into the pan.

Continues overleaf

You will need
200ml pudding moulds
x 8, greased, then
dusted with flour and
base-lined with a disc
of baking paper
deep-sided roasting tray
baking tray, lined with
baking paper

9. Place the pan over a low–medium heat, stirring continuously with a whisk until the custard has thickened enough to coat the back of a spoon. Pass the custard through a sieve, gently stir through the saffron threads, then cover the surface with a piece of baking paper to stop a skin forming, and set aside.

10. Make the caramel sauce. Add the sugar and 50ml of water to a small saucepan and place the pan over a high heat. Bring the mixture to the boil, then continue to boil until it turns into a dark golden caramel (about 6–7 minutes). Remove the pan from the heat and carefully whisk in the double cream, followed by the butter. Continue to whisk until the butter has melted and fully combined into the sauce, then cover and set aside.

11. Make the decorations. Melt two thirds of the white chocolate in a microwave in 10 second bursts, or in a heatproof bowl set over a pan of barely simmering water. Once melted, add the remaining one third of the chocolate and stir until all of the chocolate has melted.

12. Dip the fig quarters halfway into the white chocolate. Place them on the lined baking tray and sprinkle over some chopped pistachios and dried rose petals, then leave the chocolate to set (you can place the figs in the fridge for 5 minutes to speed up the setting, if you like).

13. When you're ready to serve, run a small, sharp knife around the edges of the puddings to loosen them from the tins, then turn them out onto serving plates and gently shake them to release. Top each one with two white-chocolate fig quarters and serve with the custard and caramel sauce alongside for pouring over.

Pistachio Melting Moments

The pistachio buttercream gives these melt-in-the-mouth little sandwich biscuits a delicately resinous tone that's offset by the zing of lime zest and the milky sweetness of the white chocolate.

Makes: 16
Hands on: 45 mins + chilling
Bake: 14 mins

For the biscuits
75g shelled unsalted
  pistachios
200g unsalted butter,
  cubed and softened
75g icing sugar, sifted
½ tsp pistachio extract
200g plain flour
½ tsp baking powder
25g cornflour
pinch of salt
finely grated zest of
  ½ unwaxed lime
1 tbsp whole milk

For the filling
75g unsalted butter,
  cubed and softened
150g icing sugar, sifted
finely grated zest of
  ½ unwaxed lime

To decorate
100g white chocolate,
  broken into pieces

You will need
2 baking sheets, lined
  with baking paper
small piping bag fitted with
  a medium plain nozzle

1. Make the biscuits. Finely grind the pistachios in a mini food processor. You need 50g of ground pistachios for the biscuit mixture – set aside the rest to use in the frosting and to decorate.

2. Beat the butter, icing sugar and pistachio extract in a stand mixer fitted with the beater, on medium speed for 2–3 minutes, until pale and creamy. Sift in the flour, baking powder, cornflour and salt. Add the 50g of ground pistachios, along with the lime zest and milk and mix to combine. Cover and chill for 30 minutes, until firm.

3. Pinch off cherry tomato-sized pieces of dough (about 15g each) and roll them into neat balls. You should have about 32 balls in total. Arrange these on the lined baking sheets, spacing them evenly apart, then slightly flatten the tops with your fingers. Chill them for 20 minutes while you heat the oven to 180°C/160°C fan/Gas 4.

4. Press the tines of a fork into the top of each ball of biscuit dough. Bake the biscuits on the middle shelf for 14 minutes, until firm and just starting to turn golden at the edges. Leave to cool on the baking sheets.

5. Make the filling. While the biscuits are cooling, beat the butter until pale and light. Add the icing sugar, lime zest and all but 2 teaspoons of the reserved ground pistachios and mix again until smooth and combined. Set aside.

6. Make the decoration. Melt the white chocolate in a heatproof bowl set over a pan of barely simmering water, stirring until smooth. Remove from the heat and leave to cool for 1 minute.

7. Dip the edge of 16 of the biscuits into the melted chocolate to coat about one third, scatter with a light dusting of the remaining ground pistachios and chill for 20 minutes, until the chocolate sets.

8. Finish the biscuits. Spoon the buttercream into the piping bag fitted with the medium plain nozzle and pipe the buttercream over the underside of each plain biscuit. Sandwich with the chocolate-edged biscuits to make 16 melting moments in total.

Chocolate & Hazelnut Entremets

Hazelnuts and chocolate share a creaminess that makes these decadent desserts simply to die for. Rich praline chocolate mousse sits on top of crisp chocolate and hazelnut meringue, all wrapped in joconde sponge and topped with ganache.

Makes: 6
Hands on: 4 hours + chilling
Bake: 40 mins

For the dacquoise sponge
50g blanched hazelnuts
75g caster sugar
5g cornflour
5g cocoa powder, sifted
2 egg whites
pinch of salt

For the joconde chocolate paste
30g unsalted butter, cubed and softened
30g icing sugar
1 egg white
25g plain flour
10g cocoa powder

For the joconde sponge
100g blanched hazelnuts
100g icing sugar, sifted
50g plain flour
3 eggs
25g unsalted butter, melted
3 egg whites
pinch of salt
25g caster sugar

For the praline chocolate mousse
50g caster sugar
50g blanched hazelnuts
1 platinum-grade gelatine leaf
175g 70% dark chocolate, broken into pieces
250ml double cream
2 tbsp hot espresso coffee

Continues overleaf

1. Make the dacquoise sponge. Heat the oven to 180°C/160°C fan/ Gas 4. Tip the hazelnuts into a baking tray and toast for 4 minutes, until golden, then leave them to cool. Reduce the oven temperature to 150°C/130°C fan/Gas 2.

2. Finely grind the cooled hazelnuts in a food processor. Tip them into a bowl and add 25g of the caster sugar, and the cornflour and cocoa powder and mix to combine.

3. Using an electric hand whisk, whisk the egg whites with the pinch of salt in a large mixing bowl until they form firm peaks. Add the remaining 50g of sugar and continue to whisk until you have a smooth, glossy meringue.

4. Fold the dry ingredients into the meringue with a large metal spoon or spatula until thoroughly combined. Spoon the dacquoise mixture onto the centre of the lined baking sheet, then spread it out with a palette knife into a 25cm square (about 4mm deep). Bake the sponge for 20 minutes, until set and starting to crisp. Remove the sponge from the oven and leave it to cool on the baking sheet. Increase the oven temperature to 200°C/180°C fan/Gas 6.

5. Make the joconde chocolate paste. In a small bowl, cream the butter with the icing sugar for 1 minute, until pale and creamy. Add the egg white, a little at a time, beating well between each addition until combined. Sift the flour and cocoa powder into the bowl and beat until smooth. Spoon the mixture into the small piping bag and snip off the end to a fine writing point.

6. Pipe fine diagonal lines, 5mm apart, across each baking sheet lined with a silicone mat to fill a rectangle about 35 x 25cm. Place the mats (on the baking sheets) in the freezer for 15 minutes, until the chocolate paste sets solid.

Continues overleaf

For the ganache
100g 70% dark chocolate, finely chopped
40g milk chocolate, finely chopped
140ml double cream
1 tbsp golden syrup

For the tuiles
40g unsalted butter
2 tsp golden syrup
50g caster sugar
25g plain flour
25g blanched hazelnuts, roughly chopped
10g cocoa nibs
pinch of salt

You will need
baking sheet, lined with baking paper
small piping bag
2 baking sheets, lined with silicone baking mats
8cm diameter baking rings x 6 (about 4cm deep)
25 x 6cm acetate strips x 6
6.5cm plain cutter
small baking tray, lined with baking paper or silicone mat

7. Make the joconde sponge. While the paste is setting, finely grind the hazelnuts in a small food processor, sift in the icing sugar and plain flour and blitz briefly to combine. Tip the mixture into a mixing bowl and add the whole eggs and melted butter. Whisk to combine.

8. In a separate bowl, whisk the egg whites with a pinch of salt until they form stiff peaks. Add the caster sugar and continue to whisk for another minute until smooth, frothy and thoroughly combined. Using a large metal spoon or rubber spatula, fold the egg-white mixture into the hazelnut mixture.

9. Using a palette knife, spread half of the joconde sponge mixture over the chocolate paste stripes on one silicone baking mat, taking care not to disturb or soften the lines of chocolate, and filling the space between them evenly. Repeat with the remaining sponge mixture on the second silicone baking mat. Bake for 7 minutes, until the sponge is set and just firm when pressed lightly with your finger, and it starts to turn golden at the edges. Remove from the oven, leave to cool for 5 minutes, then turn out the sponges onto clean sheets of baking paper and carefully remove the silicone baking mats.

10. Assemble the entremets. Line the inside of each baking ring with a strip of acetate and place them on the lined baking sheet. Trim the joconde sponges and, using the 6.5cm cutter, stamp out 6 discs and set aside. Cut the remaining joconde into 6 strips, each about 23 x 5cm. Place one strip into each acetate-lined baking ring to line the sides, making sure the striped side of the cake faces outwards. Using the 6.5cm cutter, stamp out 6 discs of dacquoise sponge and place one in the bottom of each joconde-lined baking ring to make a base.

11. Make the praline chocolate mousse. Dissolve the caster sugar in 1 tablespoon of water in a small saucepan over a low heat, without stirring. Increase the heat slightly, bring the syrup to the boil and cook for 2 minutes, until you have a golden caramel. Stir in the hazelnuts to coat and continue to cook until the caramel turns amber and the nuts are toasted. Quickly tip the hazelnut caramel onto the lined baking tray and leave it to cool and set to a praline. Once set, break the praline into small pieces, then tip it into a small food processor and blitz it for 3–4 minutes, until very finely chopped and it starts to form a paste. Set aside.

12. Meanwhile, soak the gelatine in a bowl of cold water for 5 minutes, until soft. While the gelatine is soaking, melt the chocolate in a heatproof bowl set over a saucepan of barely simmering water, stirring until smooth. Remove the pan from the heat and leave the chocolate to cool slightly. Whip the double cream in a large mixing bowl until it holds firm peaks.

13. Drain the gelatine, shake off any excess water and stir it into the hot coffee until melted. Add the melted chocolate, praline paste and coffee mixture to the whipped cream and fold until the mixture is smooth and thoroughly combined. Divide the mousse between the joconde-lined rings and spread it level. Place a reserved joconde disc on top of each mousse, cover the tops and chill for 30 minutes.

14. Make the ganache. While the mousse is chilling, put both chocolates in a heatproof bowl. Heat the cream and golden syrup in a small saucepan until just boiling. Pour the hot cream mixture over the chocolate, leave for 1 minute, then stir gently until the chocolate is melted and smooth. Spoon the ganache equally over the top of the entremets, spreading it level each time. Cover the entremets and return them to the fridge to set (about 4 hours).

15. Make the tuiles. Melt the butter with the golden syrup and caster sugar in a small saucepan over a low–medium heat. Combine the flour, hazelnuts, cocoa nibs and salt in a bowl. Add the melted butter mixture and beat until smooth. Leave to cool for 15 minutes. Meanwhile, heat the oven to 170°C/150°C fan/Gas 3.

16. Arrange 3–4 cherry-sized balls of the tuile mixture on the lined baking sheet, leaving plenty of space between each one to allow for spreading during baking. Bake for 8 minutes, until golden brown and bubbling. Remove from the oven and leave to cool for 1–2 minutes. Carefully lift each disc off the paper with a palette knife, mould each into a curved shape around a rolling pin and leave it to crisp up on a wire rack. Repeat to make 12–14 tuiles in total.

17. To serve, take the entremets out of the fridge 20 minutes before serving. When you're ready, place each ring on a serving plate, lift off the baking rings and carefully peel off the acetate. Decorate the top of each entremet with a tuile to finish.

Rye & Beer Bread

Rye flour and ale give this loaf a deep golden colour and a nutty flavour. Amber ale makes the bread's flavour warm and rounded, while stout makes it slightly smoky. The loaf tastes even better a day after baking, once the flavours have had time to mellow out.

Serves: 1 large loaf
Hands on: 20 mins + rising
Bake: 40 mins

───────────────

400g strong white
    bread flour
175g wholemeal rye flour
3g fast-action dried yeast
1 tsp salt
300ml amber ale or stout
75–100ml hot water
1 tbsp barley malt extract
    or runny honey
1 tbsp rapeseed oil

You will need
large baking sheet, lined
    with baking paper
oiled proving bag
baker's cloche or cast-iron
    Dutch oven (optional)

1. Mix both types of flour with the yeast and salt in a stand mixer fitted with the dough hook until combined.

2. Mix the ale or stout, 50ml of the hot water, the barley malt extract or honey and the oil in a jug and pour the mixture into the dry ingredients. Mix on low speed to combine, adding more of the hot water if the mixture looks dry. Increase the speed to medium and knead for 7 minutes, until the dough is smooth and elastic.

3. Tip out the dough onto a work surface and shape it into a ball. Lightly oil the bowl, return the dough, cover it with a clean tea towel and leave it to rise at room temperature for 1½ hours, until doubled in size.

4. Tip out the risen dough onto a lightly floured work surface and knead it gently for 20 seconds to knock it back. Shape the dough into a neat, tight ball and place the ball on the lined baking sheet with the seam on the underside. Slide the baking sheet into the proving bag and leave the loaf to prove at room temperature for 1–½ hours, until doubled in size.

5. Heat the oven to 220°C/200°C fan/Gas 7 and heat the baker's cloche or cast-iron Dutch oven, if using, at the same time.

6. Dust the top of the risen loaf with white flour. Using a sharp knife, lame or razor blade, cut 3–4 slashes in the top of the loaf, then either slide the dough quickly into the oven on the baking sheet, or place the loaf in the hot cloche or Dutch oven. Cover with the lid.

7. Bake the loaf for 35–40 minutes, until deep golden and risen, and the underside of the loaf sounds hollow when tapped. Leave to cool completely on a wire rack before slicing.

Maisam's Pistachio Croissants

I am in love with croissants. I also love mild, creamy pistachios, which remind me of the pistachio trees we had when I was growing up in Libya. These croissants have everything I could wish for – the puffy crunch of the pastry, and the creamy white chocolate and pistachio ganache inside.

Makes: 9
Hands on: 1½ hours
 + overnight chilling
Bake: 25 mins

For the croissant dough
280g strong white
 bread flour
30g caster sugar
1 tsp salt
7g fast-action dried yeast
85ml whole milk
200g block of chilled
 unsalted butter

To glaze
1 egg, beaten

For the pistachio ganache
75g shelled unsalted
 pistachios
100g white chocolate,
 chopped
100ml double cream

You will need
2 baking sheets, lined
 with baking paper
2 oiled proving bags
medium piping bag fitted
 with a jam nozzle

1. Make the croissant dough. Mix the flour, caster sugar, salt and yeast in a stand mixer fitted with a dough hook until combined. Add the milk and 85ml water and knead on low speed for 8–10 minutes, until the dough is smooth and elastic. Place the dough in a clean bowl, cover with a clean tea towel and leave to rise for 1 hour, until doubled in size. Knead the dough gently for 20 seconds to knock back and shape roughly into a rectangle, wrap and chill for 12 hours.

2. While the dough is chilling, place the butter between 2 sheets of baking paper and tap with the end of a rolling pin to flatten into a 15cm square. Keep the butter wrapped in the baking paper and chill with the dough until firm.

3. Once rested and chilled, remove the dough and butter from the fridge and set the butter aside to bring up the temperature slightly while you roll out the dough. The butter must be pliable and warm enough not to crack, but cool enough not to melt when rolled out.

4. Lightly flour the work surface and roll out the dough to a rectangle, about 30 x 15cm. Place the butter block in the middle of the dough and fold each side of the dough over to cover the butter and meet in the middle, pinch the edges together to seal.

5. Roll out the dough (with the butter sealed inside) away from you into a rectangle, about 45 x 15cm, with one of the short sides facing you. Brush away any excess flour, then fold the bottom third of the dough up to cover the middle third, then fold the top third down on top so that you have three layers, and a seam of dough facing you. Give it a quick light roll to compress and even out the surface, then wrap and chill for 30 minutes.

6. Place the dough back on the floured surface with the seam facing you, then rotate it 90 degrees clockwise so that the seam is now on the left. Repeat the rolling out and folding from the previous step and chill for at least 30 minutes before you shape the croissants.

Continues overleaf

7. Once the dough has rested, roll it out as neatly as possible into a rectangle of about 40 x 28cm. It's best to roll it out slightly larger, then trim to size to remove any uneven edges. Divide one of the long sides of the rectangle into 8cm lengths, marking each point with a small cut. Repeat on the opposite side, but making the first mark at 4cm, then the rest at 8cm, so the cuts on either side are staggered. Once you have marked the points on the dough, use a large sharp knife and ruler to cut it into 9 triangles, using the marks as the start and end points.

8. Shape the croissants. Take each triangle of dough and gently stretch it out to make it slightly longer. Place 1 triangle on the work surface and make a small cut in the middle of the triangle base. Starting with that side, roll up the dough into a croissant, shaping it slightly into a crescent. Repeat for all the triangles of dough. Place the rolled croissants onto the lined baking sheets with the pointed end of the triangle tucked underneath. Slide the baking sheets into the proving bags and leave the croissants to prove for 1–3 hours, until doubled in size. The proving time will depend on the temperature of your room.

9. When the croissants are almost ready, heat the oven to 220°C/200°C fan/Gas 7. Gently brush the croissants with the beaten egg, taking care not to deflate them. Bake for 10 minutes, then reduce the temperature to 190°C/170°C fan/Gas 5 and bake for a further 15 minutes, until golden brown. Leave to cool completely on a wire rack.

10. Make the pistachio ganache. While the croissants are baking, blitz the pistachios in a mini processor to a smooth paste and set aside.

11. Put the chocolate in a heatproof bowl and set aside. Gently heat the double cream in a small pan until almost boiling, then pour the cream over the chocolate and let it sit for 2 minutes. Stir the cream and chocolate together to form a smooth, glossy ganache, then stir in the pistachio paste. Cover the surface and leave to cool for 30 minutes, until thickened (this makes the ganache easier to pipe).

12. Fill the croissants. Spoon the ganache into the piping bag fitted with a jam nozzle. Poke 2 holes into the bottom of each croissant. Insert the piping nozzle into one of the holes, squeeze the bag and move the piping tip around slightly to fill one side, then repeat with the second hole to ensure the croissants are evenly filled with the ganache. Repeat to fill all 9 croissants.

Beetroot, Butternut & Feta Galette

This free-form tart is a veritable flavour bomb. A pastry case of earthy spelt flour and nutty parmesan is filled with bittersweet roasted beetroot and butternut squash, and intense sweet–sour pomegranate molasses, salty sharp feta, and sticky caramelised onions. And that's before mentioning the citrussy sumac in the salsa.

Serves: 6–8
Hands on: 1 hour + chilling
Bake: 1 hour 35 mins

For the pastry
150g plain flour
50g wholemeal spelt flour
¼ tsp salt
¼ tsp caster sugar
175g unsalted butter,
  cut into 1cm cubes
  and chilled
25g parmesan, finely
  grated
100ml chilled water
1 tsp cider or white
  wine vinegar

For the filling
about 5 satsuma-sized
  beetroot, washed,
  unpeeled, roots and
  stems trimmed
½ butternut squash,
  peeled, deseeded and
  cut into 5mm slices
4 tbsp olive oil
2 red onions, sliced
2 garlic cloves, crushed
1 tsp dried oregano
1 tbsp pomegranate
  molasses
150g feta, crumbled
1 thyme sprig,
  leaves picked
1 tbsp whole milk
salt and freshly ground
  black pepper

Continues overleaf

1. **Make the pastry** at least 2½ hours ahead to give it plenty of time to rest. Mix both types of flour with the salt and sugar in a large mixing bowl. Lightly rub in the butter and parmesan with your fingertips, just enough to knock the corners off the butter pieces. Add the chilled water and vinegar and quickly mix with a palette knife to bring the dough together into a ragged ball.

2. Lightly flour the work surface, tip the dough out of the bowl and flatten it into a square. Roll out the dough to a rectangle that is three times as long as it is wide, about 36 x 12cm, with one of the short ends closest to you. Fold the top third of the dough down to the middle and the bottom third up to cover it to create a three-layered square of dough. Wrap the dough and chill for 1 hour.

3. Lightly flour the work surface and roll out the dough to a rectangle, about 45 x 15cm, with one of the short ends closest to you. Fold the top edge down to the middle and the bottom edge up to meet it in the middle. Turn the dough 90 degrees clockwise and fold the dough in half, much like closing a book. Wrap and chill the dough for another 1 hour, or until you're ready to bake. Heat the oven to 190°C/170°C fan/Gas 5.

4. **Make the filling.** Place the whole beetroots into the lined roasting tin. Cover tightly with another sheet of foil and roast the beetroots for 1 hour, until tender when tested with the point of a knife. Leave to cool, then peel and cut into 5mm slices. Season with salt and pepper.

5. Tip the butternut squash onto a large baking tray, then add 1 tablespoon of the olive oil and season well with salt and pepper. Turn the squash to coat it in the seasoned oil and roast alongside the beetroot for 30 minutes, until tender and just starting to brown at the edges. Leave to cool. Turn the oven off for now.

Continues overleaf

Beetroot, Butternut & Feta Galette *continued*

For the salsa
small bunch of flat-leaf
    parsley, leaves picked
    and roughly chopped
4 tbsp extra-virgin olive oil
25g walnut pieces, toasted
2 tsp red wine vinegar
½ tsp sumac

You will need
small roasting tin,
    lined with foil
large baking sheet, lined
    with baking paper

6. Add the onions to a large frying pan with 2 tablespoons of the olive oil and a pinch of salt and cook over a low–medium heat, stirring often, for 15 minutes, until tender and just starting to brown at the edges. Add the garlic and oregano and cook for a further 1 minute. Season well, stir in the pomegranate molasses and cook for another 1 minute, until the onions are lightly caramelised and sticky. Leave to cool.

7. Assemble the galette. Lightly flour the work surface, roll out the pastry and cut it into a 30cm disc, about 3mm thick. Carefully transfer the pastry to the lined baking sheet.

8. Spoon the onion mixture onto the pastry, leaving a 3cm border around the edge. Arrange the slices of beetroot and butternut squash and the crumbled feta on top, overlapping the vegetable slices and tucking the feta in between. Drizzle with the remaining olive oil and scatter with the thyme leaves. Fold and pleat the edge of the pastry slightly over the vegetables to create a border, then brush the pastry border with milk. Chill the galette for 20 minutes while you heat the oven to 200°C/180°C fan/Gas 6, then bake it for 30–35 minutes, until the pastry is crisp and golden.

9. Make the salsa. While the galette is baking, add the parsley leaves and olive oil to a mini food processor, season with salt and pepper and whizz until finely chopped. Tip in the walnuts and whizz again to finely chop. Add the vinegar and sumac and mix to combine.

10. Serve the galette warm, cut into wedges, with the salsa drizzled over the top.

Paul's Red Velvet Cake

A tender, tangy buttermilk sponge is the foundation for this cake's striking red interior. The colour can depend on the cocoa you choose: Dutch process cocoa, which is washed with a potassium carbonate solution to neutralise its acidity, produces a darker, more red cake; natural cocoa is lighter in colour. Flavourwise, though, you'll be met with the same deliciousness.

Serves: 12–16
Hands on: 1½ hours
Bake: 25 mins

For the sponge
280g unsalted butter, cubed and softened
245g golden caster sugar
3 eggs, beaten
25g cocoa powder, sifted
2 tsp vanilla extract
2 tsp red food-colouring paste
6 tbsp hot water
270ml buttermilk
1 tsp salt
335g self-raising flour, sifted
1 tsp white vinegar
1 tsp bicarbonate of soda

For the filling & icing
400g full-fat cream cheese, at room temperature
250ml double cream
2 tsp vanilla extract
300g icing sugar, sifted
200g mascarpone
pinch of salt

You will need
17cm round cake tins x 3, greased, then base lined with baking paper
cake plate or stand
medium piping bag fitted with a medium closed star nozzle

1. Make the sponges. Heat the oven to 200°C/180°C fan/Gas 6. Beat the butter and sugar in a stand mixer fitted with the beater, on medium speed for 3–5 minutes, scraping down the inside of the bowl from time to time, until pale and creamy. Add the eggs, a little at a time, beating well between each addition until combined.

2. In a small jug, mix the cocoa powder, vanilla, red food colouring and hot water together to form a paste. Add this to the bowl and mix well until combined.

3. Combine the buttermilk and salt in a jug. Mix one third into the bowl, then add one third of the flour. Continue to mix in the buttermilk and flour alternately until thoroughly combined.

4. In a small bowl, mix the vinegar and bicarbonate of soda together, then add this to the bowl and beat gently until the mixture is smooth.

5. Divide the mixture equally between the lined tins and spread it level. Bake the sponges on the middle shelves for 20–25 minutes, until risen and a skewer inserted into the centres comes out clean. Leave the sponges to cool in the tins for 5 minutes, then carefully turn them out onto a wire rack to cool completely.

6. Make the filling and icing. Whisk the cream cheese, cream, vanilla, icing sugar, mascarpone and salt in a stand mixer fitted with the whisk until the mixture is smooth and holds stiff peaks. Divide the icing equally between two bowls, then chill it until needed.

7. Assemble the cake. Remove one bowl of the icing from the fridge. Using a large, serrated knife, level the sponges, keeping any offcuts for the decoration. Slice each sponge in half horizontally so you have 6 thin sponges. Smear a little of the icing onto the middle of a cake plate or cake stand and top with the first sponge.

Continues overleaf

8. Spread one fifth of the icing over the first sponge, then top with a second sponge. Spread with another fifth of the icing, then top with a third sponge. Continue layering until you have 5 layers of icing between 6 sponges.

9. Remove the second bowl of icing from the fridge. Using a palette knife, spread half of the icing over the outside of the cake to seal and neaten. Clean the palette knife and smooth off any excess icing to create a smooth even icing layer.

10. Using half of the remaining icing, spread a second thin, even layer over the top of the cake and smooth it with a palette knife.

11. Spoon the remaining icing into the piping bag fitted with a medium closed star nozzle and pipe 8 rosettes around the top edge of the cake.

12. Crumble the reserved offcuts of sponge and gently press these up the bottom third of the cake. Sprinkle a few crumbs over each piped rosette to finish.

Sarah Bernhardt Cookies

These macaron, ganache and chocolate-coated Danish cookies are named after the French actress, who was said to have loved them when she visited Denmark to promote her autobiography in 1911. The toasty, nutty notes of chocolate are brilliant with almonds.

GLUTEN-FREE
Makes: 36
Hands on: 1 hour
Bake: 14 mins

For the macarons
150g ground almonds
150g icing sugar, sifted
2 egg whites
½ tsp almond extract
pinch of salt
25g flaked almonds

*For the chocolate
crème filling*
175g 70% dark chocolate,
    broken into pieces
2 egg yolks
50g caster sugar
75g unsalted butter,
    cubed and softened

For the coating
150g 70% dark chocolate,
    broken into pieces
2 sheets of gold leaf
    (food grade), optional

You will need
2 medium piping bags
    each fitted with a
    medium plain nozzle
2 baking sheets, lined
    with baking paper

1. Make the macarons. Heat the oven to 170°C/150°C fan/Gas 3. Whizz the ground almonds and icing sugar together in a food processor for 30 seconds to combine.

2. In a medium mixing bowl, whisk the egg whites and salt with an electric hand whisk until they form stiff peaks. Add the ground almond mixture and almond extract to the egg whites and fold them in gently with a rubber spatula until thoroughly combined.

3. Spoon the egg-white mixture into a medium piping bag fitted with the medium plain nozzle and pipe 36 mounds, each 3–4cm in diameter, onto the lined baking sheets, leaving space between each mound to allow for spreading during baking. Sprinkle the top of each macaron with flaked almonds and bake on the middle shelf for 14 minutes, until slightly puffy, crisp and golden. Leave the macarons to cool on the baking sheets.

4. Make the chocolate crème filling. While the macarons are cooling, melt the chocolate in a heatproof bowl set over a pan of barely simmering water. Stir until smooth and remove from the heat.

5. Whisk the egg yolks in a stand mixer for 1 minute, until slightly paler in colour.

6. Meanwhile, place the caster sugar in a small saucepan and add 50ml water. Set the pan over a low heat to dissolve the sugar. Bring to the boil, stir, then reduce the heat slightly and simmer for 30–60 seconds, until the syrup thickens slightly.

7. Whisking continuously, pour the hot syrup onto the egg yolks. Continue whisking for 2–3 minutes, until the mixture cools, becomes pale and thick, and leaves a ribbon trail when you lift the whisk.

Continues overleaf

8. Using a rubber spatula, fold the melted chocolate into the egg-yolk mixture until nearly combined, then gently beat in the softened butter, a little at a time, until the filling is silky smooth. Scoop the chocolate crème into the second piping bag and pipe kisses or bulbs of the chocolate mixture on top of each macaron. Chill for 20 minutes, until firm.

9. Make the coating. While the macarons are chilling, melt the chocolate in a heatproof bowl set over a pan of barely simmering water. Stir until smooth, then transfer to a small, deep bowl or teacup.

10. Finish the macarons. Dip the top of each macaron in the melted chocolate to coat the chocolate crème, then leave to cool and set firm. Decorate with a little gold leaf, if using, before serving at room temperature. (The cookies will store in an airtight box in the fridge for about 7 days.)

Triple-layer Dark Chocolate Peanut Butter Brownies

Raw peanuts have a grassy flavour, but roasting them triggers a chemical reaction within the peanut that forms pyrazines, compounds that give the richer, nuttier flavour that is just like roasted cocoa beans. It's no wonder, then, that peanut and chocolate are so good together.

Makes: 16
Hands on: 45 mins + chilling
Bake: 35 mins

For the brownie
200g 54% dark chocolate,
   broken into pieces
150g unsalted butter, cubed
1 tbsp cocoa powder
3 eggs
150g caster sugar
50g light brown soft sugar
1 tsp vanilla extract
125g plain flour
½ tsp baking powder
pinch of salt
100g salted peanuts,
   roughly chopped, plus
   extra to decorate
50g salted caramel popcorn

For the peanut cheesecake
180g full-fat cream cheese
40g caster sugar
75g crunchy peanut butter
1 egg, lightly beaten
1 egg yolk
1 tsp vanilla extract

For the glaze
100g 54% dark chocolate,
   finely chopped
50ml whole milk
50g unsalted butter, cubed
1 tbsp honey, golden syrup
   or liquid glucose

You will need
23cm square cake tin,
   greased, then lined
   (base and sides) with
   baking paper

1. Make the brownie. Heat the oven to 170°C/150°C fan/Gas 3. Melt the dark chocolate with the butter and cocoa powder in a heatproof bowl set over a pan of barely simmering water, stirring from time to time. Remove from the heat and leave to cool for 3–4 minutes.

2. Whisk the eggs, both types of sugar and the vanilla in a stand mixer fitted with the whisk, on medium speed for 3 minutes, until well aerated and paler in colour. Add the melted chocolate mixture and mix until just combined.

3. Sift the flour, baking powder and salt into the bowl and fold them in with a rubber spatula until almost smooth. Add the peanuts and mix until thoroughly combined.

4. Spoon the mixture into the lined tin and spread it level. Bake the brownie on the middle shelf for 25 minutes, until it is just set, and the top is lightly risen and starting to crack.

5. Make the peanut cheesecake. While the brownie is baking, in a small bowl beat together the cream cheese, caster sugar, peanut butter, beaten egg, egg yolk and vanilla until smooth. Spread the mixture on top of the brownie in an even layer and return the brownie to the oven for 10 minutes, until set. Remove from the oven and leave to cool in the tin.

6. Make the glaze. Put all the glaze ingredients in a small saucepan over a low heat, stirring gently until melted and thoroughly combined. Spoon the glaze over the peanut cheesecake brownie, spread it out evenly and leave it to cool.

7. Scatter the top with the popcorn and extra peanuts, pressing them gently into the glaze, then chill the brownie for 1 hour, until the glaze sets. Cut the brownie into 16 equal squares to serve.

Rebs's Simit

Pronounced 'smit', these chewy sesame bagels are inspired by my travels to Turkey, where you'll find them for sale on stalls around every corner. I first made them for my Turkish boyfriend's dad during lockdown when he was missing his homeland, and they've quickly become a staple in my house. They have a malty sweetness from the sesame seeds, which if you have a sweet tooth like me, is perfect with jam. Alternatively, smoked salmon or hummus works instead.

Makes: 12
Hands on: 1 hour + rising
Bake: 20 mins

For the dough
750g strong white
   bread flour
1 tbsp salt
1 tbsp caster sugar
450ml lukewarm water
14g fast-action dried yeast

For the sesame topping
200g white sesame seeds
3 tbsp runny honey

For the blackberry jam
200g blackberries
150g jam sugar
juice of ½ lemon
3 tbsp gin or water

You will need
2 baking trays, lined
   with baking paper
2 oiled proving bags
sugar thermometer

1. Make the dough. Sift the flour, salt and sugar into a large mixing bowl, stir to combine, then make a well in the centre. Pour in the lukewarm water and sprinkle over the yeast. Bring the mixture together with a metal spoon into a rough dough.

2. Lightly flour the work surface and knead the dough for 8–10 minutes, until smooth and elastic, and no longer sticky. Shape the dough into a ball, place the dough in the clean bowl and cover it with a clean damp tea towel. Leave it to rise in a warm place for 1 hour, until doubled in size.

3. Make the sesame topping. While the dough is rising, toast the sesame seeds in a large, dry frying pan over a medium heat for 5 minutes, until golden. Make sure you stir the seeds, so they toast evenly. Set aside to cool on a plate.

4. Gently warm the honey with 3 tablespoons of water in a small pan, stirring, for 2 minutes, until the honey melts. Set aside to cool.

5. Shape the dough. Knead the risen dough gently for 20 seconds to knock it back, then divide it into 12 equal pieces, about 100g each. Working with one piece at a time, roll the dough with your hands into a 50cm-long sausage. Fold the dough sausage in half and, holding one end, twist the two strands together to look like a rope. The dough will now have a loop at one end. Thread the joined end through the loop to form a ring shape and squeeze firmly to join the two ends. Repeat to shape all 12 pieces of dough.

6. Carefully dip both sides of each dough ring into the cooled honey mixture, then into the toasted sesame seeds until coated all over. Place the simit on the lined baking trays, making sure

Continues overleaf

they have space to rise. Slide the baking trays into the proving bags and leave the simit to prove for 45 minutes, until puffed up.

7. Make the blackberry jam. While the simit are proving, put the blackberries, jam sugar, lemon juice and gin or water in a saucepan fitted with a sugar thermometer. Stir over a low heat until the sugar dissolves, then increase the heat to medium-high and bring the liquid to the boil. Stir regularly to help crush the blackberries and prevent the jam sticking to the bottom of the pan. Cook until the mixture reaches 105°C on the sugar thermometer, then remove the pan from the heat and pour the jam into a serving bowl or sterilised jar and leave to cool.

8. Bake the simit. As the simit finish rising, heat the oven to 210°C/190°C fan/Gas 6–7. Then, bake them for 16–20 minutes, until golden and crisp on the outside. Place the baked simit on a wire rack and cover them with a clean tea towel to stop them drying out. Eat the simit immediately (best this way); or store them, then reheat them in the oven to refresh.

Pistachio & Elderflower Éclairs

These choux slippers are filled with a pistachio cream and topped with a musky, fruity elderflower cordial icing. If you can't find pistachio paste, make your own by whizzing blanched pistachios in a food processor – they will give you a bright green colour and an intensely clean, nutty flavour.

Makes: 20
Hands on: 1½ hours
+ chilling
Bake: 30 mins

For the pistachio crème
2 egg yolks
75g caster sugar
25g cornflour
1 tsp vanilla paste
250ml whole milk
50g white chocolate, finely chopped
75g unsalted butter, at room temperature
75g pistachio paste
25g shelled unsalted pistachios, finely chopped, plus extra to decorate
finely grated zest of ½ unwaxed lime

For the choux pastry
75g unsalted butter, cubed, at room temperature
100ml whole milk
1 tsp caster sugar
pinch of salt
125g strong white bread flour, sifted
4 eggs, lightly beaten
icing sugar, for dusting

Continues overleaf

1. Make the pistachio crème. Whisk together the egg yolks, caster sugar, cornflour and vanilla in a mixing bowl until smooth. In a small saucepan, heat the milk until just boiling. Pour the hot milk onto the egg-yolk mixture, whisking continuously until smooth. Return the mixture to the pan and cook it over a low heat for 3 minutes, whisking until thickened and you can no longer taste the cornflour.

2. Strain the mixture through a sieve into a clean bowl. Add the white chocolate, then stir it until smooth and melted into the crème. Cover the surface to prevent a skin forming and leave the crème to cool to room temperature.

3. In another bowl, beat the butter until pale and light. Gradually, add the beaten butter to the cold crème, mixing well between each addition. Add the pistachio paste, chopped pistachios and lime zest and mix to combine. Cover and chill for 1 hour, or until ready to use.

4. Make the choux pastry. While the crème is chilling, melt the butter with the milk, sugar, salt and 100ml of water in a saucepan over a medium heat. Stir, then quickly bring the mixture to a rolling boil. Immediately slide the pan off the heat, quickly add the flour and beat vigorously with a wooden spoon or rubber spatula until smooth. Return the pan to a low heat and cook, stirring continuously, for 1 minute, until the mixture is glossy and cleanly leaves the sides of the pan. Tip the mixture into a large mixing bowl and leave it to cool for 5 minutes. Heat the oven to 190°C/170°C fan/Gas 5.

5. A little at a time, add the eggs to the mixture, beating well between each addition with a wooden spoon or spatula until the batter is silky smooth and reluctantly drops off the spoon in a V-shape – you may not need to add the last tablespoon of egg.

Continues overleaf

Pistachio & Elderflower Éclairs *continued*

To fill & decorate
250g raspberries
150g icing sugar, sifted
3 tbsp elderflower cordial
green food-colouring paste

You will need
large piping bag fitted
    with a medium closed
    star nozzle
large baking sheet, lined
    with baking paper
medium piping bag fitted
    with a medium closed
    star nozzle
small piping bag fitted
    with a large plain nozzle

6. Scoop the mixture into the large piping bag fitted with a medium star nozzle. Pipe the choux into 20 neat 12cm-long éclairs on the lined baking sheet. Chill them for 10 minutes.

7. Dust the top of the éclairs with icing sugar and bake them on the middle shelf for 30 minutes, until golden brown, crisp and puffed up. Leave them to cool on the baking sheet.

8. Fill and decorate the éclairs. Using a serrated knife, cut each éclair in half horizontally. Spoon the pistachio crème into the medium piping bag fitted with a medium star nozzle and pipe it over the bottom half of each éclair, then top it with 4 raspberries and gently press on the lid. Repeat with the rest of the éclairs.

9. To decorate, whisk together the icing sugar and elderflower cordial and add a tiny dot of green food-colouring paste to make a thick-but-spreadable pale green icing. Spoon the icing into the small piping bag fitted with a large plain nozzle and pipe a neat, smooth line over the top of each éclair. Leave to set for 2 minutes, then scatter with a few finely chopped pistachios. Leave the icing to set completely before serving.

Praline & Apricot Cake

Delicate génoise sponge leaves the apricot filling to sing in this elegant cake. Apricots (especially dried) are well known for their intense sweetness, which makes a great bedfellow for rich vanilla buttercream. Pecans are a good match, too – naturally sweet and rich, they complement the fruit while also bringing out its nuttiness. Pecans are the fattiest of all the nuts, but in a good way – the high level of oil adds bags of flavour.

Serves: 12
Hands on: 2 hours
Bake: 20 mins

_____

For the apricot filling
200g dried apricots
about 200ml
   just-boiled water

For the German buttercream
2 egg yolks
100g caster sugar
2 tbsp cornflour
2 tsp plain flour
115ml whole milk
115ml double cream
2 tsp vanilla paste
165g unsalted butter,
   softened

For the génoise sponges
6 eggs
190g caster sugar
2 tsp vanilla paste
190g plain flour
40g unsalted butter,
   melted

For the pecan praline
75g pecan halves
75g caster sugar

For the buttercream
250g unsalted
   butter, softened
500g icing sugar, sifted

Continues overleaf

1. Begin the apricot filling. Add the dried apricots to a small saucepan and pour over enough just-boiled water to fully cover them, then set aside to soak while you make a pastry cream.

2. Begin the German buttercream. Whisk together the egg yolks, sugar, cornflour and plain flour in a large bowl, and set aside.

3. Place the milk, cream and vanilla in a medium saucepan over a medium heat and bring the mixture to boiling point. Then, immediately pour a little of the hot milk mixture into the bowl with the egg mixture to temper it, and whisk to combine. Whisk in the remaining milk, then transfer this mixture back into the saucepan and place it back over a medium heat. Bring to the boil, stirring continuously, and then cook for about 1 minute, until you have a smooth, thick pastry cream. Transfer the pastry cream to a tray or shallow, wide container, cover the surface with a sheet of baking paper and set aside to cool completely.

4. Continue with the apricot filling. Cover the apricot pan with a lid and simmer over a low–medium heat for about 5 minutes, until the fruit is soft. Then, drain the apricots and, using a hand-held stick blender, blitz them to smooth purée. Transfer the purée to a shallow dish or container and set it aside to cool completely. Meanwhile, heat the oven to 190°C/170°C fan/Gas 5.

5. Make the génoise sponges. Add the eggs, caster sugar and vanilla to the bowl of a stand mixer fitted with the whisk attachment and whisk on high speed for about 3–4 minutes, until tripled in volume and the mixture leaves a ribbon trail when you lift the whisk.

6. Sift in the flour a little at a time, using a rubber spatula to fold in each batch gently. Once you have added all the flour, fold in the melted butter.

Continues overleaf

Praline & Apricot Cake *continued*

You will need
20cm round cake tins x 3, greased, base-lined, and the sides dusted with flour
baking tray, lined with baking paper
large piping bag fitted with a large plain nozzle
cake-decorating turntable

7. Divide the mixture equally between the prepared tins and bake the sponges for about 15 minutes, until golden, firm to the touch, and a skewer inserted into the centre of each comes out clean. Allow the sponges to cool in the tins for 10 minutes, then turn them out onto a wire rack to cool completely.

8. **Make the pecan praline.** While the sponges are cooling, tip the pecan halves into a baking tray and roast them in the oven for about 3–4 minutes, until fragrant.

9. Tip the sugar into a large, heavy-based saucepan and cook it over a medium heat, stirring if necessary, until all of the sugar has melted and you have a golden caramel. Remove the caramel from the heat and stir in the pecans, then tip out the mixture onto the lined baking tray and leave it to cool and set. Once set, transfer it to a food processor and blitz it to a crumb consistency. Set aside.

10. **Finish the German buttercream.** In the bowl of a stand mixer fitted with the beater, beat the softened butter on medium speed for about 3–4 minutes, until pale and fluffy. With the mixer running, a spoonful at a time, add the pastry cream, beating continuously until you have added it all and the mixture is light and fluffy. If your buttercream appears very soft, transfer it to the fridge to chill for about 30 minutes before assembling the cake.

11. **Make the second buttercream.** In the bowl of a stand mixer fitted with the beater, mix the softened butter and icing sugar together on a low speed for about 1 minute, until combined. Then increase the speed to high and beat for 3–4 minutes, until you have a light and fluffy buttercream. Transfer the buttercream to the large piping bag.

12. **Assemble the cake.** Place 1 sponge on a serving plate or cake board and transfer it to the cake-decorating turntable. Pipe a ring of buttercream around the outside edge of the top of the sponge. Spoon half the apricot purée inside the ring of buttercream and spread it level with a palette knife. Spread half of the German buttercream on top of that. Sprinkle over one third of the praline crumb, then place the second sponge on top. Repeat the ring of buttercream, the apricot purée and the layer of German buttercream. Top with the remaining sponge.

13. Pipe the rest of the buttercream around the top and sides of the layered cake and, using the turntable to help you, smooth it out with a palette knife to give an even coating all over. Then, hold the tip of the palette knife against the surface of the buttercream at the base of the cake and rotate the turntable with your other hand as you gradually move the palette knife up the cake to create a swirl effect around the side (if you create a lip at the top, that's fine). Do the same on top of the cake, then sprinkle with the remaining praline crumb to finish, inside the top edge and around the base.

Root Vegetable Mini Loaves

Carrots, parsnips and butternut squash make these little loaves extra-moist, while maple syrup, cinnamon and nutmeg add layers of spicy sweetness.

VEGAN
Makes: 12
Hands on: 45 mins
Bake: 30 mins

───────────────

For the sponges
270g plain flour
1 tsp baking powder
1 tsp bicarbonate of soda
¼ tsp salt
2 tsp ground cinnamon
½ tsp grated nutmeg
100ml vegetable oil
150g light brown soft sugar
50ml maple syrup
100ml almond milk
½ tsp apple cider vinegar
1 tsp vanilla paste
100g each: grated carrot,
    parsnip and squash
1 small apple, peeled,
    cored and grated
60g sultanas
80g pecans, chopped
40g unsweetened
    desiccated coconut

For the maple drizzle
3 tbsp coconut cream
75g light brown soft sugar
1 tbsp maple syrup
¼ tsp vanilla paste
½ tsp cornflour

For the frosting
400g icing sugar, sifted
125g vegan spread
1 tsp vanilla paste
2 tbsp vegan cream cheese
few chopped toasted pecans
    and pumpkin seeds

You will need
12-hole mini-loaf tin, oiled
medium piping bag fitted
    with a medium plain nozzle

1. Make the sponges. Heat the oven to 180°C/160°C fan/Gas 4. Sift the flour, baking powder, bicarbonate of soda, salt and spices into a large mixing bowl and stir to combine.

2. Whisk the oil, sugar, maple syrup, almond milk, vinegar and vanilla paste in stand mixer fitted with the whisk, on medium speed for 1–2 minutes, until combined.

3. Remove the bowl from the mixer, then sift in the flour mixture and gently fold it in with a metal spoon to make a thick batter. Fold in the grated vegetables, and the apple, sultanas, pecans and desiccated coconut until thoroughly combined, but do not over-mix.

4. Divide the mixture equally between the holes in the prepared tin. Bake for 20–25 minutes, until the sponges are golden and risen, and a skewer inserted into the centre of each comes out clean. Leave the sponges to cool completely in the tin.

5. Make the maple drizzle. Meanwhile, place 1 tablespoon of the coconut cream in a small bowl and set aside. Then, place the remainder in a small saucepan with the sugar, maple syrup and vanilla. Warm the mixture over a low heat, stirring, until the sugar dissolves. Mix the cornflour into the reserved coconut cream to a creamy paste, then, using a balloon whisk, whisk this into the warm sauce until combined. Bring the mixture to the boil, then reduce the heat and simmer for 5 minutes, until the drizzle reduces to a thick, syrupy consistency. Leave to cool.

6. Make the frosting. Put the icing sugar, vegan spread and vanilla in a mixing bowl and whisk with an electric hand whisk until combined. Add the vegan cream cheese and whisk until light and creamy, adding a splash of coconut cream, if needed, to make a pipeable frosting. Spoon the frosting into the medium piping bag.

7. Turn the loaves out of the tin and pipe the frosting in a zig-zag motion along the top of each loaf. Using a teaspoon, drizzle the sauce over and sprinkle with the pecans and pumpkin seeds.

Maxy's Lamb Patties

Lamb is my favourite meat. When you mix it with lots of onion and sweet peppers, as well as earthy paprika, fragrant thyme and the flavour explosion that is the Scotch bonnet chilli, you just can't go wrong. I promise, every bite of these pastry turnovers delivers.

Makes: 18
Hands on: 1½ hours
   + chilling
Bake: 30 mins

For the rough puff pastry
450g strong white
   bread flour
1 tbsp ground turmeric
2 tsp medium curry powder
2 tsp fine sea salt
1½ tbsp caster sugar
450g unsalted butter,
   cubed and chilled
180–200ml chilled water

For the lamb filling
500g minced lamb
1½ tsp onion powder
1½ tsp paprika
2 tsp all-purpose seasoning
1 tsp ground white pepper
1 tsp garlic powder
1 tsp stock powder
1 tsp salt
⅓ Scotch bonnet chilli,
   deseeded and finely
   chopped; or 1 tsp dried
   chilli flakes
1 tbsp olive oil
1 onion, finely diced
3 spring onions,
   finely sliced
3 garlic cloves, minced
5 thyme sprigs, leaves
   picked and chopped;
   or 1 tsp dried thyme
⅓ red pepper, deseeded
   and finely chopped

Continues overleaf

1. Make the rough puff pastry. Sift the flour, turmeric, curry powder, salt and sugar into a large mixing bowl and mix to combine. Add the butter and lightly toss the cubes to coat them in the dry ingredients. Pinch the butter between your fingertips, flattening the cubes to incorporate them into the flour mixture until crumbly with some larger visible flecks of butter.

2. Make a well in the centre and add the chilled water, a little at a time, mixing with a palette knife until it starts to come together into a rough dough (you may not need all the water), then tip the dough onto the work surface and gather it into a ball with your hands. Flatten the dough into a rough square, then wrap and chill it for 30 minutes.

3. Lightly flour the work surface, then roll out the dough in one direction until tripled in length to make a long rectangle, about 1cm thick, with the one of the short ends closest to you. Brush away any excess flour, then fold the top third of the dough down to the middle and the bottom third up over the first so that you now have a three-layered piece of dough with a seam running along the top. Give the dough a quarter turn clockwise so the top seam is now on the right. Repeat the rolling and folding, give the dough a quarter turn and repeat again, so that you have rolled and folded three times in total. Wrap and chill the dough for at least 20 minutes.

4. Make the lamb filling. While the dough is chilling, add the minced lamb to a large bowl and sprinkle in the onion powder, paprika, all-purpose seasoning, pepper, garlic powder, stock, salt and chilli. Mix the seasonings into the mince, then set aside until ready to use.

5. Heat the olive oil in a large frying pan over a medium heat. Add the onion and sauté for a couple minutes to soften slightly. Add the spring onions, garlic, thyme and both peppers and

Continues overleaf

1/3 yellow pepper,
   deseeded and
   finely chopped
2 tbsp plain flour

For the egg wash
1 egg, beaten
pinch of salt

You will need
14cm pastry cutter
   or side plate
2 baking sheets, lined
   with baking paper

cook for 5 minutes, until softened. Add the seasoned mince and cook for 5 minutes, stirring often until browned. Sprinkle over the flour and pour in 2 tablespoons of water. Cook for a few more minutes, stirring until the liquid thickens. Transfer the filling to a bowl and set it aside to cool. Heat the oven to 180°C/160°C fan/Gas 4.

6. Lightly flour the work surface, then roll out the dough to 3mm thick (you may find it easier to do this half at a time). Using the pastry cutter or a side plate, cut out 18 discs, re-rolling the pastry as necessary. Place a heaped tablespoonful of the cooled filling into the centre of a pastry circle. Repeat for all the discs of pastry.

7. Make the egg wash. Beat together the egg and salt with 1 teaspoon of water, then brush it around the edge of each pastry disc.

8. Finish the turnovers. Fold over the pastry to create a half-moon shape and enclose the filling, then press down with a fork to seal the edges. Place the turnovers on the lined baking sheets, brush with the egg wash, then prick the top of each one with a fork. Bake for 25–30 minutes, until puffed up and golden.

Toasted Coconut Shortbread

Buttery shortbread from snowy Scotland is paired with coconut from the sunny tropics in this trans-continental biscuit with snap. Quickly heating the desiccated coconut in a pan coaxes out its nutty flavour.

Makes: 18
Hands on: 1 hour + chilling
Bake: 12 mins

For the shortbread
75g desiccated coconut
150g unsalted butter,
    softened
75g caster sugar
225g plain flour
finely grated zest of
    1 unwaxed lemon
pinch of salt

For the royal icing
500g icing sugar
2 egg whites
red, green and yellow
    food-colouring pastes

You will need
7–8cm flower cutter
2 baking sheets, lined
    with baking paper
4 small paper piping bags
cocktail stick or
    wooden skewer

1. Make the shortbread biscuits. Add the desiccated coconut to a frying pan set over a low heat and toast it for about 3–4 minutes, stirring occasionally, until golden. Remove the pan from the heat and set the coconut aside to cool.

2. Add the softened butter and the sugar to a large bowl and cream them together with a spatula or wooden spoon until the sugar is dissolved. Add the toasted coconut, and the flour, lemon zest and salt and mix to fully combine to form a dough. If the dough feels very soft, chill it for about 30 minutes, before moving on to the next step (if it's manageable, you can skip the chilling and keep going).

3. Roll out the dough on a lightly floured work surface to about 7–8mm thick. Using the flower cutter, stamp out about 18 flower shapes, re-rolling the trimmings as necessary.

4. Place the shortbread flowers on the lined baking sheets and place the baking sheets in the freezer to chill the shortbread for about 10 minutes. Meanwhile, heat the oven to 180°C/160°C fan/Gas 4.

5. Bake the chilled biscuits for about 10–12 minutes, until just turning golden at the edges, then remove them from the oven and leave them on the baking sheets to cool completely.

6. Make the royal icing. Sift the icing sugar into a large mixing bowl. Add the egg whites and 1 tablespoon of cold water and whisk for about 2 minutes using a balloon whisk until the icing is smooth and thick and will just hold a ribbon trail.

7. Spoon 2 tablespoons of icing into each of 3 small bowls. Tint the icing in one of the bowls very pale pink using a dot of red food-colouring paste. Turn the second bowl green and the third yellow, then cover each bowl and set aside.

Continues overleaf

8. Using the red food-colouring paste, tint the remaining icing in the mixing bowl dark pink – add a tiny amount at a time to achieve the desired colour. Spoon 4 tablespoons of the dark pink icing into one of the piping bags and snip the end to a fine writing point. Cover the remaining icing to prevent it drying out. Pipe a neat, continuous outline around the edge of each flower-shaped shortbread and leave it to dry for 30 minutes.

9. Add a drop more water to the dark pink icing to loosen it up enough to just run smoothly off the spoon. Working on one biscuit at a time, spoon 1 rounded teaspoon of dark pink icing into the middle of each biscuit and, using a teaspoon or small palette knife, tease the icing into the flower shape to fill the outline smoothly.

10. Spoon the green, yellow and pale pink icings each into another of the piping bags. Snip the ends to a fine writing point. Pipe a dot of green in the middle of the flower. Pipe a circle of yellow icing around the green dot. Pipe a pale pink dot in the middle of each petal and using the cocktail stick or skewer, feather the icing out from the middle of each flower starting at the green centre and into the pale pink dot, using the photograph as a guide. Pipe 6 tiny dots of pale pink icing in between each petal and in the middle of each flower.

11. Repeat to decorate the remaining flower shortbreads and leave them until the icing has set firm before serving.

Ginger & Caramel Squares

These light joconde sponge squares are flavoured with creamy ground almonds. The result is a delicate backdrop that leaves the salted caramel buttercream and peppery ginger syrup to be the stars of the show.

Makes: 12
Hands on: 1½ hours
   + chilling
Bake: 12 mins

For the salted caramel
55g caster sugar
25g dark muscovado sugar
200ml double cream
5g sea-salt flakes

For the joconde sponge
185g golden caster sugar
5 large egg whites
5 large eggs
185g ground almonds
45g plain flour
¼ tsp salt
30g unsalted butter, melted

For the ginger syrup
finger-sized piece of fresh
   ginger, finely grated
finely grated zest of
   1 unwaxed lemon
75g golden caster sugar
75g dark muscovado sugar

*For the Italian
meringue buttercream*
3 large egg whites
155g granulated sugar
½ tsp juice from
   1 unwaxed lemon
250g unsalted butter,
   cubed, at room
   temperature
150g salted caramel
   (see above)

Continues overleaf

1. Make the salted caramel. Add the sugars to a medium saucepan, and the cream to a separate small pan. Melt the sugars on a medium heat until fully dissolved, then cook to a dark caramel, stirring with a wooden spoon if necessary to help the caramel cook evenly. Meanwhile, gently heat the cream over a low heat to just remove the chill – but don't let it boil.

2. Once the sugar is caramelised, remove the pan from the heat and carefully pour the warmed cream into the caramel, whisking continuously to combine. Then, mix in the salt. Pour the caramel into a tray with a lip or into a wide, shallow container and set it aside to cool completely. Once cooled, set aside 150g for your buttercream and transfer the rest to the small piping bag without the nozzle.

3. Make the joconde sponge. Heat the oven to 200°C/180°C fan/ Gas 6 and measure out 65g of the golden caster sugar. Set the remaining 120g aside. Place the egg whites into the bowl of a stand mixer fitted with the whisk and whisk on high speed until the egg forms soft peaks, then continue to whisk and gradually spoon in the 65g of sugar to create a light, stiff meringue. Transfer the meringue to a clean bowl and set aside.

4. Tip the whole eggs into the bowl of the stand mixer (no need to fully clean it), along with the remaining 120g of sugar and the ground almonds. Switch to the beater and mix on medium–high speed for 3–4 minutes, until thick and airy, and the mixture leaves a ribbon trail when you lift the beater. Meanwhile, in a separate bowl, sift together the flour and salt and set aside.

5. Using a rubber spatula, fold one quarter of the meringue into the almond and egg mixture, then add the rest of the meringue in two stages, gently folding to combine, and taking care not to knock out too much air. Once fully combined, gently fold the sifted flour and salt into the mixture, followed by the melted butter.

Continues overleaf

To assemble
3-4 pieces of stem ginger
    in syrup, drained and
    finely chopped

To decorate
2-3 pieces of stem ginger
    in syrup, drained and
    finely sliced

You will need
20 x 30cm traybake tins
    x 2 (at least 2.5cm deep),
    greased, then lined
    (base and sides) with
    baking paper
sugar thermometer
2 small piping bags,
    1 fitted with a medium
    closed star nozzle
ruler

6. Divide the mixture between the two prepared traybake tins and gently smooth the tops with a palette knife. Bake the sponges for 10-12 minutes, or until they are just brown on top and just firm to the touch. Leave to cool in the tins for 5 minutes, then carefully turn them out onto wire racks to cool completely.

7. **Make the ginger syrup.** While the sponges are baking, put the ginger, lemon zest, sugars and 225ml of water into a small saucepan. Place the pan over a medium-high heat, bring the mixture to the boil, then cook for about 10-15 minutes, until slightly reduced, but thin enough to be able to absorb into the sponge. Pass the syrup through a sieve into a clean bowl and set aside to cool.

8. **Make the Italian meringue buttercream.** Place the egg whites into the clean bowl of a stand mixer fitted with the whisk.

9. Pour the sugar and 85ml of water into a medium saucepan and place the pan over a medium-high heat to bring the syrup to the boil. Use a wet pastry brush to brush down any sugar crystals that form on the inside of the pan, if necessary.

10. When the syrup reaches 110°C on the sugar thermometer, switch the stand mixer to medium-high speed to begin whisking the egg whites – you're aiming for stiff peaks by the time the sugar reaches 117°C.

11. When the sugar reaches 117°C, immediately remove the pan from the heat and reduce the speed of the stand mixer to medium. Gradually pour the hot syrup down the inside of the mixer bowl in a steady stream, taking care not to pour it directly onto the whisk. When you have added all the syrup, add the lemon juice and turn the speed back up to high to whip it to a glossy Italian meringue. Continue to whisk until both the meringue and the bowl feel cool (about 10 minutes).

12. With the mixer running, add the butter a few cubes at a time, waiting until each addition is fully incorporated before adding the next. Pause to scrape down the bowl occasionally.

13. Once you've added all the butter, you should have a light, glossy buttercream. Stop the mixer and scrape down the bowl, then add the salted caramel and whisk again on a medium speed until the caramel is fully incorporated into the buttercream.

Place 100g of the buttercream into the small piping bag fitted with the medium closed star nozzle and set this aside for the final decoration. Use the remaining buttercream to assemble the cake.

14. Assemble the cake. Place one of the sponges on a chopping board. Using a pastry brush, coat both of the sponges generously with the ginger syrup and then spread the sponge on the chopping board with half of the remaining buttercream, smoothing it out into an even layer. Sprinkle the finely chopped stem ginger over the buttercream, then place the second sponge on top, syrup side up. Cover this sponge layer with the remaining buttercream and smooth it over as neatly as possible with a palette knife. Chill the cake in the fridge for about 30 minutes (this makes it easier to slice).

15. Use a ruler to mark out 12 equal squares on the cake (each is about 6 x 6cm with a little cake to spare around the edges). Then, using a large sharp knife, slice the sponge into equal portions and discard (or eat!) any offcuts.

16. To decorate, snip a small hole in the end of the piping bag containing the salted caramel and pipe lines of caramel diagonally across the top of the cakes, in a sweeping motion. Pipe a rosette of buttercream onto the middle of each square and top each with a thin slice of stem ginger.

Peanut Cookies

Short and sweet, this recipe proves that even simple bakes can pack in flavour. Roasting the peanuts before mixing the biscuit dough triggers the Maillard reaction (see page 14) to open a Pandora's box of grassy, meaty and rich deliciousness.

VEGAN
Serves: 18
Hands on: 35 mins
Bake: 12 mins

255g blanched peanuts
255g plain flour
pinch of salt
65g icing sugar, sifted
170ml peanut or
    groundnut oil
about 200g smooth or
    coarse peanut butter,
    according to preference
about 100g homemade
    raspberry jam (see p.270)

You will need
**2 large baking sheets,
    lined with baking paper**
cocktail stick

1. Heat the oven to 190°C/170°C fan/Gas 5.

2. Spread out the peanuts over a baking tray and roast them in the oven for about 10 minutes, until they are fragrant and starting to brown. Set them aside to cool completely. (If you can't find blanched peanuts you can roast them with the skins on and then, once cool, rub them between your fingers to remove the skins.)

3. Tip the cooled peanuts into the bowl of a food processor and blitz them to a medium or fine-ground consistency, according to preference, then set them aside.

4. Add the ground peanuts, flour, salt and icing sugar to the bowl of a stand mixer fitted with the beater. Mix on low speed to combine, then add the oil, mixing until just combined.

5. Divide the dough into 36 equal pieces (each about 20g). Roll each piece between your hands to form a little sausage and place the sausage shape onto one of the lined baking sheets. Pinch the middle of the sausage to narrow it a little and flatten the dough at either end – you're aiming to shape the cookies to resemble monkey nuts. Use the cocktail stick to score lines horizontally and vertically over the surface of each shaped dough to create the monkey-nut texture. Repeat for all the dough pieces, spacing them well apart over the baking sheets.

6. Bake the cookies for 11–12 minutes, or until brown at the bottom and around the edges, then leave them to cool on the trays.

7. Once cool, turn half of the cookies base upwards and spread each with 2 teaspoons of peanut butter and 1 teaspoon of raspberry jam. Sandwich with the remaining cookies, then serve.

Chocolate, Caramel & Tahini Tart

The tahini in the pastry case for this tart provides an underlying nuttiness that matches so well with the caramel layer and is picked up again by the tahini in the rich chocolate filling. A final flourish of crunchy sesame seed brittle completes the flavour explosion.

Serves: 8
Hands on: 1½ hours
  + chilling
Bake: 20 mins

For the pastry
100g unsalted butter,
   cubed, at room
   temperature
25g icing sugar, sifted
25g tahini
1 egg, lightly beaten
200g plain flour
pinch of salt

For the caramel
75g caster sugar
1 tbsp hot water
25g unsalted butter
100ml double cream
1 tbsp golden syrup
1 tbsp toasted white
   sesame seeds
pinch of salt

For the filling
350g 54% dark
   chocolate, chopped
100g unsalted
   butter, cubed
75g light muscovado sugar
2 eggs
1 tsp vanilla paste
pinch of sea salt
2 tbsp tahini
150ml double cream

Continues overleaf

1. Make the pastry. Beat the butter, icing sugar and tahini in a stand mixer fitted with the beater, on medium speed for 2-3 minutes, scraping down the inside of the bowl from time to time, until pale and creamy. Add the egg and mix until combined.

2. Sift the flour and salt into the bowl and mix again briefly until the dough starts to clump together, taking care not to overwork it. Tip the dough out onto the work surface and lightly knead it to bring it together into a neat ball. Flatten the dough into a disc, then wrap it and chill it for at least 1 hour, until firm.

3. Lightly flour the work surface and roll out the pastry into a neat disc, large enough to line the base and sides of the tart tin and about 2mm thick.

4. Using the rolling pin, lift the pastry into the tin, pressing the pastry neatly into the base and the grooves in the sides. Trim the excess pastry from the top with a sharp knife and chill the tart case for at least 20 minutes.

5. Heat the oven to 180°C/160°C fan/Gas 4. Place a baking sheet on the middle shelf of the oven as it heats up.

6. Prick the base of the tart case with a fork, line it with baking paper and fill it with baking beans or rice. Place the tart on top of the hot baking sheet and bake it on the middle shelf for 15 minutes, until the top edge starts to turn crisp and pale golden. Remove the paper and beans or rice and return the tart case to the oven for 5 minutes, until the base is crisp. Leave to cool.

7. Make the caramel. While the case is baking and cooling, heat the caster sugar with the hot water in a small saucepan over a low heat until the sugar dissolves. Increase the heat to medium, bring the syrup to the boil and cook, without stirring, for 3 minutes, until it is a rich, amber-coloured caramel. Slide the pan off the heat and carefully add the butter, cream and golden syrup. Return

Continues overleaf

For the sesame brittle
50g caster sugar
12g mixed black
    and toasted white
    sesame seeds
pinch of salt

To decorate
200ml double cream

You will need
20cm fluted tart tin
    (about 3.5cm deep)
2 baking sheets, 1 lined
    with baking paper
baking beans or rice
medium piping bag fitted
    with a medium closed
    star nozzle

the pan to a low heat and simmer, stirring for 1 minute, until the sauce is smooth and thick. Remove the pan from the heat and stir in the sesame seeds and salt. Pour the caramel into the baked pastry case, spread it level and leave it to cool. Then, chill it for 30 minutes, until set.

8. Make the filling. Melt the chocolate with the butter in a heatproof bowl set over a pan of barely simmering water. Stir until smooth. Remove the bowl from the heat.

9. Using a balloon whisk, combine the muscovado sugar, eggs, vanilla and sea salt in another heatproof bowl. Set the bowl over a pan of simmering water and whisk continuously for 5 minutes, until the mixture thickens slightly. Remove from the heat and leave to cool for 2 minutes.

10. Pour the melted chocolate into the whisked egg mixture, stirring gently until just combined. Add the tahini and cream and mix again until silky smooth. Pour the mixture over the set caramel layer in the pastry case and spread it out evenly. Leave the filling to cool to room temperature, then cover the tart and chill it for 4 hours, until the filling has set.

11. Make the sesame brittle. While the tart is chilling, heat the caster sugar with 1 tablespoon of water in a small saucepan over a low heat until the sugar dissolves. Increase the heat to medium, bring the syrup to the boil and cook, without stirring, for 3 minutes, until it is a rich, amber-coloured caramel. Slide the pan off the heat and stir in the sesame seeds and salt, then pour the caramel onto the lined baking sheet and leave the sesame caramel at room temperature to cool and harden.

12. Decorate the tart. Before serving, whisk the double cream until it holds soft peaks and spoon it into the medium piping bag fitted with a medium star nozzle. Pipe a ring of rosettes around the outer edge of the chocolate tart. Break the sesame brittle into shards and press the shards into or between the piped cream to finish.

EAMY

Maritozzi

A form of 18th-century Italian Lenten bun (allegedly offered as a gift to woo unmarried Italian women), maritozzi have the tang of honey and the kick of orange zest to lift the light but rich dough and complement the sumptuous vanilla cream filling.

Serves: 10
Hands on: 1 hour + rising
Bake: 12 mins

For the buns
500g strong white
   bread flour
50g caster sugar
7g fast-action dried yeast
½ tsp salt
finely grated zest of
   1 unwaxed orange
200ml whole milk
1½ tbsp runny honey
1 tsp vanilla paste
2 large eggs
1 large egg yolk
60g unsalted butter,
   cubed and softened
40g sunflower oil, plus
   extra for greasing
icing sugar, for dusting

For the glaze
1 tbsp caster sugar
1 tbsp hot water

For the filling
500ml double cream
1 tsp vanilla paste

You will need
large baking sheet, lined
   with baking paper

1. Make the buns. Combine the flour, sugar, yeast, salt and orange zest in a stand mixer fitted with the dough hook.

2. Heat the milk in a small saucepan over a low heat until lukewarm. Stir in the honey and vanilla until combined, then pour the mixture into the mixer bowl with 1 whole egg and the egg yolk. (Save the second egg for glazing.) Start to mix on low speed, add the butter and sunflower oil, then continue to mix on low for 30 seconds, scraping down the inside of the bowl from time to time. Knead the dough for 10 minutes, until silky smooth and elastic.

3. Tip out the dough onto the work surface and shape it into a ball. Lightly oil the bowl, return the dough, cover with a clean tea towel and leave it to rise at room temperature for 2 hours, until doubled.

4. Lightly flour the work surface, tip out the dough and knead it gently for 15 seconds to knock it back. Cut the dough into 10 equal pieces, each about 100g. Shape each piece into a neat, smooth ball and place the balls on the lined baking sheet, spaced well apart with the seams on the underside. Cover and leave to prove for 1 hour.

5. Heat the oven to 190°C/170°C fan/Gas 5. Lightly beat the remaining egg and use it to brush the top of each risen bun. Bake the buns on the middle shelf for 12 minutes, until golden and risen, and the underside of each bun sounds hollow when tapped.

6. Make the glaze. While the buns are baking, mix the sugar with the hot water in a small bowl. When the buns are ready, brush them with the sugar syrup while still hot, then cool on a wire rack.

7. Make the filling. Whip the cream with the vanilla until it forms medium-firm peaks, then chill it until you're ready to use.

8. Using a serrated knife, cut each bun vertically down the middle, but do not cut it all the way through. Generously fill each bun with the vanilla whipped cream, smoothing the top level with a palette knife. Dust with icing sugar to serve.

Paul's Chocolate & Raspberry Baked Alaska

Chocolate and raspberries are a loveable combination, but they really become a team when you throw in creaminess, too – here, creamy is in the form of vegan ice cream made with cashews and coconut milk. Sugary meringue is the final palate-pleaser. Make the ice cream ahead to allow time for soaking the cashews.

VEGAN
Serves: 10
Hands on: 1 hour
+ chilling + freezing
Bake: 20 mins

---

*For the raspberry
vegan ice cream*
100g odourless pure
coconut oil
200g frozen raspberries
(defrosted, drained
weight)
100g caster sugar
150g raw cashew nuts,
soaked overnight in water
250ml can of thick coconut
milk (75% coconut
extract) or coconut cream
12 drops raspberry extract,
or to taste

For the chocolate ganache
150g vegan dark
chocolate drops
150ml coconut milk
pinch of sea salt

For the sponge base
70g plain flour
½ tsp bicarbonate of soda
pinch of sea salt
125ml unsweetened
almond milk
25g odourless coconut oil
100g dark brown soft sugar
30g cocoa powder, sifted
½ tsp white wine vinegar

Continues overleaf

1. Make the raspberry vegan ice cream. Warm the coconut oil in a small saucepan over a low heat. As soon as it starts to melt, remove it from the heat and stir until melted – try not to heat it too much.

2. Purée the defrosted, drained raspberries with the caster sugar in a food processor. Pass the mixture through a sieve into a bowl, discarding the seeds in the sieve, and set aside.

3. Drain the cashews (the soaked weight should be about 200g) and tip them into the food processor (there's no need to wash it after puréeing the raspberries). Add the coconut milk and blitz for 3–5 minutes to give a smooth cream.

4. Add the raspberry purée to the food processor with the melted coconut oil and blitz for 1–2 minutes, until smooth. Add the raspberry extract, one drop at a time to taste, blending well between each addition. Pour the mixture into a shallow freezer tray and freeze for 15 minutes to chill.

5. Make the chocolate ganache. Tip the chocolate drops into a small heatproof bowl. Heat the coconut milk in a small saucepan until it just starts to bubble around the edges, then pour it over the chocolate drops. Leave to stand for 2 minutes, then stir to make a smooth ganache. Stir in the sea salt and pour the ganache into the lined 10cm hemisphere mould and leave to cool, then chill to set. Once set, freeze for 1 hour.

6. Make the raspberry ice-cream dome. Spoon the chilled raspberry mixture into the ice-cream machine and churn for 30–45 minutes, until it forms ice cream. Spoon the ice cream into the 15cm hemisphere mould, then wrap the empty 10cm hemisphere mould with a layer of cling film and place it into the centre of the ice-cream-filled bowl. Press the smaller bowl

Continues overleaf

For the Italian meringue
aquafaba from 2 x 400g
  cans of chickpeas
½ tsp cream of tartar
225g caster sugar
6.5g sachet of
  vegetable gelatine

You will need
10cm metal hemisphere
  mould, lined with
  cling film
ice-cream machine
15cm metal hemisphere
  mould, lined with
  cling film
10cm metal hemisphere
  mould, lined on the
  outside with cling film
17cm round cake tin,
  greased, then base-lined
  with baking paper
sugar thermometer
large piping bag fitted
  with a large closed
  star nozzle
kitchen blowtorch

down so the rims of both bowls are level, and the ice cream fills the space between the two bowls. Freeze for 1½ hours, until firm.

7. Make the sponge base. Heat the oven to 180°C/160°C fan/Gas 4. Sift the flour, bicarbonate of soda and salt into a mixing bowl.

8. Gently warm the almond milk in a saucepan, then remove it from the heat and stir in the coconut oil, brown sugar, cocoa powder and vinegar to make a smooth batter. Pour the batter into the dry ingredients and stir until combined and smooth. Spoon the batter into the lined cake tin and level with a palette knife. Bake for 15–20 minutes, until well risen, and a skewer inserted into the centre comes out clean. Leave to cool in the tin.

9. Make the Italian meringue. While the sponge is cooling, pour the aquafaba into a small saucepan and place it over a high heat. Bring to the boil, then boil until reduced to 150ml. Leave to cool.

10. Whisk the cooled aquafaba with the cream of tartar in a stand mixer fitted with the whisk, on medium speed until it forms soft peaks.

11. Put the caster sugar in a saucepan, add the vegetable gelatine and 5 tablespoons of water and warm the mixture over a low heat until the sugar dissolves. Increase the heat, bring the sugar mixture to a rapid boil for 4–5 minutes, until you have a thick syrup, and it reaches 120°C on the sugar thermometer. Remove from the heat.

12. With the stand mixer at full speed, slowly pour the hot syrup onto the whisked aquafaba in a thin, steady stream. Continue to whisk until the meringue is very thick and glossy and has cooled to room temperature. Spoon two thirds of the meringue into the piping bag fitted with a large closed star nozzle.

13. Assemble the Alaska. Turn out the chocolate sponge onto a serving plate. Remove the raspberry ice cream dome from the mould. Turn out the chocolate ganache and place it in the centre of the raspberry ice cream. Invert the raspberry–chocolate hemisphere onto the centre of the sponge.

14. Spread the remaining third of the meringue in an even layer over the ice-cream dome to cover. Then, pipe decorative swirls of meringue all over. Using the blowtorch, gently brown the meringue before serving immediately.

Abdul's White Chocolate & Macadamia Nut Cookies

These are my favourite kind of cookie – big and soft. I love white chocolate for its creamy sweetness, but adding savoury miso balances the flavour and adds moisture, too. My favourite nuts of all time are pine nuts, but these cookies are a chance for macadamias – my second favourite – to shine.

Makes: 15
Hands on: 25 mins + chilling
Bake: 16 mins

100g macadamia nuts
400g self-raising flour
1 tsp cornflour
1 tsp bicarbonate of soda
½ tsp salt
250g unsalted butter,
   cubed and softened
250g light brown soft sugar
100g caster sugar
2 tbsp white miso paste
2 large eggs
300g white chocolate,
   roughly chopped

You will need
3 large baking sheets, lined
   with baking paper

1. Toast the macadamia nuts in a large, dry frying pan over a low heat, tossing the pan occasionally, until they start to turn golden. Set aside to cool, then chop them into chunky pieces.

2. Sift the flour, cornflour, bicarbonate of soda and salt into a bowl and set aside.

3. Beat the butter and both types of sugar in a stand mixer fitted with the beater, on medium speed for 3–5 minutes, scraping down the inside of the bowl from time to time, until pale and creamy. Mix in the miso paste, followed by the eggs and mix until fully combined.

4. Add half of the sifted dry ingredients to the wet ingredients and mix until almost incorporated. Scrape down the inside of the bowl, then add the rest of the dry ingredients and mix again until just combined.

5. Add the white chocolate and chopped macadamias and mix until just incorporated into the dough. Cover and chill the dough for 30 minutes, until firmed up slightly – this will make it easier to form into balls.

6. Divide the dough into 15 balls (each of about 100g), then place the balls in the freezer for at least 30 minutes to firm up. This step is key to the cookies maintaining their height and not spreading too flat when they bake, so don't be tempted to skip it! Meanwhile, heat the oven to 180°C/160°C fan/Gas 4.

7. Place the cookies on the lined baking sheets, spaced well apart to allow for spreading during baking. Bake for 14–16 minutes, until golden brown and risen, but still soft in the centre. Leave to cool on the baking sheets until firmed up, then serve.

Chocolate & Speculoos Cake

This truly indulgent layer cake is made with one of the tastiest additions to the modern pantry: speculoos biscuits. Originally from Belgium, these little caramel-coloured treats are mildly spiced with cinnamon, and this cake has a double hit of them in the biscuits and in the speculoos spread in the buttercream filling.

Serves: 12
Hands on: 1 hour + cooling
Bake: 25 mins

For the sponge
75g 70% dark chocolate, broken into pieces
200g plain flour
1½ tsp bicarbonate of soda
pinch of salt
75g unsalted butter, cubed and softened
275g light brown soft sugar
3 eggs, lightly beaten
2 tsp vanilla extract
175ml soured cream
100ml just-boiled water

For the buttercream
100g 70% dark chocolate, broken into pieces
5 egg whites
200g caster sugar
pinch of salt
75g speculoos biscuits
450g unsalted butter, cubed and softened
200g speculoos spread

You will need
20cm round cake tins x 3, greased, then base-lined with greased baking paper and dusted with flour
2 medium piping bags, each fitted with a medium plain nozzle
cake scraper (optional)

1. Make the sponge. Heat the oven to 180°C/160°C fan/Gas 4. Melt the chocolate in a heatproof bowl set over a saucepan of barely simmering water, stirring until smooth. Remove the pan from the heat and leave the chocolate to cool slightly.

2. Sift the flour, bicarbonate of soda and salt into a bowl.

3. Beat the butter and light brown soft sugar in a stand mixer fitted with the beater, on medium speed for 2 minutes, scraping down the inside of the bowl from time to time, until smooth. Add the eggs, a little at a time, mixing well between each addition, then add the vanilla and melted chocolate and mix to combine.

4. Add one third of the dry ingredients and half of the soured cream to the mixer bowl and mix on low speed until just combined. Add another third of the dry ingredients and the remaining soured cream and mix again, then add the remaining dry ingredients and mix to combine, scraping down the inside of the bowl. Add the just-boiled water and mix on low speed until smooth.

5. Divide the mixture equally between the prepared tins and spread it level. Bake the sponges on the middle shelves for 25 minutes, until risen and a skewer inserted into the centre of each comes out clean. Leave the sponges to cool in the tins for 15 minutes, then turn them out onto a wire rack to cool completely.

6. Make the buttercream. While the sponges are cooling, melt the chocolate in a heatproof bowl set over a saucepan of barely simmering water and stir until smooth. Remove the pan from the heat and leave the chocolate to cool slightly.

7. Using a balloon whisk, combine the egg whites, caster sugar, salt and 1 tablespoon of water in a large heatproof bowl. Set the bowl over a saucepan of gently simmering water and whisk continuously for 5 minutes, until the mixture is hot to the

Continues overleaf

touch, thickened, and leaves a ribbon trail when you lift the whisk. Scoop the meringue into the bowl of a stand mixer and whisk on medium speed for 5 minutes, scraping down the inside of the bowl from time to time, until stiff, glossy and cold.

8. Meanwhile, tip the biscuits into a freezer bag and crush them with the end of a rolling pin until they form crumbs. Set aside.

9. Gradually, add the butter to the cooled meringue mixture, whisking continuously and scraping down the inside of the bowl from time to time, until silky smooth and glossy. Add the speculoos spread and half of the melted chocolate (set aside the remaining half) and whisk again until smooth.

10. Assemble the cake. Place 1 sponge layer on a serving plate or board and spread about 6 tablespoons of buttercream over the top. Scatter over one third of the biscuit crumbs. Top with the second sponge, spread over 6 tablespoons of buttercream and scatter with another third of the crumbs. Top with the third sponge and gently press it down. Cover the top and side of the cake with a thin, smooth crumb coat of buttercream. Chill for 30 minutes.

11. Spoon 8 tablespoons of the buttercream into the remaining melted chocolate, mix until smooth and spoon the mixture into one of the piping bags fitted with a medium plain nozzle. Set aside. Spoon a further 8 tablespoons of the original buttercream into the remaining piping bag and set aside.

12. Spread the remaining buttercream in the bowl evenly and smoothly over the top and side of the cake with a palette knife. Use the tip of a palette knife to create ridges in the buttercream around the cake, working from the top of the cake to the bottom.

13. Use the buttercream in the two piping bags to pipe two-tone buttercream kisses in alternating concentric circles over the top of the cake to cover. Press the remaining biscuit crumbs around the bottom of the cake. Chill the cake for 20 minutes before slicing to serve.

Cheese & Potato Tartlets

The milky freshness of buffalo mozzarella and sour nuttiness of gruyère are mixed with sweet, caramelised onion to bring out the cheesy, creamy savouriness in the filling for these little tarts. Sprinkle them with thyme for a herby hit.

Makes: 8
Hands on: 1 hour + chilling
Bake: 20 mins

For the rough puff pastry
125g plain flour
125g strong white
    bread flour
pinch of salt
250g unsalted butter,
    cubed and chilled
1 tsp cider or white
    wine vinegar
125–140ml chilled water

For the topping
500g new potatoes,
    scrubbed
1 tbsp olive oil
1 large onion, sliced
1 large thyme sprig,
    leaves picked
4 tsp smoked garlic purée
12 bocconcini (small balls)
    of buffalo mozzarella,
    drained and halved
100g cantal or gruyère,
    thinly sliced
salt and freshly ground
    black pepper

You will need
large baking sheet

1. Make the rough puff pastry. (Do this at least 3 hours ahead to give it plenty of time to chill and rest.) Mix both types of flour and the salt in a large mixing bowl. Lightly rub in the butter with your fingertips, just enough to knock the corners off the butter pieces.

2. Pour in the vinegar and 125ml of the chilled water and mix with a palette knife to bring the dough together, adding a little more water if needed. Gather the dough with your hands and shape it into a neat square. Wrap the dough and chill it for 1 hour to rest.

3. Lightly dust the work surface with flour and roll out the dough into a neat rectangle three times as long as it is wide (about 45 x 15cm). Fold the bottom third of the dough up to the middle and the top third down to cover it to create a three-layered square of dough. Turn the dough 90 degrees and roll it out to a 45 x 15cm rectangle again and then fold it in thirds. Wrap the dough and chill it for a further 1 hour.

4. Repeat the rolling and folding again – making 4 rolls and folds altogether, twice at each stage. Wrap the dough and chill it for at least 1 hour before using.

5. Make the topping. While the dough is chilling, cook the whole unpeeled potatoes in boiling salted water for about 15 minutes, until just tender – the time will depend on the size of the potatoes. Drain, then leave the potatoes to cool, then cut them into 2mm slices.

6. Heat the olive oil in a small frying pan over a low-medium heat. Add the onion and cook, stirring occasionally, for 10 minutes, until softened and starting to caramelise at the edges. Remove from the heat, add the thyme, season with salt and pepper and leave to cool.

7. Roll out the pastry. Roll out the pastry on a lightly dusted work surface to a 40 x 20cm rectangle, about 3mm thick. Trim the edges to neaten and cut the rectangle into eight 10cm squares. Place the squares on the baking sheet and chill them for 20 minutes.

Continues overleaf

Cheese & Potato Tartlets *continued*

8. Meanwhile, heat the oven to 200°C/180°C fan/Gas 6.

9. Assemble the tartlets. Spread ½ teaspoon of the smoked garlic purée on top of each pastry rectangle and spoon the cooked and cooled onions on top. Arrange the potato slices and mozzarella on top of the onions and finish with the cheese.

10. Bake the tartlets for 20 minutes, until the pastry is crisp and golden and the cheese it bubbling. Leave the tartlets to cool slightly, then serve them hot, warm or at room temperature.

Vanilla & Cardamom Cheesecake with Rhubarb

Vanilla, cardamom and rhubarb make a good team in this beautiful cheesecake. The sweet flavour of vanilla and the floral, spicy tones of cardamom complement the sharpness of the rhubarb. Madagascan vanilla is usually the easiest to find, but if you come across them, try Mexican for a bit of spice, or sweeter Tahitian.

Serves: 8
Hands on: 2 hours + chilling
Bake: 1½ hours

For the biscuit base
125g unsalted butter, cubed, at room temperature
40g light brown soft sugar
1 tbsp golden syrup
1 tbsp whole milk
1 tsp vanilla extract
90g wholemeal plain flour
½ tsp bicarbonate of soda
½ tsp ground ginger
½ tsp mixed spice
½ tsp ground cardamom
pinch of salt
25g jumbo porridge oats or rye flakes
25g oat bran

For the filling
525g full-fat cream cheese
250ml soured cream
125g caster sugar
1 vanilla pod, split lengthways and seeds scraped out, pod reserved
¾ tsp ground cardamom
1 tbsp cornflour
3 eggs, lightly beaten
finely grated zest and juice of ½ unwaxed lemon
75g Greek-style plain yogurt

Continues overleaf

1. Make the biscuit base. Beat 75g of the butter with the light brown soft sugar and golden syrup in a stand mixer fitted with the beater, on medium speed for 2 minutes, scraping down the inside of the bowl from time to time, until pale and creamy. Add the milk and vanilla and mix again to combine.

2. Sift the wholemeal flour, bicarbonate of soda, ground spices and salt into the bowl, adding any bran left in the sieve. Add the oats or rye flakes and the oat bran, then mix briefly to combine and bring the dough together.

3. Turn out the dough onto the work surface and knead it briefly until smooth. Flatten the dough into a square, cover it with a clean tea towel and chill it for 1 hour, until firm.

4. Roll out the chilled dough on a lightly floured work surface to about 3mm thick. Cut the dough into 5cm squares and arrange the squares on the lined baking sheet. Gather the scraps together, re-roll them and cut out more squares to use up the dough. Chill for 20 minutes while you heat the oven to 170°C/150°C fan/Gas 3.

5. Bake the biscuits for 10–12 minutes, until crisp and golden, then leave them to cool on the baking sheets.

6. Once cool, weigh out 175g of the biscuits and finely crush them in a food processor or in a sealed freezer bag using a rolling pin. Tip the crumbs into a mixing bowl. (Enjoy any leftover biscuits with a cup of tea.) Melt the remaining 50g of butter in a small saucepan and mix it into the crumbs. Tip the buttery crumbs into the prepared tin and press them into a firm, even layer. Bake the biscuit base on the middle shelf for 5 minutes, until crisp, then set aside.

7. Make the filling. While the base is baking, using a balloon whisk, beat the cream cheese, 125ml of the soured cream, 100g of the caster sugar, and the vanilla seeds and cardamon in a bowl until

Continues overleaf

Vanilla & Cardamom Cheesecake with Rhubarb *continued*

For the baked rhubarb
500g forced pink rhubarb,
    cut into 3cm long pieces
100g caster sugar
juice of 1 orange
    (preferably blood orange)
reserved vanilla pod from
    the cheesecake filling
    (see above), halved

You will need
baking sheet, lined with
    baking paper
20cm springform tin,
    greased, then base-lined
    with baking paper
large roasting tin

smooth. Add the cornflour and whisk again to combine. Add the eggs and lemon zest and juice and mix again until smooth. Tap the bowl sharply on the work surface to expel any air bubbles and carefully pour the cheesecake filling onto the biscuit base.

8. Bake the cheesecake. Sit the tin in the middle of a large sheet of foil and bring the edges of the foil up to cover the sides. Place the cheesecake into the large roasting tin and pour in enough just-boiled water to come halfway up the sides of the foil-cased springform tin. Carefully place the roasting tin on the middle shelf of the oven. Bake the cheesecake for 35 minutes, or until just set. Leave the oven on, but remove the cheesecake and leave it to rest for 5 minutes.

9. Meanwhile, beat together the remaining soured cream and 25g of caster sugar, and the Greek yogurt. Carefully spoon the mixture on top of the cheesecake and return it to the oven for a further 10 minutes, until set but not coloured. Carefully remove the cheesecake from the roasting tin and leave it to cool completely before chilling it for at least 4 hours or overnight.

10. Make the baked rhubarb. Turn the oven to 180°C/160°C fan/ Gas 4. Put the rhubarb in a roasting tin or ovenproof dish and sprinkle it with the 100g of caster sugar. Add the orange juice and reserved vanilla pod. Cover loosely with foil and bake for 10 minutes, until the rhubarb is tender but still holds its shape. Leave to cool.

11. Serve the cheesecake in slices with the rhubarb and its syrupy juices spooned over the top. You can serve any remaining rhubarb and juices on the side for everyone to help themselves to more.

Japanese Milk Bread

Japanese milk bread is a rich, buttery cousin to sourdough. What makes this light-textured loaf so soft is the tangzhong, a mixture of flour and milk warmed briefly to activate the gluten in the flour.

Serves: 1 loaf
Hands on: 30 mins + rising
Bake: 30 mins

For the tangzhong
75ml whole milk
25g strong white
    bread flour

For the dough
300g strong white
    bread flour
50g '00' flour
7g fast-action dried yeast
1 tbsp caster sugar
½ tsp salt
120ml whole milk,
    at room temperature
2 eggs, lightly beaten
    (1 egg for the dough
    and 1 egg to glaze)
75g unsalted butter, cubed
    and softened, plus
    extra for greasing

You will need
900g loaf tin, greased,
    then lined (base and
    ends) with a strip
    of baking paper
oiled proving bag

1. **Make the tangzhong.** In a small pan, whisk the milk with 50ml of water and the flour until smooth. Set the pan over a low heat and cook, whisking continuously, for 30–60 seconds, until the mixture thickens to a smooth, thick paste. Spoon the tangzhong into a small bowl and leave to cool.

2. **Make the dough.** Mix both types of flour with the yeast, sugar and salt in a stand mixer fitted with the dough hook until combined.

3. Add the cooled tangzhong, the milk, 1 egg and the butter and mix on low speed to combine. Increase the speed to medium and knead for 7 minutes, until the dough is smooth, glossy and elastic.

4. Tip out the dough onto the work surface and shape it into a ball. Lightly oil the bowl, return the dough, cover and leave it to rise at room temperature for 1½ hours, until doubled in size.

5. Lightly flour the work surface and knead the dough gently for 20 seconds to knock it back, then divide it into 4 equal pieces.

6. Roll one piece of dough into a 20cm square and fold in the left and right sides to meet in the middle – the dough is now a rectangle measuring roughly 20 x 10cm. Starting from one of the short edges, roll up the dough into a neat spiral and press the seam to seal.

7. Place the spiral, seam-side down, at one end of the lined loaf tin. Repeat with the remaining dough so that you have 4 neat rolls in a row running the length of the loaf tin. Slide the loaf tin into the oiled proving bag and leave the dough to prove at room temperature for 1½ hours, until it has doubled in size and has risen above the top of the tin. Heat the oven to 180°C/160°C fan/Gas 4.

8. Beat the remaining egg with 1 teaspoon of water and lightly brush the glaze over the top of the loaf. Bake the loaf for 30 minutes, until golden and risen, then leave it to cool in the tin for 10–15 minutes. Carefully lift it out onto a wire rack and leave it to cool completely before slicing.

Muscovado & Malt Bread & Butter Pudding

Barley malt extract gives this custard a toasted, coffee and caramel flavour, which is picked up by the vanilla-caramel in the Bourbon. With all those toffee flavours going on, a sprinkling of chocolate (rather than dried fruit) makes for a perfect flavour partner.

Serves: 6–8
Hands on: 30 mins + soaking
Bake: 30 mins

300ml whole milk
300ml double cream
1 tsp ground cinnamon
½ vanilla pod, split in half
100g light muscovado sugar
2 tbsp barley malt extract
8 chocolate chip brioche
    rolls (about 350g in total),
    cut into 2cm slices
100g unsalted butter,
    softened
50g dark chocolate
    chips or caramel/blond
    chocolate, chopped
3 eggs
2 egg yolks
4 tbsp Bourbon
pinch of salt
2 tbsp demerara sugar
extra double cream,
    or custard or vanilla
    ice cream, to serve

You will need
25 x 18cm baking dish
    (about 4–5cm deep)

1. Pour the milk and cream into a saucepan. Add the cinnamon, vanilla pod, light muscovado sugar and barley malt extract and warm the mixture over a low–medium heat until just below boiling. Remove from the heat and leave to cool for 10 minutes.

2. Meanwhile, spread one side of each brioche slice with butter. Arrange the brioche in the baking dish and scatter with the chocolate chips or chopped chocolate.

3. Whisk the whole eggs, egg yolks, Bourbon and salt in a large mixing bowl until combined. Slowly pour over the infused milk mixture, whisking continuously until smooth and thoroughly combined. Strain the custard into a jug.

4. Slowly pour three quarters of the custard over the buttered brioche, cover and leave to soak for at least 1 hour or up to 2 hours, at room temperature.

5. Heat the oven to 180°C/160°C fan/Gas 4.

6. Pour the remaining custard over the soaked brioche, scatter the top with demerara sugar and bake the pudding for 30 minutes, until golden and crisp, and the custard has set but still has a slight wobble in the middle. Leave the pudding to settle for 5 minutes, then serve it with extra double cream or scoops of vanilla ice cream.

Sandro's Orange & Dark Chocolate Palmiers

Palmiers have become a bit of a recent obsession. They are so satisfying to make, and give a first, crispy, buttery bite that is beyond compare. Plus, in my opinion, you just can't go wrong when you put chocolate and orange flavours together.

Makes: 25
Hands on: 40 mins + chilling
Bake: 15 mins

For the rough puff pastry
350g plain flour
1 tsp salt
finely grated zest of
　2 unwaxed oranges
250g unsalted butter,
　cubed and chilled
120–150ml chilled water
220g caster sugar

For the chocolate dip
200g 54% dark chocolate,
　broken into pieces

You will need
3 baking sheets, lined
　with baking paper

1. Make the rough puff pastry. Sift the flour and salt into a large mixing bowl and stir in the orange zest. Add the butter and lightly toss the cubes to coat them in the flour. Pinch the butter between your fingertips, flattening the cubes to incorporate them into the flour, until crumbly with some larger visible flecks of butter.

2. Make a well in the centre and, a little at a time, add the chilled water, mixing with a palette knife until it all starts to come together into a rough dough. Tip out the dough onto the work surface and gather it into a ball with your hands. Flatten the dough into a rough square, then wrap and chill it for 30 minutes.

3. Lightly flour the work surface, then roll out the dough to a 30cm square. Then, fold in the left and right sides to meet in the middle. Next, fold the left half over the right half (like closing a book) so that the two halves sit on top of each other and make a rectangle about 30 x 7cm. Wrap and chill the dough for a further 30 minutes.

4. Place the chilled dough on the floured work surface, so that the long folded edge is closest to you. Repeat the rolling and folding from the previous step and chill the dough for a further 30 minutes.

5. Sprinkle about one third of the caster sugar onto the work surface and place the dough on top so the long folded edge is closest to you. Sprinkle another third of the sugar evenly over the top of the dough and roll it out to a 30cm square, adding half of the remaining one third of the sugar as the pastry is rolled out and becomes larger in size. Fold in the left and right sides to meet in the middle, then fold the left and right sides to meet in the middle again. Next, fold the left half over the right half so that they sit on top of each other to make a narrow rectangle made up of 8 layers. Wrap and chill the dough for a further 30 minutes.

Continues overleaf

6. Shape the palmiers. Cut the folded dough into 25 equal slices, each about 1cm wide, and place these on the lined baking sheets. Shape each one into a classic rounded palmier shape and leave enough space between them to allow them to spread slightly. Chill the shaped dough for 20 minutes while you heat the oven to 200°C/180°C fan/Gas 6.

7. Bake the palmiers. Remove the palmiers from the fridge, sprinkle them with the remaining sugar and bake them for 15 minutes, until golden and puffed, carefully turning them after 10 minutes so they bake evenly. Leave them on the baking sheets to cool completely.

8. Make the chocolate dip. While the palmiers are baking, melt the dark chocolate in a heatproof bowl set over a pan of gently simmering water, stirring until smooth. Dip one edge of each palmier into the melted chocolate, coating about one third to one half of one side, at an angle. Place each palmier back on the baking sheets until the chocolate sets, then serve.

Baked Custard Tart with Roasted Plums

Tangy crème fraîche elevates the richness of this custard, which is also flavoured with woody nutmeg and sweet vanilla. The cinnamon-roasted plums provide an astringency that bites into the creaminess of the tart to bring harmony all round.

Serves: 8
Hands on: 1 hour + chilling
Bake: 2 hours

For the pâte sablée
(pastry) case
100g unsalted butter, cubed,
   at room temperature
50g icing sugar, sifted
2 egg yolks
1 tsp vanilla extract
175g plain flour
1 tbsp double cream
pinch of salt
1 egg white, to seal

For the custard
4 whole eggs
3 egg yolks
100g caster sugar
1 tsp vanilla extract
finely grated zest of
   ½ unwaxed lemon
300ml double cream
300ml crème fraîche
good pinch of salt
freshly grated nutmeg,
   to sprinkle

To serve
8 red plums, halved
   and destoned
1½ tbsp caster sugar
½ tsp ground cinnamon
juice of ½ lemon

You will need
20cm straight-sided tart
   ring (about 4cm deep)
heavy baking sheet, lined
   with baking paper
baking beans or rice

1. Make the pâte sablée case. Beat the butter and icing sugar in a stand mixer fitted with the beater, on medium speed for 1–2 minutes, scraping down the inside of the bowl from time to time, until pale and creamy. Add the egg yolks and vanilla and mix to combine.

2. Add the flour, double cream and salt and mix again briefly until the dough starts to clump together, taking care not to overwork it. Tip out the dough onto the work surface and lightly knead it to bring it together into a neat ball. Flatten the dough into a disc, wrap it and chill it for at least 1 hour, until firm.

3. Place the tart ring on the lined baking sheet. Dust the work surface with flour and roll out the pastry into a neat disc, large enough to line the base and sides of the tart ring and about 3mm thick. Using the rolling pin, lift the pastry into the tart ring, pressing the pastry neatly into the base and up the sides. Trim the excess pastry from the top with a sharp knife and discard. Chill the pastry case for at least 20 minutes. Meanwhile, heat the oven to 170°C/150°C fan/Gas 3.

4. Prick the base of the tart case with a fork, line it with baking paper and fill it with baking beans or rice. Bake the case on the middle shelf for 15 minutes, until the top edge starts to turn crisp and golden. Remove the paper and beans or rice and return the case to the oven for a further 2 minutes to dry out the base. Lightly beat the reserved egg white until foamy and brush a thin layer over the pastry case. Return the case to the oven for 1–2 minutes, until dry and sealed. Remove the tart case from the oven, then reduce the oven temperature to 140°C/120°C fan/Gas 1.

5. Make the custard. Whisk the whole eggs and egg yolks with a balloon whisk in a large bowl. Add the caster sugar, vanilla and lemon zest and whisk to combine. Add the cream, crème fraîche and salt and whisk again until smooth.

Continues overleaf

6. Strain the custard into the pastry case, sprinkle the freshly grated nutmeg liberally all over the top to cover and bake the tart for 55–60 minutes, until the custard is just set with a slight wobble in the middle. Remove the tart from the oven, leave it to cool, then chill it for 2 hours before serving.

7. Roast the plums. While the tart is chilling, heat the oven to 200°C/180°C fan/Gas 6. Arrange the plums, cut-side up, in a roasting tin. In a small bowl, combine the sugar and cinnamon, sprinkle the mixture over the plums and pour over the lemon juice. Roast for 30–40 minutes, until the fruit is very tender, juicy and starting to caramelise at the edges. (The exact timing will depend on the ripeness of the fruit.) Leave the plums to cool to room temperature.

8. To serve, cut the tart into slices and serve with the plums and roasting juices on the side.

Triple Chocolate Mini Cakes

Ripe banana provides deep, honeyed-sweetness in these little cakes, which works well with the bitterness in the double hit of dark chocolate from both the frosting and the ganache. Choose your favourite fruit and edible flowers to cut through the richness.

VEGAN
Serves: 12
Hands on: 45 mins
Bake: 30 mins

For the sponges
200g plain flour
25g cocoa powder
1 tsp baking powder
½ tsp bicarbonate of soda
3 ripe bananas, mashed
60ml light olive oil
150g light brown soft sugar
200ml almond milk
1 tsp vanilla paste
50g vegan white chocolate,
    finely chopped
100g vegan dark chocolate,
    finely chopped

For the chocolate frosting
100g vegan dark chocolate,
    broken into pieces
400g icing sugar, sifted
125g vegan spread
1 tsp vanilla paste

For the chocolate ganache
150g vegan dark chocolate,
    finely chopped
75ml unsweetened
    almond milk

To decorate
favourite fruit, such
    as whole cherries
edible flowers and leaves

You will need
6cm round mini cake
    tins x 12, oiled
1 medium piping bag fitted
    with a large plain nozzle

1. Make the sponges. Heat the oven to 180°C/160°C fan/Gas 4. Sift the flour, cocoa powder, baking powder and bicarbonate of soda into a large mixing bowl and stir to combine.

2. Whisk the bananas, olive oil, light brown soft sugar, almond milk and vanilla in a stand mixer fitted with the whisk, on medium speed for 1 minute, scraping down the inside of the bowl from time to time, until combined. Remove the bowl from the mixer, then gently fold in the flour mixture and white and dark chocolate with a metal spoon. Do not over mix.

3. Divide the mixture equally between the oiled cake tins. Bake the sponges on the middle shelves for 25–30 minutes, until they are risen with a cracked top, and a skewer inserted into the centres comes out clean. Leave to cool completely in the tins.

4. Make the frosting. While the cakes are baking, melt the dark chocolate in a heatproof bowl set over a pan of gently simmering water, stir until smooth and remove from the heat. Leave to cool for 10 minutes.

5. While the chocolate is cooling, beat the icing sugar, vegan spread and vanilla in a stand mixer fitted with the beater, on medium speed for 3–5 minutes, until pale and creamy. Fold in the melted chocolate. Spoon the frosting into the medium piping bag.

6. Make the ganache. Melt the chocolate with the almond milk in a heatproof bowl set over a pan of barely simmering water, stir until smooth and remove from the heat. Leave to cool for 10 minutes.

7. Assemble the cakes. Run a knife or spatula around the inside rim of each sponge to loosen, then turn them out. Slice each sponge horizontally in half. Pipe frosting over the bottom halves, then top with the other halves.

8. Place a heaped teaspoon of ganache on top of each sponge. With a clean teaspoon, make a small swirl pattern in the ganache and decorate with fruit, flowers and leaves.

Cream Cheese, Chilli & Onion Bagel Loaf

There are some fabulous seasonings in this tear-and-share loaf: pickled green chillies add bite; chives give a subtle hint of onion; and the mixture of sweeter white and nuttier black sesame seeds perfectly complements the smooth, sharp cream cheese.

Makes: 1 loaf
Hands on: 40 mins + rising
Bake: 40 mins

For the dough
250g strong white
    bread flour
100g plain flour
7g fast-action dried yeast
1 tsp caster sugar
1 tsp salt
175ml whole milk
50g unsalted butter,
    softened, plus 1 tbsp
    melted to glaze
1 egg, lightly beaten
2 tsp olive oil, for greasing

For the filling
250g full-fat cream cheese
6 spring onions, finely sliced
3 pickled green chillies,
    drained and finely
    chopped
2 tbsp snipped chives
salt and freshly ground
    black pepper

For the topping
1 tbsp mixed black and
    white sesame seeds
1 tsp onion granules
1 tsp garlic granules
1 tsp poppy seeds
1 tsp sea-salt flakes

You will need
900g loaf tin, greased,
    then lined (base and
    ends) with baking paper
oiled proving bag

1. Make the dough. Mix both types of flour with the yeast, sugar and salt in a stand mixer fitted with the dough hook until combined.

2. Heat the milk to lukewarm and pour it into the dry ingredients with the 50g of softened butter and the egg. Mix on low to combine, then knead on medium for 4–5 minutes, until smooth and elastic. Tip out the dough onto the work surface and shape it into a ball. Lightly oil the bowl, return the dough, cover it with a damp tea towel and leave it to rise for 45–60 minutes, until doubled in size.

3. Prepare the filling. While the dough is rising, tip the cream cheese into a mixing bowl and add the spring onions, pickled chillies and chives. Season with salt and pepper and mix to combine.

4. Shape and fill the dough. Lightly flour the work surface and knead the dough gently for 20 seconds to knock it back. Weigh the dough and divide it into 12 equal balls. Roll each ball into a neat 12cm disc.

5. Spread 1 tablespoon of the filling onto each disc and fold the discs in half to make 12 half-moon-shaped dough sandwiches. Spread the remaining filling on top of 11 of the dough sandwiches, then stack them into pairs – one stack will not have cream cheese on the top. Place a pair of dough sandwiches into one end of the lined loaf tin, cheese-side inwards and rounded-side uppermost. Continue stacking to fill the length of the tin, ending with the dough without the cream cheese on top. Slide the tin into the oiled proving bag and leave the loaf to prove at room temperature for 45 minutes, until light and puffy and risen by at least one third.

6. Make the topping. In a small bowl combine the sesame seeds, onion granules, garlic granules, poppy seeds and sea salt.

7. Bake the loaf. Heat the oven to 180°C/160°C fan/Gas 4. Brush the top of the loaf with the melted butter and scatter with the topping mixture. Bake for 35–40 minutes, until deep golden and well risen. Leave to cool in the tin for 15 minutes, then transfer to a wire rack to cool completely before serving.

Fish & Chip Shop Smörgåstårta

There's savoury baking and then there's this astonishing smörgåstårta – a savoury cake. Beetroot bread, soured cream, curry sauce, mayo, cod, mushy peas, gherkins, capers and... yes, chips. All the flavours of your favourite British takeaway in a Scandinavian slice.

Serves: 16
Hands on: 2½ hours
  + rising + chilling
Bake: 25 mins

For the beetroot bread
700g strong white
  bread flour
2 tsp sea salt
1½ tsp caster sugar
16g fast-action dried yeast
450ml beetroot juice
25g unsalted butter, melted,
  plus 20g for spreading

For the mushy peas filling
1kg frozen garden peas
50g unsalted butter
10 large mint leaves
sea salt and freshly ground
  black pepper

For the mayonnaise
1 egg
½ tbsp white wine vinegar
pinch of sea salt
pinch of freshly ground
  black pepper
½ tsp Dijon mustard
pinch of caster sugar
125ml vegetable oil

For the fish filling
65g ghee
1kg skinless, boneless
  cod fillets
220g pickled gherkins,
  drained (pickling
  liquid reserved)
  and finely diced

Continues overleaf

1. Make the beetroot bread. Add the flour, salt, sugar, yeast, beetroot juice and melted butter to the bowl of a stand mixer fitted with a dough hook and mix on a slow speed for 1–2 minutes, until combined. Increase the speed to medium–high and continue to mix for about 12 minutes, until you have a smooth, springy dough. Shape the dough into a smooth ball and place it into a clean bowl. Cover the bowl with a clean tea towel and leave the dough to rise for about 1 hour, or until doubled in size.

2. Tip out the dough onto a lightly floured work surface and knock it back to remove any pockets of air. Re-shape the dough into a smooth ball, then transfer it to the prepared cake ring or tin, cover and leave to prove for about 30 minutes, or until almost doubled in size. Meanwhile, heat the oven to 250°C/230°C fan/Gas 9.

3. Once the dough has proved, bake it in the centre of the oven for 10 minutes, then reduce the temperature to 220°C/200°C fan/Gas 7 and bake it for a further 15 minutes, until risen and browning on top. Leave to cool in the tin for 10 minutes, then remove the bread from the tin and transfer it to a wire rack to cool completely.

4. Make the mushy peas filling. Bring a large pan of salted water to the boil, then add the peas and boil them for 5 minutes, until tender. Strain the peas and put aside 50g for the decoration. Tip the remainder back into the pan and add the butter and mint. Season with salt and pepper and, using a hand-held stick blender, blitz to a thick purée, then set aside to cool completely.

5. Make the mayonnaise. Put the egg, vinegar, salt, pepper, mustard and sugar into a narrow jug. Using a hand-held stick blender, blitz to combine. With the blender running, gradually pour in the oil until you have a thick, homogenised mayonnaise. Set aside.

6. Make the fish filling. In a large frying pan, heat the ghee over a medium–high heat. Season the cod with salt and pepper, then

Continues overleaf

2 tbsp gherkin
    pickling liquid
70g mini capers
100g dill, tender stems and
    fronds finely chopped
1 tsp Dijon mustard
100g mayonnaise
    (see above)

For the potato filling
1 litre rapeseed oil
3 large baking potatoes,
    peeled and sliced
    into 2mm slices using
    a mandoline
3 tbsp malt vinegar

For the curry sauce 'icing'
1 tbsp ghee
1 onion, finely chopped
3 tbsp curry powder
200g soured cream
800g full-fat cream cheese

To decorate
5 large baking potatoes,
    peeled and sliced
    lengthways into 2mm
    slices using a mandoline
olive oil

You will need
20cm cake ring (about
    15cm deep; use a strip
    of acetate to raise the
    side if necessary), or
    loose-bottomed tin,
    greased, then lined
    (base and sides)
    with baking paper
deep-fat fryer or cooking
    thermometer
2 baking trays, 1 lined
    with baking paper
medium piping bag fitted
    with a large star nozzle

add the fillets to the pan. Fry for about 5 minutes, then flip the fillets and fry for another 5 minutes or so, until evenly cooked through. Remove the fillets from the pan and set aside to cool.

7. Break the cooled fish into a large bowl, then add the gherkins, pickling liquid, capers, dill, Dijon mustard and mayonnaise. Season with salt and pepper and stir until well combined and the fish has broken down into small chunks. Cover and refrigerate until needed.

8. **Make the potato filling.** Pour the oil into a deep-fat fryer or a large, deep saucepan and place it over a high heat. Heat the oil until it reaches 200ºC (test it with a cooking thermometer if you're using a saucepan).

9. Add the potato slices in small batches, frying each batch for about 2 minutes, until golden brown, then removing each batch from the oil using a slotted spoon and placing it on a tray lined with kitchen paper to drain. Once you have fried all the potato slices, tip them into a bowl and toss them with the vinegar and with sea salt to taste, then set aside until you're ready to assemble.

10. **Make the curry sauce 'icing'.** In a medium frying pan, heat the ghee over a medium heat. When hot, add the onion and fry for about 5 minutes, until golden, then add the curry powder. Season with salt and pepper and fry for a further 1–2 minutes, until fragrant. Transfer the onion to a bowl and leave it to cool for about 30 minutes.

11. Spoon the soured cream into a jug and add the cooled onion. Blitz using a hand-held stick blender until smooth. Set aside.

12. Add the cream cheese to the bowl of a stand mixer fitted with a whisk and whisk for 2 minutes on a medium speed until smooth. Then, add the soured cream and onion mixture and whisk together for 1 minute, until fully combined. Refrigerate until needed.

13. **Make the decorations.** Using a sharp knife, cut out 9 fish shapes from the potato slices for the topping (discard the trimmings). Cut the remaining potato slices into strips about 1.5cm wide to resemble chips. Heat a little olive oil in a frying pan over a medium heat. Add the potato shapes and fry on both sides for about 5–6 minutes altogether, until soft and golden all over.

14. Using a fish slice, transfer the cooked shapes to the baking tray lined with baking paper and spread them out in a single layer. Cover with another sheet of baking paper and place the other baking tray on top. Set the shapes aside to cool between the trays (the tray on top stops the slices curling).

15. Assemble the smörgåstårta. Slice the beetroot bread horizontally into 2cm-thick rounds. You should have 4 even slices with the top crust of bread left over.

16. Place the base layer of bread back into the ring or tin and spread it with the 20g of unsalted butter, then spread one third of the fish filling over the top in an even layer. Place a layer of potato slices over this, leaving no gaps, then top the potatoes with one third of the mushy peas filling. Repeat this process with the next two layers and then top with the fourth slice of bread. Chill for 1–2 hours to firm up, if you have time.

17. Remove the smörgåstårta from the tin. Using a palette knife, smooth the curried cream-cheese mixture over the top and sides so that the smörgåstårta is evenly covered, then transfer the remaining 'icing' to the piping bag fitted with a star nozzle. Pipe rosettes around the top edge of the smörgåstårta.

18. Lay the fish-shaped potato slices so that they form a circle of fish, tails outwards, on the top of the smörgåstårta. Then, use the reserved peas to create spokes that fill the spaces in between. Stick the chip-shaped potato strips upright around the base of the smörgåstårta, and the remaining potato fish shape around the side, as if it is swimming.

Conversion Tables

WEIGHT

METRIC	IMPERIAL	METRIC	IMPERIAL	METRIC	IMPERIAL	METRIC	IMPERIAL
25g	1oz	200g	7oz	425g	15oz	800g	1lb 12oz
50g	2oz	225g	8oz	450g	1lb	850g	1lb 14oz
75g	2½oz	250g	9oz	500g	1lb 2oz	900g	2lb
85g	3oz	280g	10oz	550g	1lb 4oz	950g	2lb 2oz
100g	4oz	300g	11oz	600g	1lb 5oz	1kg	2lb 4oz
125g	4½oz	350g	12oz	650g	1lb 7oz		
140g	5oz	375g	13oz	700g	1lb 9oz		
175g	6oz	400g	14oz	750g	1lb 10oz		

VOLUME

METRIC	IMPERIAL	METRIC	IMPERIAL	METRIC	IMPERIAL	METRIC	IMPERIAL
30ml	1fl oz	150ml	¼ pint	300ml	½ pint	500ml	18fl oz
50ml	2fl oz	175ml	6fl oz	350ml	12fl oz	600ml	1 pint
75ml	2½fl oz	200ml	7fl oz	400ml	14fl oz	700ml	1¼ pints
100ml	3½fl oz	225ml	8fl oz	425ml	⅔ pint	850ml	1½ pints
125ml	4fl oz	250ml	9fl oz	450ml	16fl oz	1 litre	1¾ pints

US CUP

INGREDIENTS	1 CUP	3/4 CUP	2/3 CUP	1/2 CUP	1/3 CUP	1/4 CUP	2 TBSP
Brown sugar	180g	135g	120g	90g	60g	45g	23g
Butter	240g	180g	160g	120g	80g	60g	30g
Cornflour (cornstarch)	120g	90g	80g	60g	40g	30g	15g
Flour	120g	90g	80g	60g	40g	30g	15g
Icing sugar (powdered/confectioners')	100g	75g	70g	50g	35g	25g	13g
Nuts (chopped)	150g	110g	100g	75g	50g	40g	20g
Nuts (ground)	120g	90g	80g	60g	40g	30g	15g
Oats	90g	65g	60g	45g	30g	22g	11g
Raspberries	120g	90g	80g	60g	40g	30g	--
Salt	300g	230g	200g	150g	100g	75g	40g
Sugar (caster/superfine)	225g	170g	150g	115g	75g	55g	30g
Sugar (granulated)	200g	150g	130g	100g	65g	50g	25g
Sultanas/raisins	200g	150g	130g	100g	65g	50g	22g
Water/milk	250ml	180ml	150ml	120ml	75ml	60ml	30ml

LINEAR

METRIC	IMPERIAL	METRIC	IMPERIAL	METRIC	IMPERIAL	METRIC	IMPERIAL
5mm	¼ in	6cm	2½ in	11cm	4¼ in	18cm	7 in
1cm	½ in	7cm	2¾ in	12cm	4½ in	20cm	8 in
2.5cm	1 in	7.5cm	3 in	13cm	5 in	21cm	8¼ in
3cm	1¼ in	8cm	3¼ in	14cm	5½ in	22cm	8½ in
4cm	1½ in	9cm	3½ in	15cm	6 in	23cm	9 in
5cm	2 in	9.5cm	3¾ in	16cm	6¼ in	24cm	9½ in
5.5cm	2¼ in	10cm	4 in	17cm	6½ in	25cm	10 in

SPOON MEASURES

METRIC	IMPERIAL
5ml	1 tsp
10ml	2 tsp
15ml	1 tbsp
30ml	2 tbsp
45ml	3 tbsp
60ml	4 tbsp
75ml	5 tbsp

COOK'S NOTES

Oven temperatures: Ovens vary – not only from brand to brand, but from the front to the back of the oven, as well as (in a non-fan oven) between the top and bottom shelves. Invest in an oven thermometer if you can. Always preheat, and use dry oven gloves.

Eggs: Eggs are medium and should be at room temperature, unless specified. Some recipes may contain raw or partially cooked eggs. Pregnant women, the elderly, babies and toddlers, and people who are unwell should be aware of these recipes.

Butter: In the recipes, 'softened butter' means to soften to room temperature, unless otherwise specified. You should be able to leave an indentation with your fingertip when you press down.

Herbs, vegetables and fruit: Use fresh herbs and fresh, ripe medium-sized vegetables and fruit unless the recipe specifies otherwise.

Spoon measures: All teaspoons and tablespoons are level unless otherwise stated.

Waxed citrus: When a recipe calls for citrus zest, it's preferable to use unwaxed fruit. However, some citrus, such as grapefruits and blood oranges, are hard to find unwaxed. In this case, place the fruit in a colander, pour over boiling water, then dry the fruit thoroughly to remove the waxy residue before zesting.

Allergies or special diets: We want you to share these recipes with your loved ones and your community as often as possible. Please be aware, though, that some recipes contain allergens. If you are baking for others, do check before you share.

Baking Tips

Folding In
This is a way to combine ingredients gently so you don't knock out all the air. A large metal spoon or a rubber spatula is best for folding. Cut down through the mixture to the bottom of the bowl, turn the spoon or spatula upwards and draw it up, then flip it over so the mixture flops onto the surface. Give the bowl a quarter turn and repeat to combine.

Rubbing In
This is a way to combine butter and flour and add air when making pastry and simple cake mixtures. Pick up a little butter and flour mixture in your fingers and thumbs (cooler than your palms), lift and gently rub your fingers and thumbs together to combine the mixture as it falls. Keep doing this until the mixture has a crumb-like consistency.

Blind baking
Line the pastry case with the baking paper (cut to size and crumpled up to make it more flexible) and fill with ceramic baking beans, rice or dried beans. Bake as stated in the recipe (or for about 12–15 minutes, until set and firm). Remove the paper and beans, then return the pastry case to the oven and bake for a further 5–10 minutes, until the pastry is thoroughly cooked and starting to colour.

Homemade jam
For about 425g of jam (a standard jar), you'll need about 250g fruit and 250g jam sugar. Tip the fruit into a large, heavy-based pan, add the sugar and gently squash the fruit with a potato masher or the back of a wooden spoon, keeping a bit of texture. Stir the fruit gently over a low heat with a wooden spoon until the sugar dissolves. Increase the heat and boil rapidly, stirring to prevent the jam catching, until the jam reaches 105°C on a sugar thermometer. Pour the jam into a warm, sterilised jar, place a wax disc on top and leave to cool completely. Cover with a sterilised lid. Use within 1 month.

Breadmaking Tips

Kneading bread dough
Kneading develops the gluten in the flour to create a structure that stretches around the bubbles of carbon dioxide released as the yeast (or other raising agent) activates in the heat of the oven. To knead by hand, turn out the dough onto a lightly floured or oiled worktop. Hold one end with your hand and use the other hand to pull and stretch out the dough away from you. Gather the dough back into a ball again, give it a quarter turn, then repeat the stretching and gathering. As you knead, the dough starts to feel pliable, then stretchy, then very elastic and silky. Nearly all doughs need 10 minutes hand kneading. In a stand mixer, use a dough hook on the lowest speed and knead for about 5 minutes. While it's almost impossible to over-knead by hand, you can stretch the gluten too much in a mixer, which can hamper the rise. To test if the dough has been kneaded enough, stretch a small piece between your fingers to a thin, translucent sheet. If it won't stretch or it tears easily, knead it for longer.

Rising and proving
Place the dough in a moist, warm spot. A room temperature of 20–24°C is ideal – if the room

is too hot, the yeast will grow too rapidly and the dough will become distorted (and maybe develop a slight aftertaste); too cool and the yeast develops more slowly (although this can give a richer flavour and chewier crumb). Proving is the last period of rising prior to baking, after shaping a bread dough. To test whether the dough is well proved, gently prod it: if it springs back, it's not ready; if it returns to its original state fairly slowly, or if there's a very slight dent left, it's ready.

Knocking back bread dough

Knocking back or punching down risen dough happens after rising and before shaping and proving. It breaks up the large gas bubbles to make smaller, finer bubbles that expand more evenly during baking, causing a more even rise. Use your knuckles to punch down the dough. Some bakers fold or flop the dough over on itself a few times.

Perfecting a bread crust

Make sure the oven is thoroughly heated, so the dough quickly puffs (called 'oven-spring') and then sets evenly. For a crisp upper crust, create a burst of steam to keep the surface of the bread moist. To create the steam, put an empty roasting tin on the floor of the oven as it heats up. Then, immediately as you put in the unbaked loaf, pour cold water or throw a handful of ice cubes into the hot tin. Close the door to trap in the steam. For a crisp base, put a baking sheet or baking stone in the oven to heat up. Then carefully transfer your loaf onto the hot baking sheet or stone for baking.

Sourdough starter

Making a starter can take from 6 days to 2 weeks, depending on which flour you use and the ambient temperature of your kitchen. You'll need 150g organic white bread flour and 150g organic rye or spelt flour, and lukewarm (never hot) water, as well as an airtight box.

Day 1 Combine the flours and store in an airtight box or jar. Mix 25g of the flour mixture with 25ml cool water in a glass or ceramic bowl and beat to a smooth paste. Cover the bowl loosely with baking paper, securing it with a rubber band, and leave it for 24 hours at room temperature. Total weight = 50g.

Day 2 Mix 25g of the flour mixture with 25ml lukewarm water to a paste and combine it with the Day One starter. Cover again and set aside for 24 hours. Total weight = 100g.

Day 3 Discard half the mixture (50g). Add 25g of the flour mixture and 25ml lukewarm water to the remaining starter. Scoop into a glass jar. Cover loosely with the lid and set aside for 24 hours. Total weight = 100g.

Day 4 Repeat day 3. Total weight = 100g.

Day 5 Mix 100g of the flour mixture and 100ml lukewarm water to a paste and add this to the starter. Combine thoroughly, then cover loosely with the lid and leave for 24 hours. Total weight = 300g.

Day 6 Discard half the starter and add 75g of the flour mixture and 75ml water. Total weight = 300g.

Your starter should be bubbly and active and have a fresh, yeasty smell. Repeat this process for another 6 days, remembering to keep the ratio of flour to water the same at every feed. If the starter is slow after 6 days, feed it twice a day, each feed 12 hours apart. Once active, store your starter in the fridge between uses. Bring it back to room temperature and feed it the day before using it again.

Inspire Me...

Use this visual index when you need inspiration for a bake by type or special diet, or when you specifically want a judge's recipe to impress. Note that, unless they contain gelatine (in which case, use a vegetarian gelatine substitute), sweet bakes tend anyway to be vegetarian, so we've separated out savoury vegetarian recipes only into a category of their own.

BISCUITS

Janusz's Ginger Biscuits (p.49)

Bay Leaf Panna Cotta with Coriander Biscotti (p.54)

Kevin's Sourdough Crackers (p.92)

Lemon & Coconut Crackle Cookies (p.94)

Prue's Garibaldi Biscuits (p.111)

Strawberry Mousse with Hazelnut Dacquoise Biscuits (p.135)

Daisy Macarons (p.161)

Paul's S'mores (p.165)

Alfajores (p.172)

Pistachio Melting Moments (p.180)

Sarah Bernhardt Cookies (p.197)

Toasted Coconut Shortbread (p.217)

BISCUITS *continued*

Peanut Cookies (p.224)

Abdul's White Chocolate &
Macadamia Nut Cookies (p.239)

BREADS

Wild Garlic & Goat's Cheese
Gözleme (p.46)

Chai-spiced Apple Chelsea
Buns (p.50)

Fennel Seed, Chilli &
Parmesan Grissini (p.53)

Seeded Sourdough Bread
(p.73)

Ham & Pineapple Pizza (p.81)

Will's Chorizo Tear
& Share Buns (p.84)

Kevin's Sourdough Crackers
(p.92)

Savoury Fruit Loaf (p.132)

BREADS *continued*

Gulab Jamun (p.168)

Rye & Beer Bread (p.186)

Rebs's Simit (p.203)

Maritozzi (p.232)

Japanese Milk Bread (p.250)

Cream Cheese, Chilli &
Onion Bagel Loaf (p.262)

CAKES (LARGE)

Raspberry & Rose Drip
Cake (p.33)

Coffee & Ginger Layer Cake
(p.38)

Sri Lankan Fruit Cake (p.45)

Tres Leches Splatter Cake
(p.63)

Pink Grapefruit & Olive Oil
Cake (p.76)

Carole's Lemon Cake (p.87)

Buttermilk Layer Cake with
Gooseberry Curd (p.99)

Raspberry, Lemon, Pistachio
& Rose Cake (p.105)

CAKES (LARGE) *continued*

Plum Skillet Cake (p.116)

Tropical Fruit Gâteau (p.119)

Piña Colada Cake (p.125)

Blackberry, Yuzu & Passion Fruit Cake (p.129)

Apple & Almond Cake (p.137)

Rhubarb & Strawberry Crumble Cake (p.143)

Banoffee Layer Cake (p.152)

Paul's Red Velvet Cake (p.195)

Praline & Apricot Cake (p.209)

Chocolate & Speculoos Cake (p.241)

CAKES (SMALL/INDIVIDUAL)

Dawn's Halloween Cupcakes (p.57)

Sticky Toffee Cakes (p.156)

Root Vegetable Mini Loaves (p.212)

Triple Chocolate Mini Cakes (p.261)

GLUTEN-FREE

Paul's Spicy Beef Tacos (p.35)

Sri Lankan Fruit Cake (p.45)

Black Forest Pavlova (p.79)

Sticky Toffee Cakes (p.156)

Sarah Bernhardt Cookies (p.197)

JUDGES' RECIPES

Paul's Spicy Beef Tacos (p.35)

Prue's Lemon Meringue Pie (p.70)

Prue's Spring Rolls (p.97)

Prue's Garibaldi Biscuits (p.111)

Paul's Pain aux Raisins (p.141)

Paul's S'mores (p.165)

Paul's Red Velvet Cake (p.195)

Paul's Chocolate & Raspberry Baked Alaska (p.235)

PUDS AND DESSERTS

Bay Leaf Panna Cotta with Coriander Biscotti (p.54)

Prue's Lemon Meringue Pie (p.70)

Black Forest Pavlova (p.79)

Passion Fruit Trifle (p.113)

Plum Skillet Cake (p.116)

Raspberry & Custard Tart (p.147)

Strawberry Mousse with Hazelnut Dacquoise Biscuits (p.135)

Ginger Treacle Tart (p.155)

Gulab Jamun (p.168)

Fig & Date Steamed Puddings (p.175)

Chocolate & Hazelnut Entremets (p.183)

Chocolate, Caramel & Tahini Tart (p.227)

Paul's Chocolate & Raspberry Baked Alaska (p.235)

Vanilla & Cardamom Cheesecake with Rhubarb (p.247)

Muscovado & Malt Bread & Butter Pudding (p.252)

Baked Custard Tart with Roasted Plums (p.257)

Inspire Me . . .

SAVOURY

Paul's Spicy Beef Tacos (p.35)

Syabira's Swirled Curry Puffs (p.41)

Wild Garlic & Goat's Cheese Gözleme (p.46)

Fennel Seed, Chilli & Parmesan Grissini (p.53)

Aromatic Beef Slab Pie (p.59)

Seeded Sourdough Bread (p.73)

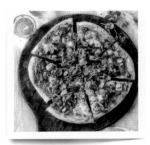
Ham & Pineapple Pizza (p.81)

Will's Chorizo Tear & Share Buns (p.84)

Kevin's Sourdough Crackers (p.92)

Prue's Spring Rolls (p.97)

Apple, Shallot & Blue Cheese Tarte Tatin (p.107)

Savoury Fruit Loaf (p.132)

Rye & Beer Bread (p.186)

Beetroot, Butternut & Feta Galette (p.191)

Rebs's Simit (p.203)

Maxy's Lamb Patties (p.215)

SAVOURY *continued*

Cheese & Potato Tartlets (p.243)

Japanese Milk Bread (p.250)

Cream Cheese, Chilli & Onion Bagel Loaf (p.262)

Fish & Chip Shop Smörgåstårta (p.265)

SWEET PASTRY & PÂTISSERIE

Prue's Lemon Meringue Pie (p.70)

Blackcurrant Millefeuille (p.89)

Paul's Pain aux Raisins (p.141)

Raspberry & Custard Tart (p.147)

Ginger Treacle Tart (p.155)

Daisy Macarons (p.161)

Maisam's Pistachio Croissants (p.189)

Pistachio & Elderflower Éclairs (p.205)

Inspire Me . . .   279

SWEET PASTRY & PÂTISSERIE *continued*

Chocolate, Caramel & Tahini Tart (p.227)

Maritozzi (p.232)

Sandro's Orange & Dark Chocolate Palmiers (p.255)

Baked Custard Tart with Roasted Plums (p.257)

TRAYBAKES

Victoria Sandwich Traybake (p.122)

James's Salted Pretzel Caramel Brownies (p.159)

Congo Bars (p.171)

Triple-layer Dark Chocolate Peanut Butter Brownies (p.200)

Ginger & Caramel Squares (p.221)

VEGAN

Raspberry & Rose Drip
Cake (p.33)

Syabira's Swirled Curry
Puffs (p.41)

Seeded Sourdough Bread
(p.73)

Kevin's Sourdough Crackers
(p.92)

Lemon & Coconut Crackle
Cookies (p.94)

Rhubarb & Strawberry
Crumble Cake (p.143)

Banoffee Layer Cake (p.152)

Peanut Cookies (p.224)

Paul's Chocolate & Raspberry
Baked Alaska (p.235)

Triple Chocolate Mini
Cakes (p.261)

VEGETARIAN SAVOURY

Syabira's Swirled Curry
Puffs (p.41)

Wild Garlic & Goat's Cheese
Gözleme (p.46)

Fennel Seed, Chilli &
Parmesan Grissini (p.53)

Seeded Sourdough Bread
(p.73)

Kevin's Sourdough Crackers
(p.92)

Apple, Shallot & Blue Cheese
Tarte Tatin (p.107)

Savoury Fruit Loaf (p.132)

Rye & Beer Bread (p.186)

Beetroot, Butternut & Feta
Galette (p.191)

Rebs's Simit (p.203)

Cheese & Potato Tartlets
(p.243)

Japanese Milk Bread (p.250)

Cream Cheese, Chilli &
Onion Bagel Loaf (p.262)

Index

This book is published to accompany the television series entitled *The Great British Bake Off*, broadcast on Channel 4 in 2022

The Great British Bake Off® is a registered trademark of Love Productions Ltd

Series produced for Channel 4 Television by Love Productions

The Great British Bake Off: Favourite Flavours

First published in Great Britain in 2022 by Sphere

10 9 8 7 6 5 4 3 2 1

A CIP catalogue record for this book is available from the British Library.

ISBN: 978-1-4087-2698-3

New recipes developed and written by:
Annie Rigg and Lisa Sallis

Commissioning Editor: Fiona Rose and Ruth Jones
Design & Art Direction: Smith & Gilmour
Project Editor: Judy Barratt
Copyeditor: Nicola Graimes
Recipe Tester: Sophie Garwood
Food Photographer: Ant Duncan
On-set GBBO Photography: Mark Bourdillon and Smith & Gilmour
Food Stylist: Annie Rigg with Holly Cowgill
Assistant Food Stylists: Hattie Arnold, Hattie Baker, Valeria Russo, Sonali Shah and Susanna Unsworth
Props Stylist: Hannah Wilkinson
Production Manager: Abby Marshall
Cover Design: Smith & Gilmour

Publisher's thanks to: Hilary Bird, Coralie Dorman, Hugh Dowdall, Sarah Epton, Uyen Jackson and Jon Leigh; and to Cal and Ed for the rhubarb

Typeset in Neutraface
Colour origination by Born Group
Printed and bound in Italy by L.E.G.O. SpA

Papers used by Sphere are from well-managed forest and other responsible sources.

Sphere
An imprint of Little, Brown Book Group, Carmelite House, 50 Victoria Embankment, London EC4Y 0DZ
An Hachette UK Company
www.hachette.co.uk www.littlebrown.co.uk

WITH THANKS

Love Productions would like to thank the following people:
Executive Producer: Jenna Mansfield
Food & Challenge Producer: Katy Bigley
Home Economist: Becca Watson
Love Executives: Letty Kavanagh, Rupert Frisby, Kieran Smith, Joe Bartley
Publicists: Amanda Console, Shelagh Pymm
Comissioning Editor: Vivienne Molokwu

Thank you also to: Paul, Prue, Noel and Matt. *And to the bakers for their recipes:* Abdul, Carole, Dawn, James, Janusz, Kevin, Maisam, Maxy, Rebs, Sandro, Syabira and Will